Race, Place, and the Law 1836–1948

RACE,

PLACE,
and the LAW
1836–1948

David Delaney

University of Texas Press ⤛ Austin

To the memory of Eleanor,

to the promise of Irene,

and to Michele, for more than I can remember.

Requests for permission to reproduce material from this work
should be sent to Permissions, University of Texas Press, Box 7819,
Austin, TX 78713-7819.

♾ The paper used in this publication meets the minimum
requirements of American National Standard for Information
Sciences—Permanence of Paper for Printed Library Materials,
ANSI Z39.48-1984.

Library of Congress Cataloging-in-Publication Data

Delaney, David.
    Race, place, and the law, 1836–1948 / David Delaney.
        p.   cm.
    Includes bibliographical references and index.
    ISBN 0-292-71596-x (cloth : alk. paper).—ISBN 0-292-71597-8
(pbk. : alk. paper)
    1. Race discrimination—Law and legislation—United States—
History.   2. United States—Race relations—Philosophy.   I. Title.
KF4755.D45   1998
305.8'00973—dc21   97-36989

Contents

Preface

This book is about two aspects of social reality in the United States and their relationship. The first aspect concerns the central position that geography has occupied in the unfolding dynamics of African American history. More specifically, it examines the significance of conflicts over space in the historical politics of race relations between blacks and whites. By geography I mean, as a first approximation, the shifting arrangements of social space, the creation and transformation of real places, and the differing experiential geographies of real people. Mine is an interpretation of the importance of geography to U.S. history that, I believe, has not been offered before. Its value is in relating otherwise separate events in a common story. I hope that in illuminating the complex connections between space, power, and experience that are at the heart of this story, we will come to understand better the ways in which the worlds we live our lives in have been racialized.

The second aspect concerns the involvement of a specialized but highly significant set of social practices in the historical geopolitics of race and (antiblack) racism. These are the practices associated with formal legal argument and judgment. To refer to legal argument—the creation and manipulation of legal meaning through procedures known as legal reasoning—as a social practice is to recognize it simply as something that people *do*. It is an activity, a craft, a practice. In studying the role played by legal reasoning in the construction and revision of inherited geographies of race and racism, we can see how a certain sort of meaning has been inscribed onto lived-in landscapes. We can see how the spatial configurations that reflect and reinforce racist ideologies have been justified as right, reasonable, and preferable to other arrangements. We can also see how these geographies have been challenged, criticized, and occasionally reshaped by these same legal practices. But, as we will see, the point of argument is usually not simply to justify or critique; the point is to make something happen. The point is to actually change the world (or to prevent change) by enlisting the power of law.

Chapter 1 provides an orientation to the general themes that are developed and explored in subsequent chapters. Here I discuss ideas such as geographies of race and racism, the geopolitics of race, and the legal landscape. I also present a way of understanding legal practice as a kind of (geo)political practice. In the following five chapters these general notions are used to make sense of historical events.

Chapters 2 and 3 treat roughly the same period of time. Each also pivots on spatial, racial, and legal transformations wrought by the Civil War. Chapter 2 looks at the on-the-ground geographies of race that characterized and were integral to slavery in the United States and at the changes in these geographies that followed abolition. The main themes here are the politics of space and the shifting connections between space, power and experience. In chapter 3 we shift our focus to formal legal practice. Here, through an analysis of a series of cases directly concerned with the spatiality of race, we examine the moves and countermoves of attorneys and judges who were participating in the geopolitics of slavery and emancipation. Our principal theme here is the politics of the creation of legal meaning.

While chapter 3 analyzes a series of cases over a long period of time, chapters 4 and 5 focus on events leading up to a single case, *Buchanan v. Warley*. Chapter 4 looks at the phenomenon of classical Jim Crow segregation. We begin with a rather general exploration that focuses on the political significance of using law to shape social space in this way. This is followed by a closer look at the emergence of a popular social movement advocating something like municipal apartheid laws in many U.S. cities in the early twentieth century. Finally, we study in some detail how the politics of segregation and antisegregation played out in Louisville, Kentucky.

Like chapter 3, chapter 5 shifts from the messy world of politics and power to the seemingly controlled and reasonable world of legal argument. After analyzing how segregation ordinances were handled by various state courts I undertake a detailed examination of the briefs presented to the U.S. Supreme Court by both sides in the case of *Buchanan v. Warley*. These arguments reveal strikingly divergent views of the connections between space, race, and law. They also represent contrasting visions of desirable worlds. The arguments in *Buchanan* illustrate the different ways that the idea of race itself was understood by white people at the time. Particularly interesting for us is how connections between race, class, and sexuality were given expression in legal argument and how understandings of these connections were used to ground legal distinctions.

Chapter 6 again shifts to a different level of analysis, this time from a single case to a single doctrine—the doctrine of changed conditions—as it was developed in a number of cases in the thirty years following *Buchanan*. The focus of dispute in these cases was racially restrictive covenants or private contracts among white property owners that excluded people of color from most neighborhoods of U.S. cities in the twentieth century. Here I trace the micromoves of argument and the small increments of legal meaning that went into shaping the geographies of race and racism that we have inherited. Of some significance here are the ways in which political conflicts over social space were transformed into specialized debates about the spatiality of a rule. In a section on the judicial construction of place, which studies a series of cases all concerning a single neighborhood in Washington, D.C., I try to demonstrate how these micromoves and countermoves mattered to real people. Chapter 7 is an epilogue.

My gratitude to many of the people who helped this work come into being can only be hinted at. I'd like to thank Bob Sack, Dirk Hartog, Dave Trubek, Gerry Kearns, Marilyn Little, and Bob Ostergren for helping me turn my ideas into a dissertation that, in turn, became this book. I also have unpayable debts to Donna Baron, Tim Cresswell, Carol Jennings, Helga Leitner, Drew Ross, Eric Sheppard, and Steve Silvern for providing me with friendship and intellectual community. At crucial points along the way the help, encouragement, and example of Nick Blomley have been of immeasurable importance. My colleagues Lawrence Douglas, Tom Kearns, Austin Sarat, Martha Umphrey, and Jean Zilewicz provided a wonderfully supportive environment during the period that the manuscript was under revision. Discussions with my students in "Race, Place, and the Law" at Amherst College allowed me to greatly clarify and simplify my approach to the questions I raise in this book. I was extremely fortunate in having worked with as careful, sensitive, and intelligent a copyeditor as Letitia Blalock. Shannon Davies at the University of Texas Press has been tremendously supportive and encouraging. Without her initiative, goodwill, and expertise, this book might not have been written at all. By far the most important contributor to what is of value here is my friend, companion, and fellow Watervlietian, Michele Emanatian. She has given me the intellectual, emotional, and material support that I needed throughout the long period that this was a work in progress. I thank her especially for trying to convince me that the ideas were worth sharing.

1 Orientations

In the summer of 1836, a six-year-old girl from Louisiana known only to us as Med found herself in Massachusetts. We don't know much about her experiences in the North that summer or about what she thought of her journey. We do know that her impending return to the South generated a good deal of controversy.[1] The reason was that in Louisiana Med was considered to be a slave—legally speaking, someone's property. Attorneys for the Massachusetts Female Anti-Slavery Society argued that she could not be compelled to return because, at least while she was within Massachusetts, she was free. Forcing her to go back to the plantation in Louisiana therefore not only would mean returning her to bondage but, perhaps more alarming, could only be done by recognizing that the person who claimed to own her in the South "owned" her in Massachusetts as well. Otherwise, by what right could he compel her to return? In the view of abolitionists, such a recognition would amount to the reestablishment of slavery in a state from which, they believed, it had been eliminated. The return of Med could only be accomplished by the expansion of slavery.

This claim was answered by an attorney for Med's "owner" with the no less plausible—in legal terms—argument that Med was, by Louisiana law, simply an object of property like any other, and that it was both sound policy and settled judicial practice that the property rights of the citizens of the several states of the Union be recognized and protected by the sister states. In legal terms, he argued that comity be granted by the courts of Massachusetts to the laws of Louisiana. He invited the court to imagine the consequences should the citizens of any state feel insecure in their possession of property when traveling outside their home state. In any event, the owner was simply asserting a limited and qualified right of removing the property in question. This hardly constituted the reestablishment of slavery in New England. Grant comity, he argued, and the problem quite literally will go away. These arguments about Med's travels through the antebellum United States were made before a judge who complimented each of the attorneys on the quality of his presentation. The question in this case was not simply what was to happen to Med but about the meaning of slavery, of comity, of property, and so on. What was to happen to Med, in fact, *depended* on the answers given to these other—peculiarly legal—questions. For the judge, some of the considerations that went into the determination of Med's fate were the circumstances of her arrival in Massachusetts in the first place (did she escape or was she brought by someone else?), the differences between natural law and positive law as they related to the case at hand, and decisions by other judges in similar cases.

More than one hundred years later, in the 1940s, Clara Mays and her family, after a long and difficult search for housing in wartime Washington, D.C., bought a house on First Street not far from Howard University. Soon after moving in, Mays received a letter from a prominent local attorney advising her that if she and her family did not vacate the premises quickly, legal action would be initiated that would compel her to leave. Having participated in many similar proceedings, the lawyer felt confident in assuring her that the law was unquestionably on his side.[2] The previous owners of the property had signed a contract—a restrictive covenant—with their neighbors agreeing not to sell any property in the neighborhood to "Negroes." There being no doubt that the Mayses were Negroes, their occupancy was in violation of that contract. The deadline for voluntary compliance passed and the threat was acted upon. At trial the plaintiffs—neighboring "Caucasian" property owners—prevailed and the Mayses were ordered to leave the neighborhood. Mays, assisted by attorneys associated with Howard Law School, appealed.[3] Among the arguments offered by her attorneys was that the neighborhood in question was so different in 1944 compared to what it had been like in 1926 when the contract was drawn up that "the doctrine of changed conditions" should apply. This doctrine, essentially a rule of judicial interpretation, allowed judges to decline to enforce the terms of a contract if, because of changes in the relevant circumstances, enforcement would be unfair. Attorneys for the neighbors argued that conditions had not changed, or at least not so much as to render the contract unenforceable. Attorneys in this case disagreed about what those conditions were, what circumstances were or were not relevant, how much change counted as change in the technical sense, who was responsible for the change that had occurred, and much more. The judges who decided the case also had strikingly divergent understandings of what sort of rule the doctrine of changed conditions was and whether and how it ought to be applied. Nevertheless, as in Med's case, a decision was reached and lives were affected.

These cases, along with others, will be examined in detail in subsequent chapters. Before revealing the outcomes, I would like to draw attention to some elements common to these cases. Perhaps most obvious, each of these cases illustrates the crucial role played by lawyers and judges in shaping the contours of what is sometimes called race relations in U.S. history. To put it bluntly, the kinds of things that lawyers and judges do—argue, interpret, categorize, create, and manipulate legal meaning—have occupied an important place in efforts both to maintain and to challenge racial subordination.[4] Perhaps less obvious, each of these events also illustrates the centrality of "space," "place," or geography in the historical constitution of race. Both of these cases were about space, the meaning of space, and what it means to cross a line. Both of these cases, and many others to be explored, have been about making connections between race, space, law, and, considering the significance of the events for Med and Clara Mays, experience—or what it's like to be in the world. Both of these events, separated as they are by generations, are links in a chain of events that I'll call the geopolitics of race and racism. In each case African Americans were not where some white people wanted them to be. More particularly, each event demonstrates the place of legal reasoning and argument in the unfolding of the geopolitics of race.

In the following pages, I will introduce a number of basic concepts that, taken together, can illuminate these and many other events. More important than understanding these episodes, however, is beginning to see how such events have contributed to shaping the world that we inhabit. Contemporary geographies of race and racism bear the traces of these earlier conflicts.[5] If, as seems likely, these configurations persist and mutate long into the twenty-first century, they will bear the marks of our occupancy as well. Our orientation to this way of looking at the world begins with us: with experience.

Geographies of Experience

If we ever consider the idea that each of us has a biography or life story, we most likely imagine first how our lives unfold through time. Day after day or year following year, time or temporality gives whatever structured coherence our lives seem to have as chains of events.[6] Narratively we may announce episodes by saying "first" or "and then." We tell stories of before and after and change. Our lives are, in a sense, made out of time. But we are also physical, corporal, mobile beings. We inhabit a material, spatial world. We move through it. We change it. It changes us.

Each of us is weaving a singular path through the world. If you are sitting in a room reading this book, retrace your steps. As we think back in time—an hour ago, last week, three birthdays ago—we also think back in space. The paths that we make, the conditions under which we make them, and the experiences that those paths open up or close off are part of what make us who we are. In this sense they are constitutive of our being. Different paths, different experiences, different lives. They are fundamental conditions of what it's like to be in the world.

These *geographies of experience*, as I'll call them, are in important ways irreducibly unique. Each is as singular, exceptional, and improbable as the biography it helps form. And yet while there is no typical biography, there are of course significant commonalities among lives deriving from shared experiences. We all share some experiences as sentient, corporal human beings. Members of a common culture may confer shared meaning on experience. People share times and places. Paths crisscross, converge, diverge. We are not singular atoms bouncing through a void. There are commonalities among people who inhabit a place at the same time or who do things together. People may be categorized by common spatial experiences—the prisoner, the refugee, the exile, the fugitive, the homeless, the alien. These commonalities plus the elements that are irreducibly individual all contribute to making us—you, me, us—who we are.

The spatial organization of the society—how the material, social world is put together—is a basic condition of one's experiential geography. This is perhaps a more familiar sense of the term *geography*. Our world—call it turn-of-the-century United States, or perhaps simply turn-of-the-century Earth—is a very different place than was, say, pre-Columbian America or medieval Europe. It looks different. It would feel different to be in or of those other worlds. Among the fundamental elements of humanly created places that can vary from culture to culture or from era to era are how the world of everyday life is carved up into meaningful spaces and the kinds of culturally specific spatial codes which condition basic experiences of access, exclusion, and protection.

Geographies of Power

To consider phrases like "how the world is carved up into meaningful spaces" raises interesting questions about, for example, who is doing the "carving." To what end or purpose is this carving done? Under what conditions? What kinds of "meaning" are assigned to spaces? Consider ethnographic accounts of gender or age-based spatial exclusions.[7] Consider apartheid. Consider again the spatial conditions required for us to make sense of being a prisoner, a refugee, a fugitive. To call to mind the *experience* of access granted or denied, of exclusions and expulsions enforced, of protection or sanctuary respected or violated, is to become conscious of the social relations of power. A fundamental element, therefore, of any human world, including ours, is what I will be calling *geographies of power*.[8] Consider these reminiscences by literary critic Blyden Jackson of a world not too distant, in time, from ours:

> Through the veil I could perceive the forbidden city, the Louisville where white folks lived. It was the Louisville of downtown hotels, the lower floors of the big movie houses, the high schools I read about in the daily newspapers, the restricted haunts I sometimes passed, like white restaurants and country clubs, the other side of windows in banks, and of course, the inner sanctums of offices where I could go only as a humble client or a menial custodian. On my side of the veil everything was black: the homes, the people, the churches, the schools, the Negro Park with the Negro park police. . . . I knew that there were two Louisvilles and in America, two Americas. I knew, also, which of the Americas was mine.[9]

Jackson, of course, was recalling his experience navigating a landscape constructed according to segregationist or white supremacist conceptions of power. This is a world that Clara Mays and millions of other Americans found familiar. For our immediate purposes, geographies of power can be thought of as those spatial configurations that reflect and reinforce social relations of power.

The connections between space and power—and so their connections to experience—can be manifest in any number of ways and can involve any number of the basic elements of social space such as location, distance, spatial networks, routes, centralization, marginalization, and so on. One fundamental way in which the connections between space and power are expressed is through territoriality.[10] *Territoriality* can be thought of as the assignment of a particular sort of meaning to lines and spaces in order to control, at first glance, determinable segments of the physical world. Upon further reflection, however, it is clear that the objects of control are social relationships and the actions and experiences of people.

Complex territorial configurations are basic though often invisible elements of everyday experience. Retrace your steps again. Examine how many "meaningful spaces" in this sense you enter into and pass out of as you make your way through the world—the number of meaningful lines you cross and what it means to cross them. Examine the proliferation of public and private spaces to which you have access. Consider the complex of spaces around you from which you are excluded and how it would feel to cross the lines and enter these forbidden spaces. Ours, of course, is a highly privatized world. The landscapes that we inhabit are derived, in large part, from a set of ideas centered on the concept of property in all its variety and complexity.[11] A world carved up according to different principles would not be our world. The connections between space and power would be so dissimilar that the experience of living in the world would be different. We would not be us.

Of basic importance for the arguments to be developed in this book is the idea that complex territorial configurations—and the codes of access, exclusion, and inclusion of which these configurations are the physical expression—are inseparable from the workings of large-scale power orders such as those associated with, in our world, gender, race, and class. These are in addition to those associated with explicit legal-political notions such as the state, governance, sovereignty, jurisdiction, and the like. Many of the spatial configurations through which we each make our way are constructed according to various ideologies of domination and subordination, hierarchy, and inequality. Much of what power is and how it is experienced is bound up with how it is *spatialized.* For example, much of our common understanding of the spatialization of public and private reflects and reinforces inherited conceptions of gender hierarchies.[12] And though the experiential differences between "men's world" and "women's world" are less

severe than in previous generations, they have by no means been obliterated. This is especially so when we consider the spatialization of men's work
and women's or the differential geographies of fear at night. It makes sense,
therefore, to think about geographies of gender or geographies of patri-
archy *not* as maps of where men and women are—whatever that would
mean—but rather as those spatial configurations that reflect and reinforce
social relations of power or inequality based on conceptions of gender or
of patriarchal ideologies. In this way we can understand social space itself
as being gendered. Similarly, the experiential geographies in Louisville and
elsewhere were strongly conditioned by geographies of power reflecting
and reinforcing white supremacy. This is so with respect to many other dimensions of social difference such as age, wealth, labor relations, and sexual orientation. We all live within all of these geographies of power and
others. Indeed, there is no "outside" of them.

Another principal argument of this book is that such spatial configurations are not incidental to power relations such as those predicated on race
but are integral to them. This means, first, that such relations are what they
are because of how they are spatialized. The long struggle against racial
segregation demonstrates that the spatiality of racism was a central component of the social structure of racial hierarchy, that efforts to transform
or maintain these relations entailed the reconfiguration or reinforcing
of these geographies, *and* that participants were very much aware of this.
Space and power are so tightly bound that changing one necessarily entails
changing the other. In fact, many contemporary human geographers argue
that it doesn't make sense to think of them as "separate" at all. Space can
often be seen as the embodiment of power; power as the point of spatial
differentiation.[13]

Before looking at some specific features of geographies of race and racism,
I'd like to introduce two additional elements of our orientation to geographies of power: history and politics. I said above that geographies of power
are integral to the maintenance and revision of social relations of power.
To speak of the maintenance and revision of power is to introduce time,
change, process, and history into our understanding. It is also to implicate
social practice or human action. I'll treat each of these in turn.

Geographies of power in all of their complexity are historical and dynamic.[14] They are historical in the sense that they come to us from the
past—or, more accurately, we (any generational "we") inherit them from

previous generations. We are born into a world. We change it simply by living our lives. We pass it on to those who follow bearing the marks of our occupancy. Geographies of gender, for example, are inherited, revised, reworked, and bequeathed generation after generation. We can see this kind of process unfold rather clearly and dramatically in the context of twentieth-century geographies of race and racism. If you were born in the southern United States before the mid-1950s, you inherited a racialized landscape that was in crucial respects similar to the world described by Blyden Jackson. If you were born there in the 1970s, after the events known as the Civil Rights movement, the geographies of race and racism that you inherited and inhabited were, in crucial respects, strikingly different. They had been transformed. Geographies of power are dynamic and in continual flux, even if they appear in any time or place to be immutable and stable. They change. They are changed. They are in motion. Most important, as with history more generally so far, there is no once and for all.

As reference to the Civil Rights movement also suggests, such changes or transformations are often the result of deliberate actions. They are the products of what I will call the *geopolitics of social life* or of everyday life.[15] Such actions are rooted in the practical recognition of the connections between space, power, and experience by people whose lives are shaped by geographies of power, that is, by their inhabitants. Images of the Civil Rights movement also call to mind the strong reactions to such attempted changes in the prevailing order.[16] By saying that geographies of social life reflect power, we mean that they are the objects of contestation and the products of actual struggles. Viewed as the products of political conflicts, they may retain elements of tension or contradiction born of compromise. These kinds of geographical configurations may also be seen as having been constructed and revised according to various ideologies or common visions of power. They may be understood as the unsteady products of uneasy resolution among various competing ideologies.[17] Consider Med's journey through the complex geographies of freedom and slavery or Clara Mays' navigation through geographies of race and private property. In the cases to be examined we can see various versions of racism, liberalism, federalism, and other ideologies mapped or inscribed in uneasy accommodation or tension with one another onto real landscapes, real places. The points, here, are that key aspects of geographies of experience are the products or result of political actions, and that these geographies of power are extremely complex and potentially unstable ideological constructions.

Geographies of Race and Racism

The connections between space and power are probably illustrated no more clearly than in the context of the historical politics of race and racism in the United States. It is hard to understate the central significance of geographical themes—space, place, and mobility—to the social and political history of race relations and antiblack racism in the United States. Consequently, we cannot underestimate the importance of the historical geography of race to United States history more generally. It's obvious, for example, that segregation, integration, and separation are spatial processes; that ghettos and exclusionary suburbs are spatial entities; that access, exclusion, confinement, sanctuary, forced or forcibly limited mobility are spatial experiences. Some of the cleavages and conflicts within black political thought through the generations have concerned divergent views of both the desired and possible connections between space and power. Nineteenth-century debates about the merits of emigration or colonization, twentieth-century debates about the practical meaning of integration, and recurrent strands of separatism and black nationalism that have found expression in the stated desire for—or necessity of—a black nation in North America or community control of inner-city neighborhoods all have been directed at imagining and creating alternative geographies of race.[18] More pervasively, what has been called the politics of black mobility has been an enduring and often explosive theme in U.S. social and political history.[19] Finally, in conventional political discourse the perceived "problems" of race have been rhetorically spatialized as the "southern problem" or the "urban problem." In innumerable ways, then, the history of race relations in the United States has been the history of conflicts over spatial relations. The geographies that we all live in tell the tale.

It is a basic premise of this book that the history and dynamics of race and racism are not marginal but integral to an understanding of the political construction of U.S. landscapes more generally. The close connections among race, space, and power have been most obvious with respect to the urban and metropolitan landscapes of the twentieth century and to many of the Southern rural landscapes of the eighteenth and nineteenth centuries. If we want to understand the historical construction of geographies of race and racism in the United States, it seems we have to do more than map changing distributions of "black people"—as if the geographies of race were in principle no different than the geographies of cotton or the blues or the AME Church. We will instead examine the ways in which racism as a set of ideologies contributes to the shaping of geographies of power.[20] We will look at the spatial configurations that make race relations what they are at any time and place. Our aim is to explore the creation and re-creation of part of what Toni Morrison has called "the wholly racialized world."[21]

The Geopolitics of Race

Our focus here, then, is on the social practices that contribute to this shaping and reshaping of geographies of race as instances of both geographies of power and geographies of experience. *The geopolitics of race* can be conceived of as a single but complex process that in the United States began with European contact with indigenous peoples—and the resultant racialization of the Western Hemisphere—and continues to the present day.[22] With respect to the geopolitics of European American and African American race relations, the process took root with the introduction of slavery and, again, can be projected deep into the twenty-first century.[23] The geopolitics of race refers to a complex chain of events. We can regard it in the broad sweep of U.S. history as a story of continuity and change from generation to generation. In subsequent chapters, for example, we will look at the geopolitics of slavery, abolition, emancipation, segregation, and desegregation. We will also examine specific illustrative events and particular strategic encounters and the actual practices that contributed to the formation of the geographies of race which we have inherited.

Geopolitical Practices

By geopolitical practices I mean, most generally, those social and political actions oriented toward reshaping the spatial conditions of social life. In the context of race relations, these have included such practices as firebombing, lynching, picketing, demonstrating, schooling, and preaching. Perhaps more commonly they have included evicting or denying access to housing in certain neighborhoods, posting Whites Only signs over doorways, ignoring such signs, passing statutes authorizing or mandating racial exclusions, and issuing judicial opinions and decrees validating or voiding these statutes. That is, many of the most significant practices which constitute the geopolitics of race are what we think of as specifically *legal* practices. Likewise, much of the meaning that is mapped onto lived-in land-scapes is specifically *legal* meaning. This book is largely about how this meaning is arrived at and how this mapping is accomplished. To shift the emphasis somewhat, we want to know how connections between law and space or between meaning and power are made and unmade in practice.

Before examining these ideas more closely, consider this event from every-day life. On the morning of Friday, November 14, 1913, W. D. Binford, a superintendent in the mechanical department of the Louisville *Courier-Journal*, went to the Hotel Henry Watterson to address a luncheon of the Real Estate Exchange of Louisville.[24] He came to tell the fifty or so as-sembled realtors that Louisville had a problem, that he had a solution, and that they had an opportunity to be part of that solution. The problem iden-tified by Binford concerned the consequences of the ongoing "invasion" of Louisville's "white residential districts" by Negro "mercenaries."

According to Binford, the Negro was moving into the "best and most exclusive squares in the city" and waiting for neighboring property owners to make an offer "large enough to induce him to leave." Among the ob-servable consequences of this invasion were a "migratory movement of whites from pillar to post," a precipitous decline in property values, and a growing preference among whites to rent their homes rather than buy. If unchecked, he claimed, this state of affairs would lead to racial disturbances and would "make a provincial city of our much boasted 'Gateway to the South.'"[25]

Binford's solution was a municipal segregation ordinance modeled on one enacted in Baltimore in 1911.[26] The objective of the ordinance was the maintenance of racially segregated residential districts throughout the city. The ordinance would include procedures for the identification and map-ping of "white blocks" and "colored blocks" and would penalize members of the two recognized races for residing in the territory assigned to the other.

Binford had done his homework. Giving the legislative and judicial his-tories of the Baltimore ordinance—as well as those enacted in other mu-nicipalities—he suggested ways that Louisvillians could avoid some of the difficulties that Baltimore segregationists had encountered. He also noted the beneficial effects such an ordinance would have on the Negro: it would help to maintain "the most friendly feeling" that white Louisvillians, as southerners, had for "the colored man and brother"—a feeling that the in-

vasion of mercenaries had begun to jeopardize. Speaking both to the organization and to the assembled individuals as realtors, Louisvillians, property owners, and white men, he urged his audience not to remain passive
and to lend support "at the proper time." However, Binford cautioned that
if Louisvillians were to avoid the exacerbation of the problem that had characterized the Baltimore campaign, then supporters of the segregation ordinance must act quickly and quietly.

According to press accounts, the president of the real estate exchange,
J. D. Wright, disagreed with Binford's assessment of the problem as well as
with the efficacy of his proposed solution. Wright voiced his opposition to
any undue discrimination, stating that Louisville and Washington, D.C.,
were the only two U.S. cities in which "the negro has an ample chance
to elevate himself." Moreover, an ordinance such as the one proposed, he
believed, would be more likely to "make the negro rebellious" than to create conditions conducive to harmony. In any case, he felt that the real estate exchange should not take any action until public opinion was clear. On
the other hand, another realtor, J. E. Dawkins, seems to have been convinced that the law would "help the negro" and that the real estate exchange
should endorse Binford's proposal. The *Courier-Journal* reported that "a
resolution to make the question a special order of the next meeting was
defeated, Pinkney Varble contending that the resolution violated a rule
against business at social meetings."[27]

Binford and the others mentioned in this story were all participants
in the geopolitics of race. They and countless others were contributing to
the shaping of the landscape that Blyden Jackson would recall years later.
The geopolitics of race can take place anywhere. We can find it at a Friday
business luncheon, on street corners, at kitchen tables, or in schools and
churches. We find expressions of it in the press. It happens in city council
chambers, mayors' offices, and courtrooms. It takes place locally, nationally, and internationally, in private and public. It is important to note here,
though, that the instrument Binford advocated in his project to reshape
the geography of race in Louisville was a law, a set of rules. More specifically, he urged the city government to put certain restrictions on property
owners—to limit those to whom one could sell or rent real property. He
sought to modify in a small but potentially significant way the legal meaning of property, of what it means to own. As I'll now discuss, he sought to
change (or maintain) inherited geographies of race by reshaping the legal
landscape.

On the Legal Landscape

In the following pages we will be looking more closely at some specifically legal kinds of practices. We want to see how the kinds of activities that go into crafting legal arguments (and judgments) are involved in the geopolitics of race. This requires at least a cursory examination of questions about law, language, and politics. We will begin, however, on the ground.

In the modern world—or in that segment of it that we call the United States—all geographies of power and experience are embedded within and take much of their meaning from what I will be calling the legal landscape. It is helpful to think of the *legal landscape* as the complex ensemble of lines and spaces—territorial configurations—that give legal meaning to determinable segments of the physical world or actual lived-in landscapes. Again, begin with where you are. The landscape within which you are situated is composed of innumerable "legal spaces" which in aggregate constitute systems of sociospatial differentiation. They effect a spatial distribution of power conceived of in terms of "rights." Work outward from the room you're in to the building and its configuration of authorized and unauthorized spaces; to the institution or neighborhood within which the building is set. The walls and fences, the gates and doors, tell only a fraction of the story. Consider the complex mapping of public and private. We live, after all, in a sea of property, a dense grid of spatialized power. Consider the legal meaning contributed to the landscape by the specific deeds, leases, contracts, and licenses drawn up with reference to these spaces. Now add in the jurisdictional spaces, the municipality, county, and state spaces. In the United States we must also take account of the complex spatiality of federalism according to which formally distinct states are considered to occupy the same physical space.[28] As we can see, legal meaning saturates lived-in landscapes. Does it matter?

In our world there is no "outside" of the legal landscape. There is no point in the terrestrial world that is void of legal meaning. Every point of land is "owned" in some sense, every "where" is within multiple, overlapping legal jurisdictions. This means that every location may refer back to or implicate a number of social relations—actually, a network of relations of power. Think of the space of a single residential apartment. The legal meaning that it carries may refer to relations among tenants and landlords, management companies and employees, previous tenants and neighbors, mortgage holders, city, state, and federal housing authorities, the police, and so on. In fact—and this is of primary significance for the geopolitics of social life—every such territorialized segment of the world has, potentially, a surplus of legal meaning. Consider now the complexity of a landscape saturated by these legal spaces.

The experiential meaning that law inscribes on the physical world is often conceptualized and *felt* in terms of rights or obligations, or what kinds of actions, under what conditions, are permitted, prohibited, or mandatory in relation to whom.[29] That is, the meaning of social space is, in large part, about social relations of power. Experientially, as we move through the world in the course of a given day or year, we pass into and out of innumerable legal spaces. We cross over lines or refrain from crossing. As we move, "rights," "duties," and so on become attached or fall away. Some become rather firmly attached; others are rather ephemeral. This suggests that rights are often contingent on space. What rights we feel we have or feel obliged to recognize others as having often depend on our location in the legal landscape. Again, when we speak of rights we speak of constellations of social relations conceptualized in terms of the language of law or "legal discourse."

As I indicated above, most often in our experience the legal meaning of social space—not simply a single, isolated space but an extensive ensemble of spaces—is obvious enough. Indeed, one of the things that is entailed by being socialized into one's culture is that such meaning can be largely taken for granted. If you have ever deliberately trespassed, you know what that *feels* like. Occasionally, however, it may be a significant part of a group's geopolitical project to call into question that which seemingly had been obvious: to challenge the received connections between meaning, space, power, and experience in such a way as to engage in a reinscription or remapping of meaning onto lived-in landscapes. Consider squatters, participants in the sit-in phase of the Civil Rights movement, and participants in the Sanctuary and Anti-Apartheid movements.[30] What follows tracks such moves through an exploration of legal reasoning and the geopolitics of race.

On Legal Practice

In our legal culture the phrase "legal practice" is most often taken to refer to the activities of professional legal actors such as lawyers and judges. In this book the doings of these kinds of people are, indeed, of primary significance. However, it is important to recognize that what we might call everyday legal practices or nonprofessional legal common sense is equally—in some ways more, in some ways less—important to how we understand how law works and how legal meaning shapes experience.[31] For example, when W. D. Binford addressed the realtors of Louisville to enlist their support for a segregation ordinance, he made a number of legal claims. He was, after all, speaking in support of a law. He spoke about rights and justice, about property and contract, about legislative authority, judicial practice, and constitutional validity. Although Binford was a mechanic, his understanding of these legal issues was shared by many people generally considered more competent to discuss such matters. Gilbert Stephenson, a graduate of Harvard Law School and author of the prestigious *Race Distinctions in American Law*,[32] public officials in various municipalities—including Louisville's city attorney Stuart Chevalier—and state court judges all more or less endorsed Binford's views on law. On the other hand, just as doubts were raised at the realtor's meeting, so was Binford's take on things legal directly challenged by black citizens of Louisville as well as by attorneys—including, eventually, a past president of the American Bar Association and counsel for the National Association for the Advancement of Colored People, Moorfield Storey—and other state court judges.[33] Claims and counterclaims about law were made by different people in differing situations in order to shape the unfolding of events, in efforts to shape local geographies of race.

In this book we are concerned with legal practice primarily as an aspect of political practice. Politics is always about something. If politics is broadly—and charitably—conceived of as involving conflicting assessments of how social life is organized, how it should be organized, and how to narrow the gap, then clearly legal practices have been an important component of political action for most of U.S. history. Geopolitics, in the sense used here, is about narrowing the gap between actual and desired or normative geographies of power. Familiar examples of legal practice as politics include the legal maneuvers of abolitionists and of lawyers associated with the NAACP that we will be examining in subsequent chapters.[34]

For a number of reasons, courts of law have been an important arena in which these conflicts have taken shape. However, in the process of bringing a broad social and political dispute into the legal arena, it undergoes a number of fundamental transformations. For example, the direct involvement of the state becomes a key feature of the conflict. Moreover, the formal topic of the dispute—what it is putatively about—may be changed from, say, the local geographies of race to the essential (as opposed to incidental) attributes of property (i.e., the meaning of property), the distinction between civil rights and social rights (the meaning of rights), or the relation between property relations and political authority (theories of civil society). Or the dispute may be translated into an argument about the meaning of specialized terms such as "comity" (as in Med's case) or "privity" (as in Clara Mays'). The topic of argument might shift to the intentions of "the framers," of past legislatures, of parties to contracts, and so on. It should be clear that the dispute is rendered no less political as a result of these strategic transformations and translations. However, bringing a political dispute before a court of law involves a distinct set of social practices. Specifically, it involves the purposive, creative, and interpretive practices of argument and judgment. In litigation these practices are controlled by what is taken to be a relatively distinct kind of argumentation called legal reasoning. Indeed the practice of judging often takes the form of assessments of what counts as a valid legal argument.[35]

Central to this practice are the specific acts of categorization which, woven into narrative form, constitute an argument: the assertion and denial of meaningful conceptual distinctions, and the assertion and denial of claims of implication or entailment that follow from the categories chosen. It is through these kinds of acts that meaning—specifically, legal meaning—is created and revised. In geopolitical contexts, this meaning is (provisionally) inscribed on actual landscapes. The geographies of power so constructed (and subsequently construed or reinterpreted) are of fundamental importance to how power is exercised and experienced. In the events to be described in this book, lawyers and judges looked out onto the world and presented conflicting construals of what that world was actually like. Often, I will argue, they presented interpretations of geographies that would most readily yield the desired world. Both what was seen and what was desired were, of course, strongly conditioned by views of race.

Legal Practice as Politics

Examination of the role played by legal practice in (geo)political conflicts requires some understanding of what the relationship between law and politics is supposed to be (ideally or ideologically) in our legal culture. It is not

my intention to engage in substantive debates in legal theory, only to describe important aspects of a specific set of social practices. This is important for understanding what the participants in these kinds of events think
they are doing—or feel compelled to portray themselves as doing.

We can begin by noting a distinction between what might be called conventional or mainstream legal theory and oppositional or critical legal theory.[36] For our immediate purposes we can consider conventional legal theory or jurisprudence to be what law has to say about itself and critical legal
theory to be a set of critiques on law's self-portraits. It is dangerous to reduce complex bodies of scholarship and knowledge to a few essential principles. Nonetheless, it is fairly safe to say that a belief in a rather sharp distinction between something called law and something else called politics is
fundamental not only to our legal culture but to dominant understandings
of our civilization. The core of these beliefs concerns what we can call the
Rule of Law Idea.[37] It is this distinction between law and politics that is the
primary object of critique.

In conventional legal thought the word *politics* most often refers to the
actions centered on the formation of a government—electoral politics—
and, within a government, the actions of legislators or executives—the political branches. The political is conceived of as the public realm where interests collide, deals are cut, and compromises are attempted. Politics is
about policy.[38] In contrast, law—that is, what judges do—is supposed to be
neutral and objective. Law is about principle. There is believed to be a
close connection between justice and the disinterest or neutrality of judges
and the objectivity of their approach to resolving disputes. A judicial decision is not supposed to represent how a judge wants a case to turn out;
rather, it is supposed to be a determination of what the law requires.[39] The
maintenance of this distinction between law and politics, and thus the
maintenance of the Rule of Law itself, is considered crucial to the preservation of our way of life.[40] Recognizing the importance of this distinction
is crucial for understanding what happens when a broad-scale social conflict finds its way into the legal arena.

The distinction between law and politics is to be maintained or guaran-
teed by what is considered to be a rather rigorous form of thought called
legal reasoning. Legal reasoning—what it is, how to do it, how to make
sure judges are doing it right—is what much of mainstream legal theory is
about.[41] The problem that conventional legal theories address is how to

constrain judicial interpretation—or rather, how to develop procedures of interpretation that will constrain judges. In a phrase, the problem is how to depoliticize the practice of judging. Remember that we are talking about immense power, including the power to take property and lives. In conventional legal-political thought, politicians are accountable to the people but judges are accountable to the truth.

Nearly all approaches to legal reasoning base the possibility of interpretive objectivity and judicial neutrality on some version of linguistic objectivity or the neutrality of language.[42] This, in essence, is the idea that words or concepts have rather clear, determinate, stable, meanings—that ambiguities are infrequent and that when they are encountered there is usually something outside of the judge's own preferences that will help to clarify them. If the words are in the Constitution, one might ask what the framers of the Constitution had intended; if the words are in a statute, one might look at the legislative history of the bill; if the words are in a contract, one might ask about how a reasonable person might have understood a promise, and so on. The point here is that understandings of judgment and justice are grounded in understandings about meaning and language, as is the possibility of depoliticization.

This shamefully abbreviated account of legal theory may seem familiar to you, or it may strike you as odd that anyone could seriously believe that law is not political. Our concern here is not with legal theory per se but with understanding legal practice. And while legal theory is *about* legal practice, of greater interest to us is that these central concerns of legal theory (objectivity, neutrality, rigorous reasoning, and their connection to justice) are also the concerns of practitioners themselves. A judicial opinion rarely is presented as simply what the judge wants. Whether genuinely or not, judges must portray their interpretations of law and the world as derived from something other than subjective preferences.[43] Again, truth is not what a person desires but what the law requires.

While attorneys who represent clients are not bound by the same conception of disinterest, in order to be persuasive the product of their labor—argument—must have the appearance of objectivity in the sense that it is an accurate portrayal of law and fact and the relationship between them. Ideally, the argument offered by an attorney would be adopted by a judge as *the* correct view of things. In effect, lawyers argue that their clients should prevail not simply because they want to but because the law demands it. Justice inheres in a judicial recognition of what the law objectively, clearly requires. All of this involves the rhetorical depoliticization of what, in the wider world, is inherently political.

Critics of conventional views of law see things differently. It is important to note, though, that they are in a sense asking different kinds of questions for different kinds of reasons. Their job is not to stabilize the law/politics distinction—that is someone else's job. Their job is to see if they can understand how power works in the world of experience. To that end, questioning the possibility of a sharp distinction between law and politics, critically examining *how* and why that distinction is made, and exploring the consequences of how it is made lead to a clearer understanding of how real people act in and on the world. From a critical standpoint, the depoliticization of legal practice often appears to be simply an ideological move that has the effect of legitimizing actions of powerful social agents.[44] This ideology of legalism contributes to the belief that patterns and instances of inequality are in some sense natural or inevitable and not the effects of power. Where conventional views of legal practice seek to guarantee neutrality by locating its source outside of politics in the realm of language or in "the facts" or in the process of reasoning itself, critics of legalism locate the politics of law in the practice of language use or in actual instances of interpretation. They draw attention to acts of strategic categorization and countercategorization, to the malleability of language and the fluidity or context-dependency of legal meaning.[45] They look at how claims about law are advanced through stories about power, and at how, through narrative or metaphor or rhetoric, meaning is not simply found but created. Drawing on contemporary philosophies of language which examine the mutability or plasticity of meaning and the connections between meaning and power, critics focus our attention on what is called legal discourse.

Legal Discourse

Legal discourse—or the terms, concepts, images, and stylistic and performative features characteristic of law talk in our culture—is, like geography, a cultural-historical artifact.[46] Legal discourse is something that was created piece by piece by people engaged in practical activity (recall comity). It is something that has been inherited and revised by countless generations. It can be understood in terms of continuity and change. Some elements, such as rights or law itself, are more fundamental, some less so;

some more enduring or ephemeral. Doctrines come and go and change along the way. Some elements, such as the concept of property, may appear to be stable in that there is a constancy of form over the ages. Closer examination, however, reveals profound changes in their practical significance or in their relation to other elements.[47] Again, Med's experience is instructive here. Determination of her status as someone's property or as a being intrinsically unable to be owned would have changed the practical meaning of property. Our present aim, though, is not to treat legal discourse as if it were a thing or system apart from power or social reality, but to recognize it as the complex product of transgenerational labor. We want to see how it is transformable, bit by bit, by people who do interpretive work in and on it. People change legal discourse by using it and in changing (parts of) it, they change what it refers to: social relations of power.

There are three features of legal discourse that are of particular significance for understanding the politics of legal practice and therefore the geopolitics of race. The first is the relation of legal discourse to power more generally. In Robert Gordon's words,

> these discourses . . . are, of course, discourses of power—not only for the obvious reason that law's commands are backed by force and its operation can inflict enormous pain, but to have access to these discourses, to be able to use them or pay others to use them on your behalf is a large part of what it means to possess power.[48]

This means, at least, that part of what makes formal or professional legal discourse distinctive compared to, say, everyday language is precisely its connection to power. But this distinction between legal discourse and everyday language is not absolute. As anyone who has ever been evicted or fired knows, legal discourse *in* everyday language is what power sounds like. In everyday life, to assert rights with the expectation that the assertion will be enforced is to exercize power.[49]

A second feature of legal discourse that is significant for understanding legal action as political practice is what we can call the translation effect. Critical attention here is on the tendencies of legal discourse toward abstraction and decontextualization, and on the requirement that all of social reality be able to be squeezed into the conceptual forms and categories provided by the language of law. As James Boyle writes, "It is in some sense necessary that we translate the struggles, conflicts, and politically contentious values of everyday life into the supposedly neutral semiological system of the law."[50] According to Gary Peller, "Legal discourse excludes (or suppresses) other modes of discourse, other ways of describing or conceptualizing social reality."[51] Or again, as Gordon asserts, "The commonplace legal discourses often produce such seriously distorted representations of social life that the categories regularly filter out complexity, variety, irrationality, unpredictability, disorder, cruelty, coercion, violence, suffering, solidarity, and self-sacrifice."[52] The assumption here is that any social state of affairs is amenable to a multiplicity of plausible characterizations or descriptions, and that specifically legal descriptions are not only partial and impoverished but distorted and distorting. Critics focus not simply on this translation effect but, more important, on what is lost—or added—in translation.

The third feature of the critique of legal discourse that I will note here follows from consideration of the translation effect. This is the ideological skewing that is integral to legal discourse as historical (political) artifact. Legal discourse is seen to be inherently ideological. This is especially (but not only) so with respect to the role it plays in directly legitimizing or justifying actual inequality.[53] Critics also note, though, the contestable and, in fact, contested social visions that are built into and structure legal categories and doctrines themselves. Whole areas of law such as contract, family law, real property, criminal law, constitutional law, and international law are seen to presuppose and project onto the world the vision of social reality, social relations, and social identity that is assumed by various strands of liberal political theory.[54] In particular, liberal discourse takes as normal a world of men conceived of as bounded, self-knowing, self-directed, autonomous individuals endowed with (liberal versions of) reason, will, and passion. This notion of what it means to be human is used in law as a standard against which to assess the actions of real people. To the extent that this vision is inaccurate, or at best partial, it distorts reality in ways that tend to maintain inherited hierarchies of power.

Legal discourse is also considered to be inherently ideological in the assumptions it embodies about itself—about law, legal practice, and legal reasoning as a distinct and autonomous way of knowing. As discussed above, in order for law to do what is required of it, it must plausibly be seen as a neutral, objective way of talking about and assessing social reality. Those considered competent in the use of legal discourse must plausibly be seen as disinterested observers of that reality. If law is ideological in the sense of being a specialized rhetoric of political discourse more generally, then it is doubly ideological precisely to the extent that it portrays itself (or users tacitly portray themselves) as otherwise.[55] It should be stressed that conventional and critical theorists are working with very different conceptions of politics.

My goal in this section has been to draw attention to some features of the raw materials, so to speak, out of which practitioners shape legal meaning and according to which inherited geographies of race are constructed and challenged. Now we will look more closely at aspects of practice itself. If legal discourse is used—or, better, deployed—in the geopolitics of race, we might want to know *how*. When we consider legal practices as particular kinds of actions by participants in some social or political event, what is it that people are actually doing? The short answer, of course, is arguing. But what is that?

Legal Argument as Political Practice

To present a legal argument is to actively participate in the process of "translation" noted above. In legal argument specialists present legal descriptions of actions, relations, events, and persons.[56] These are offered as objective determinations of what these social entities are. In legal argument, people create *renderings* of social reality in the terms received from and recognizable through legal discourse. Through analysis of actual arguments and judgments, we can examine conventional and recurring as well as novel and creative strategic moves in the making of legal meaning.

A legal argument is a piece of work, the product of deliberate interpretive labor. To engage in the practice of legal argument is to work on the raw materials provided by the inheritance that *is* legal discourse (supplemented by whatever other elements of social knowledge may be allowed). A legal argument is a complex narrative, a strategic interpretation, constructed from a particular perspective with a particular purpose in mind. The attorneys for and against Clara Mays, like those for and against the person who claimed to own Med, were trying to accomplish something. In adversarial proceedings, specialists (lawyers, including those lawyers who are judges) string together claims about reality, such as which facts are or are not legally relevant; causation and responsibility; the meaning of precedents and other cases, statutes, or constitutions; semantics and the intentions of various actors; human nature and morality; political and legal theory; reasoning and knowledge; social, political, and legal history; geography, economics, and social institutions such as courts and legislatures.[57]

Structurally these are claims about similarity and difference tied together by other claims about conditionality and entailment (a general rule: if → then; a specific application of the rule: as → therefore).[58] The resulting narratives are all strategic interpretations crafted not only to persuade or to justify or to shape someone's understanding of some state of affairs but also to make something happen. They are deliberate interventions into chains of events. They are, from our perspective, part of the events that they describe.

Where conventional views of legal argument may stress the professional search for objective truth, for an accurate description of how things really are, for the "right answer," critics emphasize the pragmatic and ultimately political aspects of practice. To examine specific performances, then, is to study actual attempts to project contested visions of social reality onto the world in order to shape the world. In litigation, lawyers try to *redefine* or *recategorize* events, relations, persons, or things in ways that, if accepted or acted upon, would most likely yield desired consequences. In the words of theorist Pierre Bourdieu, "The trial represents . . . a struggle in which differing, indeed antagonistic world views confront each other."[59]

While critics stress the politics of world-making that is inherent in *any* performance of legal discourse, these issues are sharper in those situations in which the maintenance or transformation of inherited social hierarchies is precisely the point of contention. In cases involving, for example, labor, gender, or race relations, participants must redefine these power relations in terms provided by legal discourse (for example, in terms of property, contract, or constitutional law) *while at the same time redefining the terms to fit their version of the world.*

At a finer-grained level of analysis, we can look at the specific rhetorical moves within particular argumentative performances. Here, in the examination of actual briefs and opinions, our focus is on specific claims that events, people, actions, or relations must be categorized this way rather than that, and on the rhetorical techniques through which these claims are made. To study such moves as political acts is to study the micromechanics of legal practice. This involves the examination of the precise points in an argument where, for example, contingency is portrayed as necessity, the created is portrayed as the found, the constructed as the natural or the political as the nonpolitical, and so on.[60] It is in reference to actions such as these that we can locate the politics of depoliticization within legal practice. The focus on the microtechniques of legal reasoning—tactics within larger legal-political strategies—gives substance to the idea that things could be other than they are, that is, that the possible is not exhausted by the actual. It is also to reveal the workings of culturally and historically significant acts of power in the creation or transformation of the conditions of social life. These conditions, of course, may include the spatial conditions of social life: the *spatiality* of social relational power.

Working on the Legal Landscape

As indicated earlier, legal landscapes can be thought of as geographies of power described in terms of legal discourse. The mosaic of crisscrossing lines and overlapping spaces effects a complex system of sociospatial differentiation. Geographies of race are literally coextensive with and, in a sense, embedded in these legal landscapes. As was also mentioned earlier, the component parts of the legal landscape—the lots of real estate, the areas of public space, the various units of jurisdiction, and so on—confer meaning on lived-in landscapes. To talk about legal landscapes in the sense offered here is to suggest a fusion of meaning (the meaning of power) and space (the spatiality of power). Our discussion of legal practice suggests some idea of how this fusion is attempted and provisionally accomplished. We can now ask more directly some of the central questions addressed by this book: How are the specific practices associated with legal reasoning involved in conflicts over geographies of race? How is legal meaning mapped onto the world in ways that perpetuate or weaken racism?

In order to get at these questions, I will suggest that there are, in a sense, two legal landscapes—or two aspects of a singular landscape. The first of these I've already introduced. This is the physical, visible legal landscape composed of a mosaic of territorial units such as property lots, public and private spaces, jurisdictions, and other legal spaces, as well as the lines and boundaries and borders that define the spaces. This legal landscape effects a *spatial system of differentiation*. It may be given more visible form by fences, walls, doors, gates, border crossings, and signs. This is the lived-in, on-the-ground geography of power in which you, the reader, are now sitting. The other legal landscape (or the other aspect of the legal landscape) is the conceptual, abstract—indeed metaphysical—spatiality that is integral to legal discourse itself.

This *conceptual system of differentiation* consists of concepts and categories (such as the *concept* "property"); and of conceptual boundaries or categorical distinctions (such as the boundaries between the concept "property" and the concept "state" or between "law" and "politics"). It consists also of other elements such as the boundary around the concept "equality"—manipulation of which can yield broad or narrow construals of power—or the boundary between state and federal power. This is a landscape of metaphorical limits, such as the limits of law itself, and of zones and spheres of authority or autonomy. This landscape is a conceptual configuration of metaphorical lines and spaces according to which claims of similarity and difference, *conceptual* inclusion or exclusion, are themselves made meaningful. This conceptual map is an abstract *representation* of constellations of social relations of power. It is not simply a way of talking about power but a principal way in which power is conceptualized. In those situations when the topic of a dispute or argument is the legal meaning of geographies of power then this map may be considered to be a *representation* of the spatiality of social life. This map is no less complex than are the material geographies of power in which we live our lives. It is no less *real*. It is no less the dynamic, contradictory, never finished product of intergenerational labor.

As a practical matter, the activities of legal argument and legal reasoning are among the most significant ways of "working" on this map. Interpretation is an active, creative procedure. In advancing an interpretation of the conceptual system, one works on the received categories. One manipulates conceptual boundaries—in a phrase, one draws lines. This activity is most clearly visible in the detailed strategic rhetorical maneuvers that constitute legal arguments. In the case of Med, for example, we saw how understandings of the application of comity was contingent on whether a slave was categorized as an exceptional or nonexceptional form of property, and how this categorization in turn was grounded in a distinction between natural and positive law.

The geographies of power in which lives are lived are *made* meaningful, in part, through these acts of interpretation. To ask how this meaning is made is to inquire how the conceptual system itself is maintained or transformed in practice. In those situations involving the geopolitics of social life and in those geopolitical situations in which legal action is a component of political strategy, these interpretive practices should be seen as forms of geopolitical practice. In these contexts participants create contending versions of the abstract map of the legal landscape in order to effect "on-the-ground" transformations of geographies of power. They engage in interpretive work *on the representation* in order to affect that which is represented.

Legal argument is also like cartographic mapping in that it is an attempt to reduce the complexity and ambiguity of the world to plausible, practical simplifications and clarifications. But there are many ways to simplify and clarify or to *construe*.[61] What is important for us is that divergent construals may have radically different consequences for real people, to the extent that they simplify and clarify one way rather than another. The possible construals put forth in legal argument can be considered alternative renderings of the legal landscape.

What is important for an accurate understanding of practice here is that what distinguishes each of these renderings or conceptual maps is how (or where) these metaphorical lines are drawn. Further, as there is a *translation* from a concern for actual experience and power to the abstract map of law, so there is, as a result of judgment, a *re*translation from these conceptual boundaries back to spatial boundaries—the meaning of lines and spaces on the ground.[62] This is what space means. The study of the practice is a demonstration of *how* space means or is given meaning. Because the social meaning of space is conceptualized in terms of rights, then these spatial boundaries translate to social boundaries or the limits of social actions.

So far I've been referring to argument as a piece of work or the product of reasoning and rhetoric. Arguments are crafted with the objective of persuasion in mind. What people are trying to do with argument is produce meaning. But, of course, legal argument in an adversarial system such as ours is a somewhat more specialized and peculiar endeavor. It takes place in the context of disagreement and conflict. It is, in some understandings, a substitute for violence and, in other understandings, a form of violence.[63] In any event, legal argument involves direct opposition. In any formal legal argument—i.e., litigation—there are at least two competing arguments in the sense used above. There are two contending interpretations of law and fact and their relationship. In any juridical geopolitical conflict, there are two divergent construals of the meaning of space, two incompatible renderings of the legal landscape. When read side by side, it can be seen how each takes account of the other. One version foregrounds what the other might ignore; one participant puts at the center of the argument what the opposing side would marginalize.

In terms of the structure and rhetoric of argument, our attention is drawn over and over again to the tactical practices of categorization and countercategorization, or the politics of meaning. Each one of an unmatched pair differs in what she or he proposes as the relevant categories through which reality is to be understood and in how the small set of relevant categories are related to each other. While they may agree on the relevant categories, they will differ on whether some aspect of "law" or "world" fits the category. What plaintiffs contend is a rule, defendants portray as an exception or exemption. Where one urges that crucial differences be acknowledged and distinctions drawn between the case at hand and earlier cases, the opponent stresses fundamental similarities and denies that any relevant distinction exists. If one party insists on a broad or liberal understanding of this statute or that clause in the Constitution, the other side will claim that only a narrow or strictly literal reading will be consistent with justice. Each, as we noted, is drawing lines, but they are different lines. Each is manipulating conceptual boundaries but molding them into different configurations. Each is forming meaning differently so as to produce a different conceptual map of power. But only one of these maps can be followed.

Given the real constraints on legal practice—that is, many argumentative strategies that would be possible elsewhere simply will not work in court—there remains, in theory, an infinite number of possible, plausible interpretations. In practice, though, some well-crafted arguments are less likely than others to persuade the particular audience—judges. Nonetheless, various renderings in a given case are encountered not only in the clash between attorneys for defendants and plaintiffs but also between lower court opinions and appellate court reversals and between majority and dissenting opinions in the higher courts. These are especially revealing at the Supreme Court level. While the transformation from a wider (geo)political conflict to a narrower legal dispute entails a shift in focus from the world to the map—or from the concrete to the abstract—there is more than one way to effect the translation. There is a range of plausible, practical maps. And while all participants seek to simplify the complex and to clarify the ambiguous through argument, there are a number of alternative ways of doing this too. While each legal argument necessarily distorts some aspect of reality by trying to squeeze it into what can be accommodated by a small set of legal categories, each distorts in different ways. Different bits of reality get filtered out or factored in. In our legal culture, control over meaning often yields control over (relevant parts of) the world.

The moves we want to follow are those from meaning to rules, from rules to boundaries, and from boundaries to the exercise and experience of power. But of course a fundamental aspect of power itself is the power to create meaning in the first place—the power to name.[64]

Concluding Remarks

It may seem as though this excursion into the bush of legal theory in search of the tactics of legal reasoning has taken us far from the concerns of Med, Clara Mays, and Blyden Jackson—or even W. D. Binford. In a sense it has and in a sense it hasn't. And that is the point. It seems likely that few of the inhabitants of geographies of race—or other geographies of power—care much about the subtleties of doctrine or the technicalities of legal meaning. What most of us care about is experience or what it's like to be in the world. Yet it is precisely in these subtleties and technicalities or nuances that room for maneuver is opened up or closed off. Why, one might ask, should Med's experience of being returned to bondage be contingent on understandings of the conceptual limits of comity? Why should Clara Mays' suffering depend on which of various understandings of the doctrine of changed conditions should find favor with the guy called judge? Culturally speaking, one might answer, "This is simply how we do these kinds of things here."[65] This is by no means the only method of reconfiguring social geographies, but historically speaking it is an important one. It is in the interplay between competing legal interpretations that a person will find himself categorized one way rather than another. And it is in reference to differences between categories (slave/free; owner/nonowner) that rights as a kind of social power are distributed and enforced—by authorized violence if necessary. Experiences—episodes in the biographies of real people—have been profoundly shaped by the kinds of social practices we've been discussing. What I've tried to do in this initial orientation is provide a way of thinking about connections between meaning and the world that takes history (change) and politics (power and desire) into account. It is important to emphasize, though, that legal practice has been important to efforts *both* to reinforce relations of domination and to challenge them. In the service of emancipation, practitioners of the craft of legal reasoning have used legal language to imagine a world more conducive to equality and human flourishing, and to try to bring that world, piece by piece, into being.

Geographies of Slavery
and Emancipation

In this chapter we bring the focus of our study down to earth, so to speak, by examining some of the connections between geographies of power and geographies of experience in the context of racial politics in the United States in the nineteenth century. My objective here is simply to describe key elements of the spatial configurations that were integral to slavery and to the racial order that emerged in the generation following emancipation. Our topics are continuity and change in the geopolitics of race and in geographies of race and racism. The kinds of specifically legal concerns treated in chapter 1, while in a sense ubiquitous, are a decidedly minor theme here but will be placed in the foreground in chapter 3.

Geopolitical actions can be seen here in the attempts by various people to effect spatial or geographical solutions to different social or political problems—that is, problems with or about power. Different groups of people perceived different problems and proposed different solutions. Indeed, what was seen as a solution for some was seen as a problem for others. Geographies of power and experience bore the traces of these political struggles. Of particular importance for understanding the unfolding of the geopolitics of race in this period was the interplay between (largely white) territoriality and (largely black) mobility.

The Spatiality of Slavery in the United States

This account begins on the ground, which is to say on the plantations and farms where the vast majority of black people lived and worked as slaves. It begins at a time when geographies of racism had already been

established for more than 150 years in some places, were only beginning to
be constructed in other places such as the Old Southwestern Territories of
Alabama and Mississippi, and were being substantially revised in yet others
such as the northeastern states. Moreover, these shifts should also be seen
in a more global geographical context that involved the activities of international slave traders in Africa, Europe, and the Caribbean. In addition,
by 1800 some aspects of social relations with respect to race had been almost literally "constituted" by the document that joined the several states
together in political union. One instrument for the interpretive restructuring of space that would figure prominently in the conflicts of future generations was Article 4, Section 2, of the U.S. Constitution concerning fugitives from labor and the Fugitive Slave Laws of 1793 and 1850 enacted
under this provision.[1] For the overwhelming majority of U.S. slaves, these
elements of a larger geography of slavery were of little immediate significance except to the extent that the shifting spatial morphology of slavery—
that is, the extension of slave-based agricultural production into the Southwest—stimulated domestic trade and migration. In these respects, the
geography of slavery can be seen to have been shaped by the lives of those
forced to move.

A geography of slavery in the United States has never been written. There
are, however, innumerable geographical facts implicit in the massive historical literature on the topic and thousands of geographical stories to be
found in the testimonies and narratives of those whose lives were shaped
by slavery.[2] A geographical understanding of slavery in the United States
might be reached by a number of different approaches. Here I'll sketch
three elements that would be important to such an understanding. The first
element situates U.S. slavery in a global context and considers the geographical foundations of slavery in mainland North America. It focuses on
transformations in world geographies in the seventeenth and eighteenth
centuries and rests on an understanding of the processes of European colo-
nialism and shifting patterns of international trade and traffic in slaves,
sugar, and tobacco. This is a geography of connections and commodity
flows which bound together four continents, and a changing geography of
regional specialization within the emerging world economy.[3] This is also a
geography of severance whose central fact was the involuntary migration
of, ultimately, millions of Africans. An enduring legacy of this geography
of motion was the creation of "race" along the coasts, inland waterways,

and offshore islands of what for black and white was truly the New World, and for indigenous peoples was simply the world.[4]

A second element of the historical geography of U.S. slavery describes the shifting spatial morphology of slavery. Key themes here are the gradual spread of slavery as a solution to labor problems among European Americans and the acceptance of slavery throughout the British colonies. The history of gradual dissipation in the North and consolidation in the South, coupled with the westward drift of the "frontier"—itself a color line of sorts—shows a shifting morphology of contraction and expansion. Appreciation of this morphological change is crucial to an understanding of the politics of slavery, especially in the mid-nineteenth century. It represented a central dynamic that was expressed in political terms as the "territorial question," "sectionalism," and "compromise." One attempt to crystallize this fluid morphology of slavery was expressed in political geographic terms as "the Confederate States of America."

A third, and subtler, element necessary for an understanding of the historical geography of U.S. slavery concerns the spatial variation *within* that shifting morphology. This approach was advocated and initiated by Ira Berlin in his important 1980 article "Time, Space, and the Evolution of Afro-American Society on British Mainland North America."[5] Berlin argues there that post-1960s (revisionist) historical treatments viewed slavery as a rather static and invariable social system, that they tended to hold "time constant and ignored the influence of place."[6] He demonstrates that the institution of slavery changed a great deal throughout the seventeenth and eighteenth centuries and varied significantly from place to place at any one time. Equally variable was what it meant or was like to be a slave. Recognition of this variation matters not only to how we understand the dynamics and different trajectories of place-specific versions of slavery (in his sample, New York, Chesapeake, and the South Carolina Sea Islands), but also, according to Berlin, to how we understand the historical diversity of Afro-American culture. Significant demographic variables here were local variations in the relative proportion of white to black, of free to slave, and of U.S.-born to African.

The variations that Berlin stresses in the seventeenth- and eighteenth-century coastal contexts multiplied and sharpened through the nineteenth century. At a gross level of generalization, increasing differences between the Upper and Lower South (related in part to the changing economies of tobacco, rice, sugar, and especially cotton production), between the older and newer Souths (which figured in the growth of the domestic slave trade), and between the slaveholding and nonslaveholding areas within the region led to an increasingly variegated geography of slavery. Superimposed on this geography were increasing differences in the practices of slavery in rural and urban contexts and differences in the development of black communities and race relations generally in different cities like New Orleans, Charleston, Washington, Louisville, and Baltimore.[7]

This approach to a geography of slavery in the United States can become increasingly more richly textured. The examination of interaction among these three elements of a conventional geographic perspective would bring to light a large degree of complexity and be suggestive of new insights in the dynamics of historical change. Part of what follows is, in fact, an elaboration of this project. One of the themes to be explored is the creation and control of geographical variation.

The approach to a geography of U.S. slavery that I've suggested thus far focuses on spatial networks, distributions, patterns, and forms. This is a limitation. It treats slavery as a thing, or at least the kind of thing, like cotton or magnolias, that can be easily mapped. Again, my principal purpose here is to convey some sense of the ways in which spatial configurations—meaningful lines and spaces—that were integral to slavery were constructed. Tracing the shifting frontier of slavery as a mode of agricultural production is one thing; tracing shifts in the ways in which meaning and power are spatialized is a different task altogether. Slavery was a way of doing things, a complex set of institutions. It was a system of beliefs—and of passionately conflicting beliefs. It was a way of looking at the world, an ideology, a form of consciousness, an element in one's understanding of self-identity. It was an "issue." The world of slavery was not simply a "culture region." It had—or was considered to have had—a logic which defied spatial confinement.[8] It didn't have, and for reasons to be discussed in chapter 3, could not have had, clear boundaries. The "whereness" of slavery was a question of conflicting beliefs. In a sense, slavery existed in Boston, Philadelphia, Ohio, and Minnesota in the 1850s as surely as it did in South Carolina and Texas, much to the disgust, frustration, or comfort of contemporaries. Moreover, it is important to add, this sense was a legal sense.[9]

Above all, slavery was about extremely asymmetrical relations of power. It was about the control of individual masters over individual slaves, of whites generally over the lives of blacks, and of some whites over others. The politics of control with respect to slavery could not be isolated from the politics of anything else. It entered into the politics of county agricultural societies, the politics of railroads, the politics of international relations. Moreover, as "totalizing" as the spatiality of slavery most assuredly was, it was also, as many scholars have stressed, extremely contradictory. The contradictions that infused these geographies made them complex, ambiguous, and ultimately unstable.

On the "Homeplace"

The centerpiece of the spatiality of slavery, and experientially the center of the world for most of those most intimately involved in this way of life, was the plantation or farm. While most slaveholders owned fewer than five slaves, most nineteenth-century slaves lived on plantations with from twenty to more than one thousand slaves.[10] And while the existence and experiences of scattered and isolated rural slaves, urban slaves, and free blacks created a more variegated geography of race, plantation life produced the most salient aspects of the world the slaves and slaveholders made together.[11]

The plantation—like slavery itself—was many things. It was a rural factory, it was a political institution, it was a community, it was real estate. As a legal space carved out of the world, it had characteristics of both property and state. As property it could be bought, sold, mortgaged, inherited, subdivided, or consolidated. Edgar Thompson in his *Plantation Societies, Race Relations, and the South*, however, refers to the plantation as "a miniature state" or a "submultiple of a larger state," defined in the conventional way as the conjunction of territory and a monopoly on the legitimate use of violence.[12] Consideration of the plantation as a microstate allows us to look at communities of people and more complex sets of social relations than is suggested by the simple relation of a master and a slave. This, in turn, allows us to recognize an intelligible form of politics within these relations.[13]

The internal spatial differentiation of plantations was created first and foremost with issues of control in mind. It therefore facilitated the maintenance of prevailing relations of power. However, it also accommodated some small measures of autonomy, solidarity, and self-determination on terms other than those mandated unilaterally by slaveholders. The spatial organization of plantation life—and so the social landscape of slavery— found its most immediate material expression in the arrangement of living and working spaces. The big house (which frequently was not so big), the slave quarters, the shops and outbuildings, the fields, gardens, and fences, as an ensemble of features, sustained an order of discipline and control as well as relative if tenuous security and community. The slave quarters, located away from the big house—sometimes at a distance of a few hundred yards, sometimes in different settlements scattered around the plantation—provided a measure of autonomy within which the slave community developed.[14] Most often consisting of wooden shacks, the cabins were sometimes arrayed along a tree-lined avenue. Set off from the others, in spatial expression of both social commonality and distance, might be the cabin of the driver or black foreman and his family, or the white overseer or manager.

It is important that we neither disregard nor overemphasize the significance of the spatial arrangement of the slave quarters. For while the cabins in principle were simply part of the planter's domain, most planters usually recognized that a portion of their slaves' days and a portion of the plantation belonged to them. This, at minimum, distinguishes plantation slavery from other "total institutions" like concentration camps and, beyond that, draws attention to the literal spaces which sustained family life, communal religious life, and intergenerational education. On the other hand, the degree of autonomy and stability of these communities was fixed and modified at the discretion of the planters and depended on the vagaries of paternalistic philosophy, psychological stability, and market forces for their maintenance.[15]

The spatial organization of the plantation also reflected divisions of labor which, in turn, were connected to a degree of social differentiation within the slave community. This was especially true with respect to house slaves and field hands. Again, the dimensions of this differentiation should not be exaggerated. It was important, however, that field hands generally had more opportunity to remove themselves from the direct observation of whites and that house slaves had the mixed blessing of more intimate association with the planter's family and more familiarity with the wider world. Differences in situation, in part based on a spatial-social division of labor, generated a complex politics within the paternalistic order of the plantation and engendered variations in possible forms of resistance and accommodation.[16]

As important as "everyday resistance" might have been to the social dynamics of plantation life, slavery was, after all, slavery. The overwhelming feature of the spatiality of slavery was that it was designed by whites in order to control blacks. It was a geography of discipline and confinement and, for most slaves, extremely limited mobility. Normally, slaves were confined to the plantation—or rather, to specific parts of the plantation. Occasionally they were confined to "jails" on the plantation or shipped off to local workhouses.[17] Often they were physically restrained. Such extreme physical immobilization worked to discipline "insubordinate" blacks and created an experienced contrast with the "normal" rhythms of daily life which at least permitted a relative degree of freedom of association.

These facts of life highlight the statelike features of the plantation. The planter was the creator, interpreter, and enforcer of law. And though these last two "law jobs" were frequently delegated to overseers and drivers, such delegations were sometimes codified in written regulations that Thompson has referred to as "constitutions."[18] We see here also something that looks like rights in the provisions for "appeals" of harsh or arbitrary actions of intermediaries in the plantation hierarchy.[19] Planters and slaves together also created a form of civil law in the ceremonies of marriage and in the property and contract notions that governed garden plots and self-hiring. With respect to marriage and "family law," such as it was, what the planter drew together he could and frequently did put asunder through the sale of a husband or wife. Here, finally, was perhaps the most painful of the many controls the planter could exercise over the experiential geographies of slaves: the threat of effective banishment from the community of family and friends. If a slave were sold—or traded or lent—to a nearby relative or friend, communal and emotional ties could perhaps be maintained through regular "visitations." If, however, an insubordinate slave was sold away to the speculators and traders, she might have to face another version of the middle passage and another New World.

An adequate understanding of the spatiality of slavery, and so the geopolitics of slavery, must also take account of the paternalistic ideology that shaped much of the social understandings of the participants in the regime. Eugene Genovese claims that "for the slaveholders paternalism represented an attempt to overcome the fundamental contradiction in slavery: the impossibility of the slaves ever becoming the things they were supposed to be."[20] It entered into the social construction of spatiality in the recognition that slaves did have lives—and often family obligations—beyond the bounds of the plantation, in the relative but tenuous autonomy of the quarters and in the meaning of the plantation itself as a (relative) space of protection and welfare.

Paternalism was an ideological expression of the recognition of the mutual dependence of masters and slaves. This awareness "transformed a doctrine of absolute property and absolute will into a doctrine of reciprocity."[21] As such, its inscription onto the landscape that people inhabited made geographies of power more complex. The obvious meaning of the spatiality of slavery was, in fact, somewhat more questionable.

The Wider Spatial Distribution of Power

The plantation occupied a central place in the social geography of U.S. slavery, but it was not the only place. There was a wider world beyond the fields and quarters. The geographies of power which characterized this more extensive landscape were also important influences on the conditions of social life. Situating the plantation within the wider community and the hierarchy of political-legal spaces within which it was embedded serves to illustrate the nuances and complexities of the geographies of power that slaves had to navigate. It also raises questions about the boundedness of power, the meaning of lines, and what it meant to cross a line.

Beyond the plantation itself, the most immediate elements of the geography of power were structured by the matrix of neighboring plantations and perhaps towns.[22] Together they constituted an obvious spatial distribution of power that was of critical significance to the slaves. Planters and whites generally, though, lived in a still wider world. While their lives primarily revolved around largely localized and provincial concerns, notions of their place in the universe were to a greater extent shaped by knowledge that events further afield—in county seats and state capitals, Washington, the North, foreign markets, etc.—had local consequences. In a sense whites and blacks, and especially planters and slaves, lived in different though concentric worlds. Moreover, these worlds were organized according to different principles.

The wider world in which most slaves lived was formed around the social networks that existed among slaves who lived on plantations near each other. These networks grew through the relative stability of those who had lived in a general locale for a long time. A slave on one plantation might have relatives on different neighboring plantations. Often slaves would be hired out to work for other planters, for "public work" projects such as building roads or dikes, or for other collective endeavors. Church also provided occasions for slaves from different plantations to form friendships and acquaintances. This wider world allowed relationships to be formed with whites outside of the planter's family, including other planters, merchants, and poor whites. Slaves also often had an intimate knowledge of the local physical landscape, especially those who hunted and fished or gathered wild foodstuffs and materials—either as duty or for their own ends. This then constituted a wider world of knowledge, of reputation, of connections. Even in relatively isolated areas like the Sea Islands, information and facets of oral culture could be transmitted over rather long distances. Hence references to "the grapevine" in the narratives.[23]

Among the most important features of the wider world that shaped slaves' understandings of their situation was knowledge that conditions varied significantly from plantation to plantation. Nearly everyone knew of planters who were either more lenient or more severe than their own: planters who rarely if ever used the whip, and those who used it often and arbitrarily; planters whose sense of paternalism included strong recognition of the importance of family life, and those who denied that slaves were even capable of deep emotional attachments; planters who believed that a slave's time off was her own and those who didn't; planters who generously gave permission to visit neighboring plantations and those who thought that such extravagances undermined their authority.[24] Those who didn't know of situations both palpably better and worse than their own were either extremely fortunate or unimaginably desperate. In any case, even these people knew that local plantation law varied, and that those in other situations were by degrees better or worse off than themselves. This was an intimate kind of legal geographic sense or consciousness that was attuned to variations from place to place and according to which their own place acquired meaning. It was also a politically significant kind of knowledge to the extent that it provided real and imagined "examples" of other possibilities, again both better and worse.

From the point of view of the planters, objective examples of worse conditions on neighboring plantations might be thought to underline their own beneficence in the eyes of "their people." However, the example of "free slaves," that is, those with relatively fewer restrictions, was extremely disquieting.[25] Such examples were thought to breed dissatisfaction or insubordination. And too, there was the always present fear of insurrection or individual acts of violence like murder or arson which exposure to these "examples" might inspire. Variation in what was effectively local law of plantations within a larger community was not the issue so much as what slaves made of the knowledge of that variation, that is, how it might influence the dynamics of power relations within the plantation itself. Because of this, such variation from place to place was itself perceived of as a "problem," and as such it shaped relations among the planters in the wider political world in which they lived. In the words of one planter,

> Everyone must see the evils that grow out of a want of uniformity in government on those plantations in the same vicinity. For instance, here is a planter who enforces strict discipline on his plantation, while on the other side of the cross fence is one whose discipline is loose and irregular—Negroes as free as the master. Now who does not see that the government, or rather the want of government on the part of the latter will engender discontent and subordination [sic] among the slaves of the former? [26]

The more extensive off-plantation world of slaves also created opportunities for a richer social life and for another small degree of both collective and individual autonomy vis-à-vis "their white folk." Conventionally, interplantation visits were allowed on Saturday and Wednesday nights, but again practice varied from plantation to plantation. Visiting was especially important in the case of interplantation marriages. The practice of male slaves having "broad wives" (spouses on other plantations) was widespread and, according to Genovese, may have been the most common conjugal relationship in some areas. [27] The slaves themselves related the significance of the greater freedom of movement that interplantation relations afforded. There were, of course, obvious disadvantages associated with falling in love with or marrying someone who was considered to be the legal property of another, and these were exacerbated when the relationship depended on the wills, financial stability, or luck of two planters. In many cases though, the spatial conditions of black family life cut across the rigid geography of power represented by plantation boundaries. In the words of Genovese, "the slaves had transformed the ghastly conditions under which they labored into living space within which they could love each other." [28] However, because every visit required specific permission of both slaveholders or their overseers, denial effectively meant confinement. That is, the world in which one's family lived could be opened up or closed off for any reason.

Again, for some slaveholders and whites more generally, the interplantation mobility of slaves was seen as a problem and a threat to order.[29]

There was another element to the geographies of power and experience that shaped the social life of U.S. slaves. This element derived from the embeddedness of plantations within more extensive political spaces and contributed to a more complex understanding of the boundedness of power. Before the Revolution, more or less elaborate "slave codes" had been promulgated in those colonies which had large slave populations. By the nineteenth century, they were simply an integral part of the social system of control. In some respects, the slave codes of the various states, as well as more local municipal ordinances, were directed toward mitigating these two essentially geographical problems: spatial variation in plantation law and slave mobility.

With respect to the former, slave codes represented checks on the absolute discretion of slaveholders.[30] Their prohibitions on "lenient" treatment (e.g., giving slaves relative freedom of movement, teaching them how to read and write, manumission) were more conspicuous than restrictions on cruelty. Socially, the slave codes represented a collective attempt among slaveholders to discipline their members. Spatially, slave codes can be seen as an attempt to diminish interplantation variability within a given jurisdiction or to counterpose spatial variation with a degree of uniformity over a more extensive territory. Whether or not slave codes were effective in this regard is open to interpretation. Some planters complained about the corrosive effect that the example of someone else's "free slaves" had on order and discipline. Some planters did allow slaves to become literate, to hire themselves out, or to be "effectively" emancipated without formal procedures. Other planters, though, went to considerable effort and expense to comply with the codes. And, on occasion, codes were enforced and planters were fined.[31]

Probably few slaves were aware of the existence of statutory law governing the contours of their relations with planters. However, as evinced by the prominence assigned them in their narratives, they were acutely aware of passes and patrollers.[32] The state codes required a slave to have a written pass whenever he was "beyond the limits of the plantation" on which he resided.[33] Typically, the pass was valid for a limited duration and named the bearer and the destination. The code, and particularly the pass provision, was enforced by the slave patrol. Patrols "amounted to a sort of military draft" and, in the early 1800s, members were "appointed" by the captain of the local militia.[34] In South Carolina, for example, all white males between eighteen and forty-five were eligible. In all states, shirkers could and sometimes would be fined. Patrols were organized territorially into "beats," which, according to Williamson, is still the colloquial word for townships in parts of the South.[35] It appears that the primary duties of the patrols were simply riding the roads at night looking for "suspicious slaves in suspicious places," making sure that any slave found out of bounds had a pass, and whipping any who didn't. However, formally they were also allowed to search the plantations and slave quarters themselves. Court cases cited by state historians of slavery and by Catterall indicate that patrols did occasionally go onto the plantations and that planters considered such actions to be invasions of their sovereignty.[36]

One picture that emerges from scanty secondary sources and from the views of planters is that the patrols often consisted of disorderly and drunk whites who had no respect for property, or, according to one planter, "a parcel of boys or little men, the height of whose ambition is to 'ketch a nigger.'"[37] An interesting example that shows the sometimes ambiguous boundedness of power is seen in the case of *Hervey v. Armstrong*, in which a planter sued members of a patrol for "damaging" his slaves by whipping them as they were returning from a religious meeting.[38] The patrol had been organized for Jefferson Township, but the meeting and "punishment" had both occurred in Marion Township. Armstrong had argued that by crossing the town line the patrol had exceeded its jurisdiction. The Arkansas Supreme Court agreed that the power of a patrol was "confined to the township for which it was appointed." However, it also held that Armstrong had failed to prove that his property had actually been damaged.

The picture that emerges from slave narratives is one of simple terrorism. The world beyond the plantation at night was a world of dogs and bullwhips. It was a world of white men on horses whose ferocity was unchecked by either paternalism or self-interest in protecting one's investment. And while the first-hand accounts of being whipped by the patrols while off the plantation without a pass tell us something about geographies of power and the spatial conditions of violence, they also tell us that slaves took more freedom than they were allowed and that they navigated these geographies of power according to their own lights. Some of the testimony, however, emphasizes the relative security of the plantation and differentiates the planter as protector from white terrorists more generally.[39] On this view, the line that defined the plantation also separated relative security from terror, and so reinforced the boundedness of power within. This also represented a spatialization of the ideology of paternalism.

The meaning of the line which set the plantation off from the world beyond was thus more complex than might at first be imagined. It can also be noted here that this line also marked the distinction between a merely insubordinate slave and a fugitive. Given the existence of the patrols throughout slave-holding areas and of professional slave catchers beyond, the decision to escape into the woods, into the cities, or further "into freedom" by following the North Star required a clear assessment of what risks might be entailed by crossing a line.[40]

The spatiality of U.S. slavery was centered on the plantation and was chiefly concerned with control—control of a planter over slaves, control of planters as a class over their less diligent members, and control of whites generally over the lives of blacks. Sometimes these different relations would create tensions, as between planters and the patrols or among planters. For the most part throughout the antebellum decades, these tensions were contained—at least within the worlds in which most of the participants lived—and this geography of power was remarkably stable, though not static. Other problems which threatened the stability of the social order were perceived around its edges, however. These brought into increasingly clear focus the fact that it had no sharp edges. Eventually, in the 1840s and 1850s, *the* issue in politics in the United States became precisely the boundedness of power with respect to U.S. slavery.

Many slaves also had experience in a still wider world, beyond the plantation and beyond the locale. Some slaves even in the 1850s carried with them memories of Africa; others, of Barbados or Santo Domingo. Most slaves in the nineteenth century were born in the United States, and the curtailment of the international slave trade gradually diminished the number of slaves who could recall these other worlds.[41] Many more slaves gained experience of the wider world through the domestic slave trade or by having migrated to other areas with their masters. Many of these people also carried memories of a home to which they hoped to return.[42] Still others saw more of the world by accompanying slaveholders on their travels for business or pleasure. This kind of experience was related to the division of labor in that it was limited to house servants and perhaps artisans. The scope of such travels varied with the circumstances of the planter. Travels around the South, perhaps to Charleston, New Orleans, Richmond, or Washington, were more likely than, say, trips to Boston, England, or France, but these were not unheard of.[43] However, as we saw in chapter 1 with Med, depending upon where one went, very strange things could happen.

A slave, for example, upon arriving in Philadelphia or Boston or Cincinnati could be approached and spirited away by abolitionists, or her master served a writ of habeas corpus. Within a few days she could be declared legally free. Or, believing that simply being brought across the Mason-Dixon line conferred freedom, she could refuse to cross it again and so refuse to be brought back into bondage. In a very real sense "freedom" and "bondage" were actual places in the world. Some slaves were no doubt surprised to learn that the meaning of the line wasn't always so clear, and on crossing the line between Kentucky and Ohio or Maryland and Pennsylvania (having assumed that it meant crossing from slavery into freedom), found themselves delivered back into bondage by sheriffs or magistrates.

These kinds of experiences were exceedingly rare and, compared to the numbers of those held to slavery and those other free or "quasi-free" blacks in the United States, few people were directly involved in actually shaping the margins of slavery in these ways with their lives. And while living through the ordeals of escape, recapture, kidnapping, or rescue was undoubtedly of profound biographical significance in itself,[44] the political and geopolitical significance of such stories was proportionately more significant than the numbers would suggest. What was at stake, or considered to be at stake, was what these events seemed to indicate about transformations in geographies of power and what these transformations seemed to indicate about radical changes in the conditions of social life. The geopolitics of slavery and of race in Cincinnati, Boston, and Kansas were, therefore, quite different from the geopolitics of slavery on the plantation in Arkansas, in Burke County, North Carolina, or in Louisville, Kentucky, as each in detail was different from the others. They involved the actions of different people with different interests, passions, and world views. However, all of these local geopolitical conflicts were also contiguous. It was, too, a contiguity which derived in part from claims by slaveholders that the power they held over slaves was *literally* almost boundless. This claim, in turn, was supported by an understanding of the legal landscape and of inherited geographies of power that were seen to confer affirmative duties on all citizens of the United States to recognize the rights of masters. These claims were refuted by those who sought ultimately to abolish slavery but more immediately—and as a means toward that ultimate end—to confine it to what were then called the slaveholding states.[45] In advancing these claims and in refuting them, actors were participating in the political construction of scale. The abolitionists and their tactical allies were, of course, part of one of the largest social movements in U.S. history. As will be discussed more thoroughly in chapter 3, one of the principal tools deployed by abolitionists in their attempts to shape the geography of power with respect to slavery was litigation and legal argument.[46]

All of these aspects of the late antebellum geopolitics of slavery were played out throughout the South and the North as proslavery people and their allies and antislavery people and their allies interpreted the meaning of these events—or whatever subset constituted for different people a coherent chain of events—and constructed different geopolitical scenarios according to their different understandings. The issue was precisely the changing spatial morphology of slavery and the boundedness of power which shaped and was defined by this morphology. For many white Americans, by the late 1850s the conditions under which black people lived and labored were decidedly a secondary issue. Many white northerners began to see the principal objective of the slavocracy as dominating them, just as they were seen to dominate nonslaveholding southerners.[47] They saw the spatial strategy of the South as involving, first, the obliteration of the line between freedom and slavery in the East, and so the imposition of slavery on them directly; and second, the use of the federal government, particularly the Supreme Court, to close off the territories to "free white labor," thus effecting their own policy of containment. This view became associated with and was fostered by the emerging Republican Party. Proslavery actors and their northern allies who considered the principal geopolitical question to involve the consequences of disunion regarded any interference or "intervention" as an invitation to the southern states to secede.

In whatever way the events of the late 1850s were construed and however different the ideological maps that were generated, common to all of them was a core assumption about the spatial logic of slavery in the United States: if it were contained it would die. The basis of this assumption was that control exercised by masters over slaves on the plantation depended on the exercise of control of slaveholders as a class and their allies over all of the larger spaces within which the plantations were embedded. A key element of this more extensive control involved the spatial distribution of political power in the federal government, particularly the Senate. The annexation of Texas and conquest of Mexico (with prospective admission of new states and resultant enlargement of the Senate) brought this element into sharper focus. In this context control over the plantations was seen to depend more particularly on control of the territories.[48]

In any case, people acted in accordance with their interpretation of the connections between the changing geography of slavery and desired conditions of social life. Rarely in U.S. history (with the notable exception of the "removal and pacification" of Native Americans, which was also part of the territorial questions of the day) was the construction of contending geographies of power a more explicit project. After the Republican victories in 1858 and 1860, slaveholders made the ultimate geopolitical move of inventing an *international* boundary embracing the Confederate States of America.[49] In many areas the consequences of this strategy quickly came home to the plantations and quarters. As slaveholders, overseers, and patrollers laid down the bullwhips, picked up their guns, and marched off to glory, many black people began building new geographies of power within the plantations and the larger communities. From 1861 to 1865, the line between freedom and slavery was drawn primarily by the movements of Union troops. Initially this was not the intention of those directing the movements. It was, instead, the meaning imposed on the line by black people themselves, who left nearby farms and plantations by the thousands and crossed out of slavery and into an uncertain future.[50]

In this section I've tried to sketch some of the key elements that constituted the distinctive spatiality of nineteenth-century U.S. slavery. This spatial expression of power was the complex invention of those who inhabited it. It was very much a world that slaves, slaveholders, and many others made together. A crucial part of this process of invention, of course, was the ongoing creation of meaning. It was this social relational meaning that was crafted and revised through the generations. Many of the social practices involved in the recasting of inherited social relational meaning go by the name of politics. These political actions included the formal official politics associated with legislation, but they also included the micropolitics of intra- and interplantation relations: the face-to-face negotiations and compromises, acts of resistance, brutality and kindness through which experiential meaning is formed. Much of this was conceptualized in terms of rights—that is, legal consciousness. Among planters, rights and responsibilities were derived from conceptions of property and jurisdiction. Among slaves they were the fruits of paternalism and a knowledge of mutual dependency. This spatiality was embedded within other shifting geographies of power. Problems around the edges of slavery—problems about the literal spatial limits of the slaveholders' power—were also conceptualized in terms of incompatible notions of rights. The end of this era, and so of the spatial configuration, was brought about by attempts to fashion various spatial solutions to these critical social-political problems concerning the boundedness of power and the embeddedness of the peculiar legal spaces of slavery in the larger spatial structure that was the United States. I will defer until the next chapter a discussion of the process of the translation of these social-political-spatial problems into specifically legal geographical problems. For our present purposes I should simply note that the abolition of the spatiality of slavery opened the way for new, in fact revolutionary, geopolitical practices.

The Shifting Spatiality of Emancipation

As the social relation of master and slave was first renegotiated, then disregarded, and then finally abolished in the period 1861–1865, so too the spatiality which sustained that relation was transformed. Southern blacks took the opportunity to create spatial conditions for a more desirable social life and to construct new social geographies. To a large extent they were successful. They would learn, though, that slavery and freedom did not in practice exhaust the possibilities of social, political, or legal status, just as they had known as "quasi-free slaves" that the categories weren't mutually exclusive. An intermediate status, prevalent in the North and in southern cities, that was between the no-more of slavery and the not-yet of freedom fixed their relations to others and to the world. This status was simply called black or Negro or colored. What we in hindsight and they in daily observation called betrayal, however, should not obscure the revolutionary changes in the lives of the overwhelming majority of black Americans. The most profound changes flowed directly from the fact that they were no longer regarded by others as objects of property. Whatever else freedom might or might not mean, a person would no longer be sold away from home and family, or face the humiliation of public bidding from the auction block. Gone too for most, if not all, blacks was the bullwhip.

The newly free men and women created the new social geographies initially simply by moving, by crossing lines, by redefining spaces and creating places, much as they had been doing previously but now with much greater room to maneuver. They were supported in their efforts by Union troops, members of the Freedmen's Bureau, and not a few local whites. However, they were also resisted by many in these same groups.

During the Reconstruction period a new kind of geopolitics emerged in the context of shifting forces of power and shifting relations of power between local, regional, and national actors. Out of this novel geopolitics emerged distinctive geographies of power which would be bequeathed to future generations and would shape social and political relations through the twentieth century.

As indicated, the geography of the war itself influenced the timing of self-emancipations. Many planters in the path of Union troop movements took their households away from the fighting and, in what would be the last forced migration for some black people, sent their slaves into the back country or into Texas. So too, many slaves were sold at this time to traders who were still willing to bet on a southern victory.[51] In occupied areas, however, local reconstructions had been in progress for some time before Appomattox. On the South Carolina Sea Islands, for example, the planters had evacuated and those who had worked the land now claimed it as their own.[52] Throughout the occupied South, "freedmen's" villages were built by the freed people themselves under the supervision of Union troops. However, most of these were transitory settlements. Until 1865 prudence and experience recommended that those who lived on plantations continue to work on them more or less as before.

A theme that is common to most of the WPA narratives by former slaves is how they found out about emancipation. In many cases they were told by Union officers who went from plantation to plantation "freeing" the slaves. In others the planters themselves informed them while taking the opportunity to offer new arrangements. In any case, it seemed, they had a choice— to leave or stay.[53] The line that defined the plantation changed its meaning right before their eyes. If they were to stay, it would be because—all things considered—they wanted to; if they wanted to leave, no one, it seemed, could stop them. They were free. And having lived their lives in a world in which one of the principal means of control was restraint on mobility, "free" meant free to move. In Leon Litwack's words, "Whatever else they did, that [walking off the plantation] remained the surest, the quickest way to demonstrate to themselves that their old masters and mistresses no longer owned or controlled them." [54] The vast majority continued to work the same land as before, their former master now being their employer or land-lord or both. These people began reconstructing the social geographies of the rural South by reuniting their families under a common roof. Also, they dispersed the cabins, formerly clustered together in the slave quarters, throughout the plantation. [55] Others stayed in the general area—which was, after all, their home—but found work with other employers. Still others experimented with freedom by going into the towns for a period of time, then returning to the country.

Some, however, whether immediately or after a time, left the area that they were in when they heard the news and never returned. Of these, a certain percentage, no doubt, wanted to make a clean break with a horrible past. Others, however, went back to the homeland from which they had been taken either by planters fleeing troops during the war or by pre-war migrations or trade. Still others went in search of spouses and family members from whom they had been separated, sometimes for years. Yet others, though relatively few, left the South behind.

The period of emancipation, which itself had a shifting geography to it (a "dark, dissolving, disquieting wave," as one planter put it), [56] was a time of extraordinary confusion and invention. At the center of the confusion for white, black, occupier, and occupied were basic questions of identity and social relations. The old world seemed to have collapsed and a new one was to be invented. [57] Different people had different ideas about what that world would look like. Planters, of course, wanted to reconstruct a world as much like the old world they had lost as possible. The freed people too envisioned a world which resembled the old one, in that it would be based on control over determinable slices of the landscape in the form of forty-acre farms that they would own. Freedom would mean more than simple mobility; indeed, freedom from control by their former rulers required a firmer attachment to land. [58] Clearly these were two incompatible visions, and each entailed a different geography of power. Each as well was grounded in and justified by deeply felt convictions about "rights."

Throughout 1865 there was a widespread belief among blacks that the lands which had been abandoned by or confiscated from disloyal planters were to be redistributed to them (on Christmas Day). Whether or not they were aware of debates on the topic within the Freedmen's Bureau, many felt that they who had worked the land and who needed it in order for the word *freedom* to have any meaning had far greater rights to it than did their former masters who had taken up arms against the federal government. Already former slaves on plantations that had been "abandoned" by whites had staked out forty-acre plots, sometimes on the advice of Union troops, sometimes not. More dramatic, under General Sherman's Special Field Order no. 15, issued in January 1865, freed people were given possession of abandoned and confiscated lands along the coast from Charleston, South Carolina, to Jacksonville, Florida, and had planted crops.[59] The belief in land distribution persisted even after Andrew Johnson's Amnesty Decree of May 1865 granted pardons and restored property to participants in the rebellion. While many federal and military officials as well as the planters themselves cautioned against expecting any such radical change, "the idea of 'forty acres and a mule' simply made too much sense and had become too firmly entrenched in the minds of too many freedmen for it to be given up at the first words of a bureau underling."[60]

By late autumn 1865, military officials had begun a more concerted campaign to convince some of those who had claimed a right to the land that they had been mistaken or misled.[61] This was done by enforcing the policy of restoring abandoned land to its former owners and auctioning off confiscated land to the highest bidders, often northern investors. In some cases, such as at Fortress Monroe, Virginia, former slaves were evicted from lands that had already been planted. Needless to say, they didn't go quietly. In most cases they were advised to work as wage laborers or sharecroppers for the recognized owner of the land, who frequently was the same person who very recently had claimed to own them. This advice was also accompanied by a self-help rhetoric which counseled former slaves on the virtues of the vision of hard work and saving and of someday buying their own farms.

Aside from the obvious implausibility of this self-help yeoman farmer scheme in the context of restoration, planters made other moves that facilitated the re-creation of antebellum geographies of power. For example, in some cases they made agreements among themselves not to hire laborers from neighboring plantations unless a worker could produce a certificate of dismissal from his or her former "employer."[62] This, of course, diminished the possibility of negotiating a better deal, at least in a given community. Also, laborers/tenants/sharecroppers were required to sign contracts with their employers/landlords. As it would turn out, these contracts would bind people to a given slice of land almost as firmly as had their former status as objects of property. Foreshadowing later conflicts over the geography of race, planters in some areas also formed associations whose members pledged not to sell property to blacks. While prohibitions on selling or renting land to blacks were often part of the black codes drawn up by state legislators under the period of Presidential Reconstruction (1865–1866), these provisions were overruled by military authorities. Nothing, however, prevented planters from assuming this obligation on their own.

Finally, many areas of the rural South were becoming provinces of the Invisible Empire of the Ku Klux Klan.[63] If there was a difference between the patrollers of the 1850s and early 1860s and the Klan of the late 1860s and 1870s (and presumably some members of each were the same individuals), it was measured in an increased cruelty and a decrease in protection offered by planters, now that it was free labor and not their investments that were being terrorized and "damaged."

The Geopolitics of Black Mobility

During Reconstruction a crucial element in the creation of the postslavery geography of power was the restoration of private property to the control of white planters. In the period following Reconstruction, the crucial elements were the "redemption" of state and local government to the same class of people and the reunification of the nation on terms that included allowing southern states to deal with their version of "the race problem" pretty much as they saw fit. Nonetheless, a new spatiality was to be constructed within the context of new social relations and political forces: the new spatiality of social life was to be the product of a new geopolitics of social life.

As it would turn out, this generation of southern Americans witnessed and participated in the transition from the spatiality of slavery to the spatiality of white supremacy. The key dynamic that conditioned the unfolding of this postbellum geography of race involved the interaction of (predominantly black) mobility and (white supremacist controlled) territoriality, or the geopolitics of black mobility. Within the generation, two of the most striking elements of the racial geography of the New South would be the hyperterritorialization of social life through segregation and the immobilization of black agricultural labor through the mechanisms of debt peonage. Needless to say, "law" and various forms of "legal action" figured prominently in the creation of these geographies of power.

An important dimension of the shifting geography of race of the period was the rather rapid increase in the number of black people living in urban areas of the South. This was true not only of larger cities such as Atlanta, New Orleans, and Nashville but also of smaller cities such as Selma, Alabama, Natchez, Mississippi, and Greenville, South Carolina.[64] The thousands—and by 1890, hundreds of thousands—of black people who moved into the cities of the South in the postbellum decades did so for a number of reasons. Indeed, there were as many reasons as there were people. Urbanization for many was a solution to the problems of freedom, and some of these problems had to do with the way freedom was being played out in the countryside. Voluntary migration is always related to assessments about the comparative merits of the source location and the destination. For many freed people, and especially for the first generation that came of age in the 1870s and 1880s, the cities seemed to provide comparatively greater opportunities to live freer lives. "They seemed to want to get closer to freedom, so they'd know what it was—like it was a place or a city."[65] To be sure, most black people of the period concluded from experience that it was better to live their new lives in the familiar settings of the countryside. The narratives of some of these people testify to the difficulties of their experiments with urban living and their relative satisfaction with the rural life to which they returned. To some extent, however, the fact that they could experiment at all was an expression of freedom, such as it was.

Among the motivations for moving into cities in the postwar period cited by scholars and given by the migrants themselves were comparatively greater freedom and more opportunities for self-determination. The building of the New South created a demand for nonagricultural labor, and railroads in particular offered freedmen comparatively higher wages.[66] So too a measure of comparative freedom came with the anonymity offered by city life. Cities also offered greater protection either by Union troops or officials of the Freedmen's Bureau. After Reconstruction, self-protection was more viable in the cities by virtue of a higher concentration of blacks who, as Rabinowitz stresses, did not hesitate in responding to white violence.[67] Finally, a more secure community life might be established in an urban setting. During Reconstruction, community institutions including schools, churches, voluntary associations, and businesses coalesced around the pre-existing communities established by antebellum free blacks in a number of southern cities. In addition, Republican-controlled cities such as Nashville offered a greater measure of political participation. Whatever the motivations and reservations of the different individuals, moving from the countryside to the city was seen by many to be a possible solution to the problems posed by freedom. And whether the problems are seen primarily as economic, political, or social, the solution was geographic—or, more precisely, the solution had geographical consequences.[68]

For others, that is, for many whites, this solution was itself indicative of another set of problems. Put most baldly, black people were not where different groups of white people wanted them to be, but they were where white people didn't want them to be. The increasing presence of former slaves in cities was seen as a threat to the white communities and, in some areas, as a threat to the revitalization of agricultural production. More generally, black mobility and particularly urbanization were seen as threats to, and indications of the collapse of, white control.[69]

The movement of blacks into the growing cities of the South, while particularly obvious and troubling to white residents, was only one part of the shifting spatial patterns of race. In fact, by 1890 only 15 percent of southern blacks were urban dwellers. Also important was the continuation of intraplantation labor movements and interregional migrations, especially from the seaboard states toward the Southwest. These latter, more long-distance shifts were a continuation of antebellum patterns. However, where before the war such movements were determined and directed by planters or slave traders, after the war they were determined to a larger extent by black people themselves—though facilitated by white labor agents.[70]

Yet another component of this geographical reconfiguration was various larger-scale efforts of blacks to relocate out of the South or even out of the United States. Compared to earlier and later movements, the emigration schemes of the 1870s and 1880s were more directly the result of the increasingly intolerable political and social conditions of life. In terms of rhetoric if not in numbers of people involved, the most significant of these movements were the numerous local "back to Africa" societies that had as their goal colonization in Liberia, the Kansas exodus of 1879, and the different efforts to establish all-black towns both within and outside of the South.[71] All of these movements—regardless of whether or not they were actually implemented—can be seen as efforts by black people to create the spatial conditions most conducive to an improved social (political, economic) life. For some this meant moving into urban communities; for others it meant engaging in agricultural production on their own farms away from white southerners; for yet others it meant residing in a black nation. All of these efforts were attempts to fashion geographical solutions to social problems. However, they were also regarded by others as problems in and of themselves. Black mobility was very much an issue in the last three decades of the nineteenth century, and differently situated people took actions that were intended to shape events.

Emigration and anti-emigration clubs were formed in order to investigate conditions in other places or in order to dissuade people from leaving. Meetings were held in local communities and state conventions were called in order to coordinate activity. Advocates of emigration to Liberia, Kansas, Indiana, and even Mexico circulated throughout the South.[72] Among these were people with such divergent motivations as proto-black nationalists, developers of black towns, labor and railroad agents, and politicians. In some counties of North Carolina, emigration was aided by the National Republican Committee, which wanted to relocate blacks to Indiana in hopes of tipping the balance of electoral power in its favor.[73]

Attempts to shape the changing geography of race by encouraging or discouraging black mobility employed political rhetorics of comparative geographies of power and experience. Images of a better (a freer or fairer) elsewhere coupled with denunciations of "here" were countered by images of a horrible (an inhospitable or treacherous) elsewhere coupled with praises of "here." The almost mystical status of Liberia and Kansas (fostered by, respectively, the African Colonization Society, land developers, and railroad and labor agents) contended with images of Liberia as a land of "a thousand contagious diseases, sweltering heat of a tropical sun and a poor half dead population withering like dew before the morning sun."[74] In response to a proposal made in the North Carolina House of Representatives by black representative John Williamson to instruct the North Carolina congressional delegation and senators to work for the establishment of an exclusive black territory in the West, J. C. Hill, another black legislator, voiced his opposition to "sending the Negroes away from their homes . . . to go among the uncivilized Indians and grizzly bears beyond the Missouri." North Carolina, he said, was "a good place for the development of the Negro."[75]

Against those who portrayed Kansas as a place with good land available at easy terms,[76] the *Wilmington Morning Star* warned North Carolinians against leaving "the Sunny South for the bleak winds and deep snows of Kansas."[77] Most of these images were, of course, for public and largely white consumption. It is unknown what effect such things as promotional literature, editorials, or legislative speeches had on those who might have considered moving. More influential, no doubt, were face-to-face discussions with people who claimed to have been there—wherever "there" might be. Some local emigration clubs raised money to send people scouting for suitable destinations. In order to move, people needed reliable information about distant locations; they also required transportation. Labor agents working for employers elsewhere often offered to provide both.

Beyond a political rhetoric of comparative geography, positive steps were taken by landlord-planters to limit black mobility by more decisive means. Legislatures at different times directed their attack on black mobility at different targets. In the 1870s and 1880s, most states of the former Confederacy sought to impose discipline on the planters themselves by criminalizing attempts to "entice" laborers to break their contracts.[78] These anti-enticement statutes were supplemented in some states by elements of contract law directed at the laborers themselves. These included the criminalization of the refusal to work after an advance of cash or goods had been made. Statutes such as these gave planters the option of enlisting (or threatening to enlist) state aid in keeping workers on the plantation. They also resurrected the legal category of fugitive. Another device to immobilize black labor was a series of anti-emigrant agent laws enacted throughout the period. The general thrust of these was to impose prohibitive licensing fees and taxes on out-of-state labor agents.

Likewise whites took actions to discourage urban migrations by the selective use of vagrancy laws, by withholding social services made available to poor whites, by discriminating against black people in employment and housing, by disenfranchising black voters, by police brutality, and by numerous other means. It was made clear that cities were for white people. And even though blacks continued to move to and settle in southern cities throughout the period, their presence was resented by whites who responded by making life miserable.

The various paths traced by southern black people in the generation after emancipation and the attempts by others to discourage, impede, or facilitate these movements constituted key aspects of the geopolitics of race of this era. This geopolitics, of course, was also a key aspect of the politics of social life more generally. As has been indicated—and as will be discussed in the following chapter—many of the more significant geopolitical actions and events took place in the context of formal state politics and took the form of legislation or law. The debates surrounding the constitutional amendments, including their ratification by state legislatures; the passage of federal civil rights bills in 1866 and 1875; the passing and repeal of the black codes in the states of the former Confederacy; the innumerable local municipal ordinances that shaped the details of access, exclusion, and segregation; and so many other official governmental acts all contributed to the shifting geographies of power. They all were intended to affect the legal meaning of space. They were all acts of territoriality in that they inscribed social relational meaning onto space. These kinds of acts also facilitated the development of legal action as a component of (geo)political strategy.

At least as significant in reshaping this spatiality were the innumerable daily instances of face-to-face geopolitics or the geopolitics of everyday life. Included here, for example, would be the gentlemen's agreements among planters in the countryside; the ongoing negotiations between planters and tenants or sharecroppers or between tenants and storekeepers; the acts of persuasion at meetings of emigration clubs; the accommodations reached by urban landlords and tenants or employers and employees; the moves behind the details of selective enforcement of vagrancy laws; the routine acts of discrimination in public accommodations and the departures from the routine; the acts of resistance to violence and segregation, including organized boycotts; the numerous acts of "testing" the Civil Rights Act of 1875; and the initiation of legal action. These are the kinds of actions that shaped the geographies of race and racism on the ground in the generation after slavery. Of course, not all of these kinds of actions were directly or even intentionally aimed at modifying the spatiality of social life, and not all had that effect. But because the connection between space and power had been so central to the social order that emancipation transcended, this connection remained central to conceptions of what was to follow. Many of these more face-to-face acts were intended to have spatial consequences, and many did in fact have spatial consequences. But these consequences were not necessarily those that were intended by any one party or faction.

3 Legal Reasoning and the Geopolitics of Nineteenth-Century Race Relations

The geographies of slavery and emancipation that we explored in the last chapter were constructed and reconstructed with reference to law. The common law of property and contract, local police regulations, state and federal legislation, and constitutional law were among the *sources* of legal meaning which, spatialized, contributed to the formation and reformation of geographies of power and experience. In chapter 2 discussion of the legal practices associated with litigation and adjudication was set aside in order to present a description of the on-the-ground geographies that were part of both slavery and its abolition. The present chapter returns to the theme of legal practice as geopolitics during the same time period.

With the exception of disputes about overzealous patrols, formal legal arguments about the *spatiality* of slavery within the South were rare. They were more common outside the slave-holding states. Until emancipation, slavery was in a sense beyond the formal legal order, or rather plantation law *was* the law. Trouble often arose around conflicts at and about the boundaries of slavery, at or about the boundary between the spaces of slavery and freedom. The Thirteenth Amendment abolished slavery and thereby formally erased this boundary. It brought "law"—federal constitutional law—right into the fields, workshops, and houses of the South. As we saw, however, there continued to be much dispute about what this meant in practice.

This chapter analyzes a series of legal contests about geographies of slavery, freedom, emancipation, and Reconstruction in the nineteenth century. They were all contests about what it meant to cross a line, to enter and pass out of legal spaces. This survey of cases is in no sense comprehensive, nor even representative of anything other than the specific *practices* examined. Most of the cases were, for various reasons, "landmarks" and so were taken account of, one way or another, by subsequent interpreters. What is important here, though, is what the cases reveal about the strategic political practice of legal geographic interpretation.

While in each case the opinion of the court is, of course, an important part of the story, what I want to emphasize here is the contrasting and conflicting lines of reasoning put forward by the participants. Our concern is with the translation of events into the terms of legal discourse, the shift in focus from the world of concrete experience to the map of abstract concepts and doctrines, and the crafting of alternative renderings of the legal landscape. Much of what follows is a description of these acts of categorization and countercategorization that make up the practice of legal reasoning. These actions are instances of line-drawing, or the construction and construal of conceptual boundaries in the creation of legal meaning. This is the meaning that is mapped onto lived-in landscapes. As will be seen, the biographies of real people were profoundly affected by how and where such lines were drawn.

As in chapter 2, this chapter treats both slavery and the postslavery racial order. A key theme, therefore, is change and how changes from one era to the other were understood. This necessarily involves looking at how freedom itself was understood. The pivotal political event, of course, was the Civil War. The pivotal experiential events were abolition and mass emancipation. The pivotal legal event was the constitutional revolution embodied in the Reconstruction amendments. The Thirteenth, Fourteenth, and Fifteenth Amendments were about many things. They were fundamentally concerned with race, power, and law. But they were also about federalism. "Federalism" is the name of a set of inherently spatial political-legal concepts. It is necessarily about complex connections between space and power. In the context of the United States, federalism is a way of framing questions about power. Ideas of federalism allow us to imagine two conceptually distinct "states" or "jurisdictions" that occupy the same segment of the physical world. Legal problems concerning race are often framed as questions about federalism, and problems of federalism often take the form of disputes about the *metaphorical* boundary separating and defining these two overlapping legal spaces. Much of the legal component of the geopolitics of race, especially after ratification of the Fourteenth Amendment, has taken the form of alternative renderings of the spatiality of federalism. This means that the boundaries which are the focus of questions about federalism are a key feature of the (conceptual) legal landscape.

Rendering the Spatiality of Slavery

In this period, and particularly after the 1840s, there were three principal legal-spatial issues—issues concerning what it meant to cross a line—that were fought out in courts in terms of legal discourse. These were, first, the issue of slaves in transit, or the status of slaves brought into nonslave states by their owners. The second was the issue of fugitive slaves, especially with regard to the procedures determining compliance with the constitutional mandate to "deliver up" slaves that had "escaped."[1] The third was the question of slaves in the territories, which was thought to turn on the authority of Congress to prohibit or to protect slavery in any or all of the federal territories. These were all complicated questions—or rather they were all issues that were complicated by the participants—and each raised very different legal and constitutional questions. However, they were all closely related issues. Practical understandings of each had a bearing on how the others were conceived. The first two issues, slaves in transit and the rendition of fugitive slaves, concerned the practical meaning of the boundary between the North and the South. From an abolitionist perspective, the danger to be guarded against was the extension of the institutions and relationships of slavery into the North, that is, the effective nationalization of slavery. The third issue, slavery in the territories, was similar to the slaves-in-transit issue in that arguments hinged on legal interpretations of the movements of slaveholders as slaveholders. In these cases, antislavery advocates used legal argument to attempt to confine and restrict slavery, to deny or limit its extension into free states and the territories; proslavery advocates used legal argument to resist such confinement. In their attempts to shape the geography of slavery, these actors engaged in the social practices of categorization, recategorization, and countercategorization, that is, the practice of drawing conceptual boundaries.

In the following pages I will present a brief sketch of illustrative skirmishes that highlight the involvement of these interpretive practices—the creation of meaning—in the antebellum geopolitics of slavery. No attempt is made here to give a full treatment of either the issues or the cases. My aim is only to illustrate some of the more general claims asserted so far.

Slaves in Transit: Rendering the Spatiality of Comity

As the nineteenth century progressed, geographies of race became more complex and more ambiguous. It became increasingly less certain what it meant to cross a line. This uncertainty was especially noticeable to slaveholders who entered with their slaves into states where slaveholding was prohibited. For example, the provisions in Article 4 of the Constitution which dealt with "full faith and credit" and "privileges and immunities" might have led one to expect that the property of slaveholders from other states of the Union would be protected in northern states. Common membership in the shared national space might have been thought to prohibit the denial of a slaveholder's right to movement. In fact, slaveholders and slaves did travel widely in the early national period to various resort areas and ports of the North.[2] They also passed through free states on their way west. Even if the protection of property in slaves was not *required* by the Constitution one might expect that such protection would be extended as a matter of comity.

Comity is a doctrine of international law—considered applicable to relations among the states of the Union—which concerns "the courtesy or consideration that one jurisdiction gives by enforcing the laws of another."[3] Indeed, the "full faith and credit" and "privileges and immunities" clauses of the Constitution are sometimes referred to as the "comity clauses." There are two things to note here. First, to grant comity is to give extraterritorial effect to the laws of another state. In cases concerning slavery of course, this gives extraterritorial effect to the power of masters over slaves. If comity was granted (or assumed), the slaveholder, in effect, was considered to have carried the law of the slave state with him wherever he went. If comity was denied, it was the domestic law of the nonslave state that would determine the contours of the relation, even to the point of severing the relation. That is, the relation itself—described in terms of rights and duties and such—was contingent on space, and the meaning of space was contingent on the granting or withholding of comity.

The second thing to note here is that while the Article 4 provisions are obligatory, the granting of comity is discretionary. But what events or situations are or are not covered by Article 4? The scope or applicability of these clauses is ambiguous; at the same time, comity, in the words of Supreme Court Justice Joseph Story, "is and must ever be uncertain."[4] So too then must be the geography of power that is constructed in accord with these legal concepts.

These issues were not of major significance for slaveholders in interstate travel within the South, but if a state prohibited holding other humans in bondage, how much room did a slaveholder have to maneuver? With the explicit exception of fugitives—whose status did not change as they crossed state lines as a matter of constitutional law—if the relation of master and slave was not authorized in a state, then it would seem to be impossible to be a slave in a free state. Questions often arose, then: Upon crossing a state line into a state that had abolished slavery, was a black person still a slave? Could the alleged owner still compel obedience? If the alleged slave resisted, would the owner have recourse to the state to crush the resistance? Could the alleged slave be compelled to leave the state? If in crossing into a free state the relation was severed, could this be construed as a denial of the slaveholder's freedom of movement? The problem, as one attorney for slaveholders somewhat hyperbolically put it, was that "the nonslaveholding states could pen up all the slaveholders within their States as effectively as the slave himself is confined."[5]

But if the relation was not severed by crossing the line, then not only was abolition compromised but so too, it would seem, was the sovereignty of states that had abolished slavery. This problem was recognized on the eve of the American Revolution by the English justice Lord Mansfield in the case of *Somerset v. Stewart.*[6] In ruling that a slave brought from Virginia to England by his master could not be compelled to return to Virginia, Mansfield stated that "the difficulty of adopting the relation [of master and slave] without adopting it in all of its consequences, is indeed extreme, and yet many of the consequences are absolutely contrary to the municipal law of England."[7] This is a classic expression of the "slippery slope" argument that we will encounter in many subsequent cases.[8] Was it possible to allow just a little bit of slavery? Where should one draw the line? According to the antebellum abolitionists, the line had already been drawn. For example, rhetorically addressing slaveholders, the Liberty Party in its 1844 platform said, "If you choose to cling to such a system—cling to it; but you shall not cross our line; you shall not bring that foul thing here."[9]

In the early decades of the century, a compromise of sorts had been worked out in some northern states that was based on *categories* of travelers. These categories were exceptions to prohibitions which gave degrees of qualified recognition to slavery. While slavery was (gradually) being abolished with respect to *residents*, slave property of "transients," "visitors," and "sojourners" was sometimes protected. But these distinctions were not always clear. Nor was it clear how they differed from residents. Pennsylvania in 1780 established a six-month rule to distinguish residents from non-residents. Under this rule travelers could hold slaves in the state for up to half a year, after which time the slaves would be free. In New York a similar law drew the line at nine months. In a sense, the meaning of the spatial boundary was a function of this temporal boundary as the clock began to tick upon crossing into the state. Even so, the meaning of the line depended upon the meaning of six months, and as the cases discussed by Paul Finkelman in his *Imperfect Union* demonstrate, the meaning of this was not always clear: Did it mean, for example, six continuous months or six cumulative months? Could a slaveholder merely cross out of the state and then cross back in to reset the clock? Might six *lunar* months suffice? If a slaveholder entered into the state with the intent of becoming a resident, did he have a six-month grace period, or did his residence commence with his arrival? As for "slaves," if they had been conceived in Pennsylvania but born in Maryland six months after their mother's arrival, would they be recognized as falling within the protection of the six-month rule? All of these questions were questions about the legal landscape, the boundedness of power.[10] What it meant to cross a line depended on the answers given to these questions, and attorneys and judges gave conflicting answers. To answer the question was to attach meaning to the lines that defined the legal spaces which conditioned experience.

Localizing Slavery: *Aves v. Commonwealth*

The compromise that had been worked out began to show strain in the 1830s and in the following years to disintegrate. A key turning point was reached in 1836 with the case of *Aves v. Commonwealth*[11] in Massachusetts, a state that had no statute protecting slave property of nonresidents and that had a very active abolitionist community.

Samuel Slater was a resident of New Orleans. He was also a slaveholder. Among his slaves were a six-year-old girl named Med and her mother. In May of 1836 Slater's wife, Mary, went to Boston to visit her father, Thomas Aves. Mary took Med with her on this trip, but sometime in August Mary went out of town, leaving Med in the custody of her father. It was then that Levin Harris, on behalf of the Boston Female Anti-Slavery Society, petitioned the court to issue a writ of habeas corpus to be served on Aves so that he might "show the cause of her [Med's] detention." In the court case that followed, Aves was represented in the Supreme Judicial Court of Massachusetts by Benjamin Curtis, a prominent Massachusetts attorney and a future justice of the United States Supreme Court. Curtis' job was to argue that Med was a slave whether she happened to be in Louisiana or Massachusetts, and that her rightful legal owner retained "a qualified and limited power" over her, namely, the power to bring her back to New Orleans. The court, by granting comity to the laws of Louisiana, had only to recognize that right. The opposing argument was presented by the noted abolitionist attorney Ellis Loring, with assistance by noted lawyer and future Whig senator Rufus Choate.

The arguments presented in *Aves* are analyzed in detail by Finkelman in *Imperfect Union*. His emphasis is on the historical significance of the case and the quality of the arguments presented. Loring's argument, in particular, set a standard for antislavery interpretations of comity. In fact, Curtis himself was to rely on aspects of Loring's argument in his dissent in the *Dred Scott* case more than twenty years later. It is not my purpose here to provide a thorough interpretation of the arguments, only to use key moves as illustrations of more general points concerning the practice of legal reasoning and the geopolitics of race.

Curtis' strategy was rather simple. He did not argue, for example, that the court had no authority to free Med or that the privileges and immunities clause required the court to protect Slater's property. He simply stated that the master had the "qualified and limited right [to] restrain the slave for the purposes of carrying him [*sic*] out of Massachusetts and returning to the domicile of his owner." [12] Of course, this formulation of rights assumed that Med was in fact a slave. Curtis' principal task was to fit the facts of the case into the container provided by his conception of comity—the dimensions of which were indicated by his claim that "the general principles of international law [comity] are broad enough to cover this case." [13] This he attempted to do in two steps.

First, he categorized slaves as "movable property" and cited authorities to the effect that "movable property has no locality" and that "all things which have no locality follow the person of the owner and are consequently governed . . . by the law of the place of his domicil." [14] Med's status as a slave was simply fixed by Louisiana law, as were Slater's and Aves' relation to her. Slater's rights were subject to comity.

Curtis' second move was to argue that in general the granting of comity was the rule and that though there were exceptions to this rule, the facts of this case did not fall within those exceptions. One exception to the general rule favoring comity that Curtis noted was when the foreign law to be given extraterritorial effect was "immoral." He then offered a series of arguments as to why none of the exceptions applied. The essence of this line of reasoning was that comity was ordinarily granted in cases involving movable property, and there being nothing exceptional about the property in question, there was no reason to deny comity in this case.

To rhetorically set up rules and exceptions is to implicitly advance a categorical scheme. Being "covered by the rule" or being outside the scope of the application of the rule has consequences for action. To categorize an event or situation as being inside or outside the scope of a rule (or inside the exceptions) requires the identification of some salient feature of what is being categorized that "makes the difference." In actively making or drawing these distinctions, one participates in the creation of meaning. As we will see, how this categorization takes place matters to how geographies of power are constructed.

Curtis bolstered his argument by dismissing Mansfield's slippery slope dilemma from the *Somerset* case mentioned above as being merely "theoretical" and of presenting no "practical" difficulty; by minimizing the significance of the distinction between fugitive slaves and slaves in transit; and by distinguishing the present case from *Somerset* on the basis of the different relations that held between the jurisdictions of England and Virginia on the one hand and those of Massachusetts and Louisiana on the other, pointing out that Virginia had been a dependent colony of England while Massachusetts and Louisiana were sister states.[15] All of these moves were strategic categorizations aimed at the creation of legal meaning for the purposes of maintaining the relations between Slater and Med.

Ellis Loring, arguing on behalf of the Commonwealth, countered Curtis' reading of the legal landscape. He urged the court to deny the request for comity and to recognize Med's freedom. His argument consisted of four principal moves. First, he asserted that "comity is not to be exercised in doubtful cases."[16] The fact of the argument itself, it seems, was presumptive of sufficient doubt to cause the court to "prefer the law of its own country, to that of the stranger." Next he challenged Curtis' description of the configuration of rules and exceptions. Where Curtis held that slaves were no different than any other type of property as far as comity was concerned, Loring contended that slavery was "within all [the] exceptions" to the rule. It was offensive to morals, it contravened the public policy and public law of Massachusetts and it offered a pernicious and detestable example to the citizens of the Commonwealth. Moreover, comity was founded on reciprocity between jurisdictions. Louisiana, he claimed, could not reciprocate because there were no slaves in Massachusetts that required protection and, in fact, southern states unconstitutionally denied the privileges and immunities of "colored citizens of the North." In this case, he said, "there is no room for comity." [17]

His third argument went directly to the spatiality of slavery and freedom. "Slavery," he said, "is a local institution."

Slaves are *property* . . . while they remain under the local law of slavery or when they appear in the character of fugitives. They are, on the other hand *men* . . . when they come rightfully within the limits of the local law of freedom. [18]

The critical distinction which gave meaning to the line here was whether Med had escaped or had been brought voluntarily by her master. Finally, Loring challenged Curtis' dismissal of Mansfield's slippery slope consideration and denied his opponent's distinction between the "theoretical" and "practical" difficulties that would result from the granting of extraterritorial effect to the laws of slavery. Once the limited and qualified rights requested were granted, all the other powers that masters exercise over slaves would necessarily follow. In practice, the distinction itself was merely theoretical. Loring's argument was supplemented by a brief rejoinder by Rufus Choate to Curtis' claims concerning the different relations between England and colonial Virginia on the one hand and between Massachusetts and Louisiana on the other hand—a difference that had allowed Curtis to distinguish the present case from *Somerset* and to dismiss the relevance of *Somerset* as precedent. According to Choate, the dependence or independence of the jurisdictions in question was of no concern to questions of comity. What mattered was whether there was a conflict in the local laws of the places *(lex loci)*. As a statement on the principles of international law, *Somerset* was relevant to the case at hand. [19]

What we have here, then, are contending interpretations of the legal concept comity and its applicability to the circumstances in which Med found herself. Each attorney set up the category, the exceptions that gave boundaries to the category, and the relevant attributes of the objects to be categorized, and then drew lines. All of this was to determine the spatial contingency of social relations of power described in terms of rights.

Chief Justice Lemuel Shaw, speaking for a unanimous court, agreed with Loring's interpretation of the legal landscape—but the features of the landscape that he emphasized were interestingly different. The reason that Med was *not* a slave in Massachusetts was "not so much because his [*sic*] coming within our territorial limits, breathing our air, or treading on our soil works any alteration on his *status*," but because there was simply no authority on the part of the master to restrain his slave while in the state.[20] That is, the power that a master holds over a slave cannot be assumed but must be authorized by positive law and such a law simply did not exist in Massachusetts.

The key distinction that grounded Shaw's argument was that between positive law and natural law.[21] The relation of master and slave exists in the world as a matter of positive law. As such, courts in places like Massachusetts must recognize it and not interfere with it "within the territories" of slave states or "on the high seas."[22] But the law of slavery creates a peculiar kind of property relation and a slave is necessarily an exceptional kind of property, one that is "contrary to natural right and the plain principles of justice."[23] There is in this view an implicit spatiality that corresponded to this distinction between natural and positive law. Shaw characterized Curtis' property argument as being based on the premise that "if slavery exists anywhere, and if by the laws of any place a property can be acquired in slaves, the law of slavery must extend to every place where such slaves may be carried."[24] In contrast, Shaw stated that it is necessary to "mark clearly the distinction between . . . the local law of particular states . . . and those natural and social relations which are everywhere and by all people recognized." That is, natural law is ubiquitous, positive law is local. This, however, does not by itself necessarily mean that comity cannot be extended to the laws of a slave state. What prohibits the court from granting extraterritorial effect to the limited rights requested was an inability to limit the parade of horrors represented by people who "might bring their slaves here and exercise over them the rights and power which an owner of property might exercise, and for any time short of acquiring domicil."[25] To extend comity, then, would be to establish slavery in the absence of positive law and contrary to natural law. This being simply impossible, Med was free not because Shaw freed her but because he recognized her as being not unfree.

The crucial condition to all of these categorizations was that Mary Slater had taken Med out of the positive space of slavery and into the natural space of liberty "voluntarily and unnecessarily." This deliberate act on her part was the fact in the world that distinguished the case from any concerning fugitives. The ironic result, then, was that Med was free because she found herself in Massachusetts against her will, whereas had she come of her own volition (i.e., escaped) she would be recognized as a slave—as someone lacking a will. A further irony, however, is that as a six-year-old she was recognized as not in fact having a will at all, and so was put in the foster care of the Anti-Slavery Society!

In *Aves* Benjamin Curtis and Ellis Loring advanced conflicting interpretations of the legal landscape through their divergent understandings of what it meant for Mary Slater to have crossed the line into Massachusetts with Med. In this case the larger issue of the boundedness of slavery—the confinement or extension of the institutions and relations—was answered with reference to the question "What does it mean to cross a line?" which in turn was answered with reference to interpretations of comity or extraterritoriality. The answer turned on conflicting views of the rules of application, exceptions to those rules, and whether the facts of the case better fit the rule or the exceptions. Mutually dependent or reinforcing (or circular) conceptions of property, rights, sovereignty, jurisdiction, and federalism were deployed in efforts to map out the lines of power among people in the world—including the judges themselves.

The lawyers in this case crafted complex narratives in which they carefully laid out *conceptual* boundaries. They drew distinctions and challenged the distinctions drawn by their adversaries. They generated rules and exceptions and justified these with claims about language, history, and what it means to be human. They strung together claims about the conditions under which X (for example, Med, property, *Somerset*) should or should not be categorized as Y (for example, property, exceptional property, relevant precedent) and about the consequences that followed from correct and incorrect categorizations. In doing so, they participated in the creation of legal meaning. Shaw's authoritative interpretation constituted an act of inscription of that meaning onto the physical landscape. He assigned meaning to the line, to the act of crossing the line, to the space defined by the line. The precise issue on the ground was the spatial contingency of rights and social relational power. This, then, was a crucial episode in the legal restructuring of geographies of power. The following year a Connecticut court adopted Shaw's reasoning in recognizing the freedom of those held as slaves there. In 1841 New York repealed its nine-month rule and in 1847 Pennsylvania repealed its six-month rule. By 1850 most states in the North prohibited southerners from bringing slaves into their jurisdictions.[26]

Fugitive or Kidnapped: The Spatiality of Exclusivity

The removal of state protection from slave property brought "voluntarily" into free states was a significant move in the revision of the legal landscape wrought by antislavery forces. However, that did not eliminate the existence of the institution or relations of slavery from those jurisdictions. Courts and other state agents were still obligated to recognize the status of slaves and the rights of slaveholders because of the Constitution's Article 4 clause:

> No person held to service or labor in one state, under the laws thereof, escaping into another, shall, in consequence of any law or regulation therein, be discharged from such service or labor, but shall be delivered up on claim of the party to whom such service or labor may be due.

Moreover, state agents may have had actual duties imposed on them by the federal Fugitive Slave Law of 1793. This law allowed slaveholders or their hired slave catchers "to seize or arrest such fugitives from labor."[27] But it required them to bring the seized person before a federal judge or the magistrate of a town or county, to give proof that the person was an escaped slave, and to obtain a certificate of removal that allowed them to bring the fugitive back to the state from which she or he had allegedly escaped. The fugitive slave law also provided penalties for those who obstructed the process. In the view of contemporary authorities, the fugitive slave *clause* constitutionalized, and therefore nationalized, the slaveholders' right to recaption, that is, the right of owners of slave property to capture and reclaim runaways. The fugitive slave *law* attempted to regulate how this was done.

The recognition that the fugitive slave clause and the law of 1793 gave to slavery in those jurisdictions that had abolished the relation was a considerable problem for antislavery forces. It led some to denounce the Constitution as a "covenant with hell" and to advocate "disunion" or northern secession.[28] It caused special and immediate problems for free blacks of northern states who faced the very real threat of being kidnapped by slave catchers and sold south into slavery.

In order to provide protection to their free black citizens, the legislatures of some northern states enacted regulations known as "personal liberty laws."[29] These laws were initially intended to provide more procedural safe-guards against kidnapping such as allowing a hearing for those who claimed to be free and severely penalizing the act of kidnapping. They were de-signed to "balance" the constitutionally mandated recognition of a slave-holder's right of recaption with the obligation of states to protect their citizens and the presumption that all persons were free unless proven otherwise.

In the 1820s Pennsylvania and New York strengthened their antikid-napping statutes. Pennsylvania's 1820 law, for example, increased penalties for kidnapping and prohibited most state judicial officers from hearing claims and issuing certificates of removal. This made recaption much more difficult and brought pressure on Pennsylvania from the legislature of neighboring Maryland to repeal the law and replace it with one more so-licitous of the rights of slaveholders. As a result of negotiations between the two states, the Pennsylvania legislature passed a new law in 1826 which again authorized state agents to participate in the recaption process but regulated that participation. It also stipulated that a claimant was to apply to an official for a warrant, which would be directed to a sheriff who would then seize the alleged fugitive and bring the person before a judge for a hearing. At the hearing more than the word of the owner would be neces-sary to satisfy the judge, and time would be given to the seized person to get evidence in support of a contention of freedom. Failure to follow these procedures would leave one open to prosecution for kidnapping. These legislative maneuvers were geopolitical in the sense of being oriented to-ward shaping geographies of power by assigning legal meaning to the act of crossing state lines. By the 1830s the complex issues concerning kidnap-ping, fugitive slaves, and personal liberty laws had become more contro-versial and heated. Antislavery forces fought for more stringent guarantees such as the right of seized blacks to a jury trial. Proslavery forces attacked personal liberty laws as infringements on property rights and as a denial of constitutional obligations of states. The various states of the North pre-sented claimants with a mosaic of procedures relating to the topic. The le-gal meaning of space with respect to race relations was increasingly called into question.

Nationalizing Recaption: *Prigg v. Pennsylvania*

In 1837 Edward Prigg, a professional slave catcher, was hired by Margaret Ashmore of Maryland to go to Pennsylvania and bring back to her people that Ashmore claimed to have inherited from her uncle. Margaret Morgan, the daughter of "virtually free slaves," was found in York County, Pennsylvania, with her husband, Jerry Morgan, and their children, at least one of whom had been born in Pennsylvania.[30] The Morgans had been living in Pennsylvania for five years. Prigg obtained a warrant to arrest them from a York County justice of the peace, Thomas Henderson. Prigg seized Margaret and her children and, following the procedure of the 1826 statute, brought them back to Henderson to obtain the necessary certificate of removal. At this juncture Henderson decided to have nothing more to do with the case. At that Prigg simply returned to Maryland with the Morgans and delivered them to Ashmore. He was subsequently indicted for kidnapping under the personal liberty law. The governor of Pennsylvania applied to his counterpart in Maryland for Prigg to be extradited. The request was refused. After more negotiations the legislatures of both states agreed to bring the controversy before the U.S. Supreme Court for a determinate resolution.

Again, as in *Aves* six years earlier, bringing the case to court constituted the transformation of a larger social and political conflict into a narrow legal dispute that turned on the specialized skills of lawyers. This transformation is most clear in the ways that the events themselves were translated into the terms provided by legal discourse. In the arguments and judgments that constitute the "case," there is no trace of the horror presumably experienced by the Morgan family. The face-to-face dynamics of power were squeezed out of debate as the focus was shifted to questions of the nature of federalism, the intention of the framers, the meaning of the word "claim" in the fugitive slave clause, and so on.

The case itself is a complex field of crosscutting interpretations. The arguments of three prominent attorneys were answered by the opinions of six justices, some concurring, others concurring in part and dissenting in part, and one dissenting. What was actually decided in the case of *Prigg v. Commonwealth of Pennsylvania* was a matter of debate immediately after the opinions were announced and remains a matter of historical controversy.[31] It is not my purpose here to cut through this complexity, only to focus on the treatment of central "legal" questions by way of illustrating how participants sought to restructure the legal landscape and revise inherited geographies of race.

The fact in the world that set the interpretive train in motion was Prigg capturing the Morgan family and taking them into Maryland against their will. The question was, essentially, how to characterize this event: Was it the exercise of Margaret Ashmore's right of recaption or was it an instance of kidnapping as defined by state law? There were, of course, serious consequences that followed from how this event was categorized, but the categorization itself depended on the answers to other, logically prior, questions. There are two things to keep in mind here: first, the topic was how to characterize power; and second, the crossing of a state line was of central importance in how the event would be characterized. If the act had occurred a few miles to the South it would have been classed unambiguously as recaption; if Prigg hadn't taken the Morgans to Maryland it would have been a simple kidnapping. The line made it a question: a question of the line. It also made it a *federal* question answerable with reference to the U.S. Constitution.

Schematically, the answer to the question of how to characterize Prigg's exercise of power over the Morgans depended on understandings of the capacity of the state legislature to create the category of "kidnapping" for such situations, to distinguish between "kidnapping" and "recaption," to determine what counted as each, and to assign consequences to the categorization. That is, the answer was seen to depend on the validity—the constitutionality—of Pennsylvania's personal liberty law of 1826. The answer to the question of constitutionality, in turn, depended on interpretations of federalism. The question of federalism itself was framed in terms of doctrines of *exclusivity*. For our purposes the issue was translated into the question of whether power to create legal meaning with respect to the topic was exclusively within the competence of one government—national or state— or not. There were, therefore, three options or categories. First, the power to legislate might be considered to be exclusively that of Congress; second, it could be exclusively that of the state legislatures; third, it could be concurrent or shared. The bulk of the legal arguments of attorneys were directed toward justifying the preferred categorization. In doing so they made claims about the categories, the distinctions among them, about the world, history, semantics, and so forth. Again, what follows is simply a cursory *description* of where the various participants drew the relevant lines.

Conflicting Construals

Maryland's attorney general Jonathan Merideth argued that the federal government had exclusive power to legislate on the subject of fugitive slaves.[32] Such legislation as the Fugitive Slave Law of 1793 was grounded in the "necessary and proper" clause of Article 1. A key component of his argument was the construal of "conflict" or fundamental incompatibility between the federal statute and Pennsylvania's personal liberty law. If such conflict was recognized by the justices, then the supremacy clause of the Constitution would render the state statute void. Another important and particularly spatial part of Merideth's argument was that federal exclusivity was necessary to achieve uniformity of procedures for reclaiming escaped slaves, and that the inconvenience that resulted from the lack of uniformity reduced the constitutional guarantee of the right of recaption to "a sounding phrase, signifying nothing."[33] The argument was that the avoidance of a slave catcher's inconvenience, expense, and delay required uniformity and that interjurisdictional uniformity meant that the federal government should have the exclusive authority to regulate.

In contrast, Thomas Hambly, representing Pennsylvania, argued for *state* exclusivity. His task was to challenge the constitutionality of the Fugitive Slave Law of 1793 as both a clear violation of the Ninth and Tenth Amendments and unwarranted by the "necessary and proper" clause. Crucially, he also defined the "subject matter" that was the topic of categorization differently than had Merideth. For Hambly the subject matter of the personal liberty law was kidnapping, and there was nothing in the Constitution that concerned itself with kidnapping. The power to legislate on this topic was a matter of "police and internal regulation, as much as ferries, turnpikes and health-laws."[34] He also denounced Merideth's use of the "argumentum ab inconvenienti" and urged the Court "to construe, not to legislate."[35] Unlike Merideth, Hambly did not ignore the issue of race and its connection to presumptions of freedom or servitude and, effectively, guilt or innocence.

Lastly, Pennsylvania's attorney general Ovid F. Johnson presented the argument for concurrent jurisdiction. Judicial acceptance of either Hambly's argument for state exclusivity or Jackson's argument for concurrent jurisdiction would have left the 1826 statute—and Prigg's indictment—intact. Unlike Hambly's argument, however, Johnson's did not require the risky tactic of arguing that a fifty-year-old federal law was, after all, invalid. Johnson therefore stressed the *harmonious* relationship between the federal and state laws and the lack of conflict between or among the states themselves. His main task was to deny the "conflict" upon which Merideth had based his argument for federal exclusivity. The different laws, albeit drafted for different purposes, "form together a harmonious system neither jarring nor conflicting in any part of its operation."[36] Perhaps the most interesting rhetorical aspect of Johnson's argument was his self-presentation as "the true friend of the South" who was protesting "in the name of all the states—in the name of the Union itself" the "dangerous encroachment on state sovereignty and state independence" that this application of the doctrine of federal exclusivity represented.[37]

The attorneys who presented arguments in *Prigg* advanced very different and incompatible readings of the boundary between federal and state sovereignties and the effect that this boundary had on how power did work, or should have worked, in the world. The location of that conceptual boundary was fixed with reference to how the "subject matter" was framed. From the perspective of Maryland's slaveholders, the topic was fugitive slaves; from the perspective of Pennsylvania's black citizens the topic was kidnapping. The attorneys also presented very different configurations of the relevant web of power relations connecting federal-state and interstate relations to government-citizen and citizen-citizen relations. It is crucial to note here that for Merideth of Maryland, free blacks simply did not exist.

Justice Joseph Story authored the opinion for the Court. His principal findings were that the federal government had exclusive power to legislate on the topic and that the topic was fugitive slaves. Pennsylvania's personal liberty law and others like it throughout the North were, therefore, invalid. He also ruled that while the Fugitive Slave Law of 1793 was constitutional, the participation of state officials in its workings was optional. Other justices, however, disagreed with this part of his interpretation.

I would like to note two aspects of Story's opinion that are of interest to understanding the historical geopolitics of race. First, Story accepted and elaborated on Merideth's argument that federal exclusivity was grounded in the necessity of uniformity of regulations from state to state. Interstate variation would have resulted in delays and confusion or even the outright denial of the right of recaption. "Surely," wrote Story, "such a state of things could never have been intended" by the slaveholding framers of the Constitution.[38] The problem of kidnapping was not even alluded to in Story's opinion. He construed the legal landscape solely from the slaveholder's perspective. In nationalizing the right of recaption in such a way, he obliterated the meaning of state lines as far as slave catchers were concerned. The capture and movement of escaped slaves took place in a purely national space. Story found "an absolute, positive right . . . uncontrolled and uncontrollable by state sovereignty . . . independent of comity, confined to no territorial limits." In his view, "the owner has the same security, and the same remedial justice, and the same exception from state regulation and control, through however many states he may pass with his fugitive slave in his possession, in transitu to his own domicile."[39]

Second, the spatial extension of the right of recaption (and other incidental rights) was based on the slaveholder's presumption that blackness meant servitude. Again, Story saw the world from the slaveholder's perspective without addressing the northern presumption of freedom. In doing so, he nationalized a key component of the slave law and imposed the slaveholder's ideology of race on people who had explicitly repudiated it. These were critical maneuvers in the antebellum struggle over the spatiality of race relations. In some respects the power of slaveholders not only over slaves but also over black people and nonslaveholding whites was also nationalized.

The fact of the case of *Prigg v. Pennsylvania* illustrates that in the 1840s the legal meaning of power that was inscribed on the landscape was called into question by both proslavery and antislavery forces.

Of the various alternative readings of the legal landscape that were presented, Justice Story inscribed one that he assumed would clarify and simplify the ambiguous and complex geography of power. He hoped to stabilize an increasingly unstable legal-spatial structure. In any event, he failed. The legal landscape with respect to federalism, fugitive slaves, and kidnapping was less clear than before. The decision itself was interpreted by subsequent actors in wildly incompatible ways as northern courts used it as an antislavery decision.[40] Moreover, there is the historical interpretation that resistance to the *Prigg* decision led to support in Congress for the more draconian Fugitive Slave Law of 1850, resistance to which, in turn, was a crucial factor in the emergence of the Republican Party and, ultimately, southern secession.

The Territorial Question: The Spatiality of Freedom

In the fifteen years following *Prigg*, issues involving connections between geography, law, and race relations became much more contentious and the legal landscape became, if anything, more complex and ambiguous, more open to questioning and debate. The acquisition of Oregon, the annexation of Texas, the conquest of northern Mexico, the organization of unorganized territories, and the admission of new states were, of course, geopolitical events of the first magnitude. But the expanded space of the United States caused serious problems for a number of people. What, for instance, did the acquisition of Mexican territory from which slavery had been abolished mean for the slaveholder from Arkansas who might want to migrate with his slaves to New Mexico or California? Some of these problems were, at this point, more theoretical or symbolic than practical. However, for both antislavery and proslavery forces there were serious questions about how geographies of power might change in the near future. In their attempts to confine slavery to existing spaces, antislavery advocates were seen to be "attacking slavery in places where it did not, in present, exist." To some southerners the issue seemed to be "an imaginary negro in an impossible place."[41] In 1850 various sectional issues nearly led the South to secede. Instead, the Compromise of 1850 effected a fairly radical geopolitical restructuring in order to prevent the disintegration of the Union. As a deliberate and far-reaching set of geopolitical moves, the compromise package linked such disparate issues as the admission of California, boundary changes in Texas, the reestablishment of slavery in New Mexico and new procedures for capturing fugitive slaves in the North. Thus, in some sense, the prohibition of slavery in San Francisco was related to the increase in the slaveholder's power in Cincinnati or Boston.

Different people in this period had incompatible understandings of which connections between space and meaning or geography and power did or should or must prevail. These were brought to bear in arguments concerning those nonstate spaces of the United States called the Territories and what it meant for different people to cross into those spaces from state spaces. These understandings of space and power were frequently couched—or justified—in constitutional language, that is, in the key terms of legal discourse, so that in making claims about the meaning of space, actors made claims about constitutional meaning. Each significant theory of territorial power was linked to a corresponding constitutional theory. One set of questions that shaped the territorial debate was whether Congress had the authority to prohibit slavery in the territories—as it had done since the First Congress reenacted the Northwest Ordinance—or whether, on the contrary, it had the duty to protect it in them. Were prohibitions or protections a matter of discretionary policy or constitutional imperative? If Congress did not have the power to prohibit slavery, who if anyone did?

These debates in Congress and throughout the country were not only prospective (what is to be done?) but retrospective as well. They took the form, as constitutional arguments often do, of historical arguments.[42]

In the early 1850s, that part of the original Louisiana Purchase that had not yet been carved into states was structured by the line drawn at 36°30′ which was the legal-spatial product of the events we call the Missouri Compromise of 1820. South of that line the relation of master and slave—and all that that entailed—was permitted; north of the line it was prohibited by act of Congress. In calling into question congressional power under the Constitution to prohibit slavery in the territories, proslavery and anti-antislavery advocates were calling into question the meaning of that line and the meaning of the spaces defined by that line. If it was unconstitutional for Congress to prohibit slavery in the territories, then the boundary of slavery itself would extend to Canada and to the Pacific Ocean simply by the unrestrained movement of people. In any case, the highly ambiguous Kansas-Nebraska Act of 1854—whatever else it did—effectively erased the line that had separated slavery from freedom on the white person's map of the Great Plains.[43] However, this move and the apparent resistance to the Fugitive Slave Law of 1850 made the legal landscape that much more unstable. The many questions raised about the legal meaning of space, the spatial distribution of legal meaning, and the legal structure of space were in 1857 to be given a determinate construction by the U.S. Supreme Court. This rendering—or set of renderings—would turn on interpretations of the path that Dred Scott and his family traced across the legal landscape of middle America.

There is no need to recount the complicated story of the Scotts and their travels.[44] My purpose, as in the other cases, is merely to illustrate some of the more general themes of this work. Stripped to its essential elements, the set of facts that served as a point of departure for the various legal-spatial interpretations included Dred Scott, the slave of U.S. Army surgeon John Emerson of St. Louis, having been taken by Emerson to Fort Armstrong, Illinois, in 1833 and remaining there until 1836. From the free state of Illinois, Emerson took Scott to Fort Snelling in what is now Minneapolis, Minnesota, and what was then Wisconsin Territory. Fort Snelling, though, was in the area covered by the Missouri Compromise prohibition of slavery. As a practical matter, however, it seemed that crossing the line meant nothing unless someone asserted that it meant something. At Fort Snelling, Dred Scott met and married a woman named Harriet Robinson, and over the years they had four children. John Emerson died in 1843 and the ownership of the Scotts passed to his widow, Irene Emerson. In 1846, after having traveled from Florida to Texas and back to Missouri while on "loan" to Irene Emerson's brother-in-law, the Scotts sued for freedom in Missouri under the theory that extended residence on free soil had emancipated them. Under Missouri law up to that time, this seemed to be a sound legal argument. After years of litigation and appeal, the Missouri Supreme Court found against the Scotts, ruling that whatever had been their status in Illinois or at Fort Snelling, by returning to Missouri the status of slave had become "reattached" to them.[45] In 1851, the Scotts were sold to Irene Emerson's brother John Sandford. Sandford was a resident of New York, but the Scotts remained in St. Louis. Assuming that the Scotts were free and therefore citizens, the "diversity of citizenship" between the Scotts and Sandford gave the Scotts access to federal circuit court, so once again they sued for freedom.[46] There Judge Robert Wells found the Scotts to be slaves, to have always been slaves, and therefore not to be citizens and not to have standing to sue in federal courts. It was this decision that was appealed to the U.S. Supreme Court.

Localizing Freedom: *Scott v. Sandford*

In the case of *Scott v. Sandford*, nearly all of the racial geopolitical issues of the era were translated into the terms of legal discourse. Most of the arguments were brought to bear on two principal questions. First, were the Scotts citizens, at least for the limited purpose of having access to federal courts? If the answer to this question was no, then all of the other questions would be irrelevant. The second question was: Were Dred and Harriet Scott and their children free by virtue of their residence in territories from which slavery had been prohibited? This question presented the Supreme Court with the opportunity to engage the larger geopolitical issue of the day: Did Congress have the power to prohibit or the duty to protect slavery in the territories?[47]

The Scotts' case had begun years earlier as obscure freedom suits in St. Louis. It was argued before the U.S. Supreme Court in February of 1856 but reargued in December of that year after Democrat James Buchanan had been elected president. Between February and December, it became a political issue of great significance.

Over the years of litigation, the Scotts had been represented by a number of attorneys. By the time the case reached the Supreme Court for the first time, they were being represented by Montgomery Blair, a prominent Washington attorney, native of Missouri and free-soiler. Sandford was represented by U.S. Senator Henry Geyer of Missouri and proslavery advocate Reverdy Johnson. Johnson was formerly a senator from Maryland and U.S. attorney general under President Tyler. In the words of Donald Fehrenbacher, he was "probably the most respected constitutional lawyer in the country."[48] Clearly the stakes were high. At the reargument in December, Blair was joined by George T. Curtis of Massachusetts, a brother of Benjamin Curtis, the attorney who had represented the slaveholder in *Aves* twenty-one years earlier and was now an associate justice of the Supreme Court.

In addressing the question of citizenship, Blair drew interesting distinctions. First, he asserted that "citizen" was, in federal law, synonymous with "free inhabitant." Therefore all inhabitants of the United States who were not slaves were citizens. However, he acknowledged that in a "caste" society one could be a citizen without enjoying a full range of political rights. Free blacks—as the Scotts were alleged to be —were thus in the category of "quasi-citizens." As such they had some rights, like access to federal courts, even if they lacked others, like the right to vote or serve on juries.[49]

While there was nothing particularly "spatial" about Blair's understanding of citizenship, Henry Geyer's counterargument began to suggest the important spatiality of citizenship that would be developed by Chief Justice Roger Taney in his opinion for the Court. Geyer simply denied the Scotts' right to bring suit in federal court by stressing the dual nature of U.S. citizenship: state and national. There were two ways that a person could become a citizen of the United States. One could be born a citizen or one could be naturalized. The Scotts, even if now free, had certainly not been born citizens; neither, of course had they been naturalized. They were therefore, Geyer maintained, not citizens and could not bring suit in federal courts under the diversity clause.[50]

The central issue in the case, at least as far as the Scotts were concerned, was their freedom. This turned, for Blair, on a number of points such as whether Emerson's stays in Illinois and Fort Snelling counted as "sojourning" or "residing," whether his status as an army officer constituted an exception to the rules, and whether Missouri's policy of reattachment was the last word in the matter. Blair, of course, answered the questions in a way that added up to freedom for the Scotts. But Geyer and Johnson made the politically explosive argument that the Scotts had, in fact, been slaves while at Fort Snelling because the law that prohibited slavery there—part of the Missouri Compromise legislation that had drawn the line at 36°30′—was unconstitutional because Congress did not have the authority to legislate on the topic of property in the territories. Significantly, much hinged here on the meaning of the word *territory* as found in Article 4, section 3, of the Constitution, which reads: "The Congress shall have the power to dispose of and make all needful rules and regulations respecting the Territory or other property belonging to the United States."

In order to take a closer look at this key part of the debate, I will sketch the conflicting understandings offered by Chief Justice Taney and Justice Curtis. Taney adopted an "exceedingly narrow interpretation"[51] of the territory clause, claiming, first, that it only referred to ownership or the disposal of public property and not to the "supreme power of legislation or governance." This, to his way of seeing things, had important consequences. Second, he held that it only referred to the territories that existed at the time of ratification and not to any of the territories acquired after 1798. In the latter category were the lands of the Louisiana Purchase. He also claimed that the phrase "rules and regulations" in the territories clause was meant to signify something weaker than "law," so whatever authority Congress may have possessed in the territories was severely limited and did not extend to local police powers or to property law.[52] To forbid slavery in the territories was to exercise precisely those kinds of prohibited powers. Moreover, Taney asserted, not only did Congress not have the power to forbid slavery in the territories but the Fifth Amendment created a positive duty to *protect* property. In Taney's view, slaves were no different than any other sort of property in deserving the protection of the government.[53]

According to Taney's reading of the legal landscape, the territories clause of the Constitution did not apply west of the Mississippi when the United States acquired Louisiana but the Fifth Amendment due process clause did. Much (most?) of the legislation that had been enacted over the preceding seventy years concerning life in the territories was, therefore, unconstitutional. Slavery was not prohibited anywhere in the United States except in some northern states that had taken positive action to abolish it. In a reversal of Shaw's spatiality in *Aves*, slavery as a property relation corresponded to natural law and was ubiquitous while abolition—and therefore freedom—was positive and local; slavery was the rule, freedom the exception.[54] The Scotts' stay on the Upper Mississippi had no effect on their status or their relationship with whoever claimed to own them.

Interestingly, Justice John Catron, who had been a territorial judge and who had sentenced people to death "for crimes committed where direct legislation from Congress was the only rule," could not accept that Congress had so little authority in the territories. For Catron, if it had not been possible to prohibit slavery in the Louisiana Purchase, it must have been because such a prohibition would have violated the treaty with France![55]

Justices Benjamin Curtis and John McLean, assuming what Fehrenbacher refers to as "the Republican position of interpreting the Territorial clause broadly,"[56] found, first, that this part of the Constitution necessarily entailed the full power of Congress to govern and, second, that this power was not confined by the pre-1803 boundaries of the United States. Congress therefore had the power to prohibit slavery in the territories. The exercise of that power in the legislation constituting the Missouri Compromise was, in their view, valid. The *Somerset* and *Aves* principle that slavery could not exist where it was not protected by positive law meant that, in crossing the line out of Missouri into the territories, the relation of master and slave was dissolved.

In *Scott*, as in *Aves* and *Prigg*, we can see in the practice of legal argument instances of the practice of territoriality, the creation of legal meaning and the assignment of that social relational meaning to lines and spaces in the world. It is of interest here that in *Scott* the practice of territoriality took place in the context of contests concerning constitutional theories of the territories clause of Article 4 and, ultimately, contests over the intended meaning of the word *territory*. A narrow reading of the word meant that the Scotts were still slaves, a broader reading that they were free. In speaking of the narrowness or breadth of the concept "territory," we use spatial metaphors to conceptualize the kinds of powers or authority the people called Congress were capable of exercising in relation to others. A broad reading contained more powers; a narrow reading limited the kinds of actions to fewer and less significant rules and regulations. Of course, the master concept throughout all of these arguments was power itself. The various classes of congressional power—express or implied, necessary and proper, and so on—were themselves tokens of the presence or absence of constraints on those who would be masters over those they claimed to own.

Postwar Reconstructions of the Legal Landscape

As was discussed in chapter 2, many of the questions relating to race, law, and geographies of power in this era were ultimately settled by force of arms. However, it is also true that many questions remained and many new ones arose. Many that until quite recently had been rather theoretical quickly became urgent and practical. Among these were questions of secession and disunion and those relating to slavery in the territories. In the last years of the war, the spatiality of slavery—or at least a legal description of it—was reshaped by the Emancipation Proclamation. Also, in 1863 the Fugitive Slave Law of 1850 was repealed and so slavery, though still formally in existence in the four border states of the Union, seemed at last to be doomed.

The ending of the war brought complex questions of what was to be done to the fore. Many aspects of this question had little directly to do with either race or spatiality, but because the spatiality of race relations had been central to the war, interpretations of this spatiality were of direct relevance to Reconstruction. Different and incompatible views of the inherent spatiality of power had precipitated the war. At the war's end the superiority of Union force had conferred primacy on what William Wiecek has referred to as "the Republican Nationalist anti-slavery view of power."[57] From the perspective of the Thirty-ninth Congress, the task was to solidify elements of this view. Especially in the face of continued southern defiance and presidential accommodation to Confederate and Democratic or States' Rights views of power, members of Congress felt the necessity to constitutionalize their revision of power. This move was to have significant consequences for how the geopolitics of race would be played out for the next 130 years.

The first step in this reconstitution of power was the drafting and ratification of the Thirteenth Amendment in 1865. The Thirteenth Amendment expressly abolished slavery in the United States "or any place subject to their jurisdiction" and empowered Congress to "enforce this article by appropriate legislation." In abolishing slavery the amendment erased—or at least modified—the meaning of the line that had defined the sections, i.e., the North and South. As was discussed in chapter 2, it worked its way down to the ground and modified the meaning of the lines defining plantations as legal spaces. It constitutionalized the prohibition of the confinement and immobilization that was integral to slavery. It made the practices of slavery violations of *federal* law.

The Thirteenth Amendment also seemed to work a radical reconfiguration of the spatiality of federalism, sovereignty, and the spatial contingency of rights. The previous dominant understanding—that is, the one held by all but the most radical abolitionist constitutional theorists—was that personal status and citizenship and the rights that attach to and define citizenship were all matters for the states to define, confer, and enforce. This was most clearly seen in pre-war times with respect to slavery itself. States could recognize and regulate—or they could abolish—the relation within their borders. The Thirteenth Amendment removed this power from the states as a matter of federal law. It prohibited states from establishing or protecting slavery and invalidated all of the statutes and state constitutional provisions regarding slavery. Moreover, under prevailing conceptions of sovereignty, the authority to confer rights entailed the authority and obligation to enforce and protect those rights. It thus seemed to many that the Thirteenth Amendment gave to Congress a potentially limitless amount of power over civil rights. In its effect on citizenship it seemed to some to nearly abolish the states as sovereign entities. In any case, it resulted in a radical revision of the boundary between federal and state power.[58]

While it was rather obvious to at least most people that the abolition of slavery meant that those who had been held in bondage were now free, it was no clearer than it had been in 1857 that "free" necessarily meant "citizen." Again, there were, broadly speaking, two views on the relation of the meaning of freedom to the meaning of citizenship. One view saw the Thirteenth Amendment as simply having freed the slaves and having no relationship to citizenship at all. The other—Republican, nationalist—view defined citizenship as being the status of "freemen" with "natural rights." Under the enforcement clause of the Thirteenth Amendment, Congress gave substance to this broader interpretation of abolition in the Civil Rights Act of 1866.

This act defined a U.S. citizen as anyone who had been born in the United States or had been naturalized. It further enumerated some of the rights inhering in U.S. citizenship which included the right to testify in court, to enter into contracts, to sue and be sued, to acquire and dispose of property. The act criminalized infringement of these rights of U.S. citizenship and allowed for the prosecution of infringements in federal courts. The Civil Rights Act of 1866 radically altered the cluster of notions centered on federalism, sovereignty, citizenship and rights at the heart of constitutionalism in the United States. Much of what was changed was the spatial contingency of rights. The primacy of national over state citizenship and of federal over state enforcement meant that basic civil rights were nationalized—much as the slaveholder's right of recaption had been nationalized a generation earlier.

Given the different interpretations of the effect of the Thirteenth Amendment on conceptions of citizenship, rights, and sovereignty, and given the continued resistance of many southerners to Republican and nationalist views of power, congressional Republicans recognized that the Civil Rights Act of 1866 was vulnerable to repeal by subsequent Congresses or to invalidation by the Supreme Court. To forestall that development, congressional radicals sought to constitutionalize their broad nationalist understanding of the amendment by incorporating key aspects of the Civil Rights Act into a Fourteenth Amendment. (The most significant section of this act for our purposes is section 1, which concerns national citizenship, the privileges and immunities of national citizenship, and prohibitions regarding state deprivation of rights without due process and the denial of equal protection of the laws.) The meaning of the Fourteenth Amendment was questioned in the late 1860s in Congress and in the ratification debates in the states. It has been debated ever since. Nonetheless, the amendment did seem to be an apparent reconfiguration of the spatiality of power and the spatial contingency of rights. And, unlike the Civil Rights Act of 1866, this reconfiguration seemed not to hinge on a repealable statute or on the conceptual implications of freedom but was grounded in a restructuring of constitutional federalism itself.

As a result of the Civil War, then, the legal landscape had been for at least some purposes irrefutably altered from a state-centered federalism to a nation-centered federalism. In the Thirteenth and Fourteenth Amendments, civil rights were nationalized and governmental powers were centralized in order to create a more unified and uniform legal space. Less discretion on the crucial political issues of rights and citizenship was left to the states or to local groups who might capture state power. These postwar reconstitutional moves were made expressly as qualified repudiations of the localism, decentralization, and fragmentation that had fueled sectionalism and that had permitted two incompatible legal orders to exist within one legal space. The amendments were also resources that would be used in subsequent struggles over the legal meaning of geographies of race.

Other elements of the legal reconstruction of social relations included the Fifteenth Amendment guaranteeing voting rights to black men and the Enforcement Acts of 1870 and 1871.[59] These last two were responses to the increased repression and intimidation of blacks, unionists, and Republicans in the South. They spelled out provisions for federal indictments and for the prosecution of crimes in federal courts. That is, they facilitated the assertion of national authority in local disputes and opened the way for litigation as a key component of that assertion. In general, the strategy of defendants in such cases was to attempt to relocalize aspects of racial politics by denying federal authority over civil rights.[60] In order to do this, they had to portray the enforcement of the various civil rights acts as being outside the scope of the recent amendments. In order to accomplish that they had to construct a narrow reading of the amendments so that the federal actions (prosecutions) would fall outside of them.

For all of the clarity and simplicity that the meaning of the Reconstruction amendments and legislation brought to some aspects of the legal landscape, they introduced more ambiguity and complexity to others. For all of the questions determinately closed off, others were opened up. In the 1870s there remained at least two plausible but incompatible theories of what the reconstruction of legal meaning had accomplished, of how social relations of power had been reconstituted, of how the spatiality of power had been reconfigured. On the one hand, there remained "broad" nationalist interpretations whose boundaries were set by claims of necessary implication and relatively extensive chains of inference; on the other hand, "narrow" state-centered interpretations that limited the play of implication continued to have support. For example, where the former considered the Thirteenth Amendment to have conferred extensive rights of citizenship on former slaves and to have authorized Congress to protect these rights, the latter considered it to have merely abolished the relation of master and slave. Similarly, a broad interpretation of the citizenship and privileges and immunities clause of the Fourteenth Amendment included a wide range of rights in the category of U.S. citizenship while a narrow interpretation strictly limited the rights. A broad interpretation of the Fourteenth Amendment prohibited both state action and *inaction* in the face of deprivation of the rights of citizens, and so allowed direct federal punishment of "private" acts. In contrast, a narrow interpretation held that only overt state action, or only unreasonably discriminatory acts of state legislatures, was prohibited. As there had been (at least) two plausible interpretations of the spatiality of slavery, so there were (at least) two interpretations of the revised Constitution's effect on the spatiality of citizenship and federalism. As there was also an urgent need on the ground to protect the rights of citizens, there was an imperative to get the map right.

Again, these arguments were very much about the spatiality of power. They would be refined, repeated and rehearsed far into the future. The most enduring aspect of the amendments has been their function as a framework within which to situate all subsequent claims on the topics of race, rights and federalism.

Revising the Reconstructed Spatiality of Federalism:
The Slaughter House Cases

In 1873 the Supreme Court made a critical determination of the scope of the Reconstruction amendments when by a five to four margin it endorsed the narrow, states' rights reading of the Fourteenth Amendment's citizenship and privileges and immunities clauses.[61] It was initially unclear what effect this ruling might have on the geopolitics of race because the case itself—that is, the facts in the world that attorneys had shaped into a case—did not concern race relations at all, but rather the constitutionality of a state regulation establishing a monopoly on the butchering of animals in New Orleans. The regulation was challenged under the Fourteenth Amendment by other butchers of New Orleans on the grounds that it deprived them of "property" without "due process of law." The butchers were represented in the Supreme Court by former associate justice John Campbell—who sixteen years earlier had joined Roger Taney in denying congressional authority to prohibit slavery in the territories. Campbell now argued for a broad nationalist reading of the Fourteenth Amendment which prohibited states from infringing on the rights of U.S. citizens—as the slaughterhouse regulation was alleged to have done. The state's position was argued by Thomas Durant who urged a narrow state-centered reading of the amendment.[62]

Justice Samuel Miller found that the statute did not violate the amendment because the rights that the butchers were asserting were not among those classed as rights of U.S. citizens. He did, however, acknowledge the historical vagueness and continued contestability of the boundaries in question.

In the early history of the organization of the government, its statesmen seemed to have divided on the line which should separate the powers of the national government from those of state governments, and though this line has never been very well defined in public opinion, such a division has continued from that day to this.[63]

The status of citizen of the United States and the status of citizen of a state remained distinct and separate, as did the rights that attached to the two aspects of dual citizenship and the power of these distinct sovereignties to enforce those rights. According to Miller, the framers of the Fourteenth Amendment did not intend "to transfer the security and protection of all civil rights . . . from the states to the federal government."[64] By way of illustrating where the line between national and state power was located, Miller noted that among the privileges and immunities that the federal government could protect were the right to "life, liberty and property when on the high seas" and "the right to use the navigable waters of the United States, however they may penetrate the territory of the several states."[65]

Justices Stephen Field, Joseph Bradley, and Noah Swayne and Chief Justice Salmon Chase disagreed with Miller's drawing of the line, his understanding of recent constitutional history, and his construal of the reconstructed spatiality of power. For Field, "the fundamental rights, privileges and immunities which belong to [one] as a free man and a free citizen now [after the Fourteenth Amendment] belong to [one] as a citizen of the United States, and are not dependent upon citizenship of any state."[66] Those rights were also extensive and included those enumerated in the Civil Rights Act of 1866. They included as well "the right to pursue a lawful employment in a lawful manner." The denial of this right was also forbidden by the Thirteenth Amendment's prohibition of "involuntary servitude."

Bradley also found a broad range of rights in the reconstructed version of national citizenship. Protection of those rights, though, was still left to the states "unless actually invaded by the unconstitutional acts or delinquency of the state governments themselves."[67] Swayne, in turn, distinguished fundamental rights from "certain others, local in character." The former are the privileges and immunities of citizens of the United States. However, the Reconstruction amendments were found to "trench directly upon the power of the states." In Swayne's view, the construction of the Fourteenth Amendment advanced by the majority, at least insofar as it would apply to black people, was so narrow as to turn "what was meant for bread into a stone."[68]

All of these declarations were attempts to create or limit legal meaning. Because the topic was the reconstructed meaning of federalism, and because federalism is about the spatiality of power, then each of these declarations was aimed at the reconstruction of the legal landscape.

In construing the Reconstruction amendments broadly or narrowly, the participants—here, Campbell, Durant, Miller, Field, Bradley, and Swayne—were not simply arguing about the meaning of words and phrases. They were engaging in acts of legal categorization. What kinds of situations counted as involuntary servitude? Which rights counted as the privileges and immunities of citizens of the United States and which ones didn't? Which acts counted as constituting due process or as denying it? What was it about such situations, rights, or acts that compelled their being grouped with some and differentiated from others? Where did one draw the lines? Using the amendments as a standard, the justices drew the lines in different places. In drawing the lines, in deploying and filling key categories, they were, of course, attempting to reconfigure complex relations of power. Not only those relations concerning the conceptual entities "state government" and "federal government" but also—and with direct if complicated consequences—face-to-face relations of power among actual people in real places.

According to Robert Kaczorowski, "The legal impact of the *Slaughter House* cases . . . was not immediately clear to contemporary observers."[69] After 1873, the Grant administration curtailed federal enforcement of civil rights except in the most egregious cases. Moreover, the apparent remoteness of the fate of New Orleans butchers from the daily fears of southern blacks and Republicans "permitted federal judges to interpret in contradictory ways the constitutional authority upon which efforts [of the national government to protect civil rights] depended."[70] These ambiguities, however, were soon to be (provisionally) clarified.

On the day before the Supreme Court announced its decision in the *Slaughter House Cases*, at least sixty black Republicans were killed in Colfax, Louisiana, in an election dispute known as the Grant Parish massacre. Some whites were indicted under the Federal Enforcement Act of 1870. The validity of this indictment—that is, the power of the national government to prosecute infringements of civil rights—was decided by the Supreme Court in 1876 in the case of *United States v. Cruikshank*.[71] Decided at the same time was the case of *United States v. Reese*,[72] which was triggered by attempts by city tax collectors in Lexington, Kentucky, to effectively disenfranchise blacks by refusing to accept tax payments that were a requirement for voting.

The federal government's view that enforcement was both authorized and required in these cases was argued in the Supreme Court by Attorney General George Williams. Representing the defendants was John Campbell, who had now abandoned the broad expansive view of the Reconstruction amendments that he had favored in *Slaughter House*. Campbell argued that to recognize congressional authority to punish crimes such as those committed at Colfax would lead to the "entire subversion of the institutions of the States and the immediate consolidation of the whole land into a consolidated empire." [73] Also representing the interests of state sovereignty against the invasion of the federal government were David Bryon, David Dudley Field (brother of Associate Justice Steven Field), and R. H. Marr, who declared to the Court that "the time has come when the line of demarcation between State and Federal power must be plainly defined and maintained with a steady and an even hand lest it be obliterated and utterly lost." [74]

Chief Justice Morrison Waite drew the line where Marr had suggested it be drawn. In Kaczorowski's terms, he "ignored [the] vast changes in American federalism that resulted from the Civil War and Reconstruction" and "affirmed the antebellum state's rights view of American federalism." [75] Waite emphasized the continued existence of two separate governments which were "established for different purposes" and had "different jurisdictions." "The powers which one possesses," he wrote, "the other does not." And those powers possessed by the national government were limited and defined. "Within the scope of its powers, as enumerated and defined [the federal government] is supreme and above the states; but beyond it has no existence." [76] The category of federal power did not include the protection of voting rights as spelled out in the Enforcement Act of 1870. As a result, the indictments against the leaders of the Grant Parish massacre were quashed and federal authority to protect civil rights was further limited.

Metaphorical "Invasions": The Civil Rights Act of 1875 and *The Civil Rights Cases* of 1883

In 1875, as a last effort, Congress attempted to bring what radicals considered to be the meaning of the Fourteenth Amendment down to earth. The

Civil Rights Act of 1875—passed under a broad conception of the Fourteenth Amendment after the Court had rejected this reading in *Slaughter House*—directly intervened in the geography of everyday life by prohibiting racial discrimination in "inns, public conveyances . . . theaters and other places of public amusement."[77] It therefore made access to or exclusion from such spaces a matter of federal law. The act provided for both civil damages and criminal prosecutions. This, it seemed, was a critical move in the geopolitics of race, and one aimed at the emerging or solidifying patterns of racial exclusion and segregation. It also classified some spaces as falling within its provisions while other spaces—such as schools and churches—were classed as being outside its scope.[78]

The law seemed to have had an effect on the spatial legal consciousness of at least some people. As John Hope Franklin writes, "Between 1875 and 1877 blacks in all parts of the country were seeking to enjoy the privileges granted in the new law and were demanding that the government of the United States enforce it."[79] People in Richmond, New Orleans, Chicago, New York, Philadelphia, Louisville, Wilmington, North Carolina and Winona, Minnesota, "tested" the new law and were either granted access to public accommodations or they were not; if they were not, some filed charges against those who would exclude them.

These practices were, of course, resisted by the white owners, managers, and patrons of the establishments into which black people made such unwelcome intrusions. Some circumvented the law by closing or by severely overpricing their services with generous discounts for "friends." Many simply did not comply and refused to admit or serve people of color. In those instances that led to litigation, of course, arguments were offered that either challenged the constitutionality of the act or asserted that the specific acts of exclusion were themselves excluded from its provisions. For example, Franklin cites cases in which "ice cream parlors" and "saloons" were deemed not to fall into the category of "places of amusement," and so not to be covered by the act.[80] While enforcement of the act was indifferent at best, it met with mixed results in court. In particular, again to quote Franklin, "there were sharp differences among federal judges regarding the question of constitutionality."[81] In terms of legal consciousness, there was also confusion about what would happen should someone cross the line and demand access to public accommodations or services. It was precisely this kind of ambiguity that all concerned assumed the Supreme Court would have to clarify. And while cases were certified for appeal not long after the law was passed, the Court waited until 1883 to bring order to the legal landscape in the *Civil Rights Cases*.[82]

Then it disposed of five cases that arose in different sections of the country. Four of these were criminal prosecutions. One, *United States v. Stanley*, concerned Murray Stanley's refusal to serve Bird Gee a meal in Topeka, Kansas, in 1875; another, *United States v. Nichols*, concerned W. H. R. Agee having been denied a room in a hotel in Jefferson City, Missouri, in 1876; a third, *United States v. Singleton*, concerned the exclusion of William Davis from the Grand Opera House in New York in 1879. All of these cases reached the Supreme Court on certificates of division of opinion, meaning that the justices who heard the cases at the circuit court level disagreed about the constitutionality of the law under which the defendants had been indicted. The fourth case, *United States v. Ryan*, concerned Michael Ryan's refusal to admit George Tyler to the dress circle of Maguire's Theater in San Francisco. The fifth case, *Robinson v. Memphis and Charleston Railroad Company*, was a civil case brought by Sallie Robinson to recover the $500 damages provided by the Civil Rights Act of 1875, for having been denied access to the ladies' car by a conductor on the Memphis and Charleston Railroad. All of the cases turned on the constitutionality of the first two sections of that act. It is worth noting here that with the exception of the parties in this last case, the defendants in the criminal cases were not represented by counsel. Solicitor General Samuel Phillips argued for the constitutionality of the Civil Rights Act under both the Thirteenth and Fourteenth Amendments.

As framed by both the majority and dissenting opinions, the issue was whether or not Congress had the authority to pass a law that prohibited racial discrimination—exclusion or denial of access to blacks by whites—in inns, theaters, public conveyances, and places of public amusement. The question of constitutionality, then, was answered with reference to how "rights" were categorized: how those who were denying those rights were categorized, how the power to prohibit those acts of denial was categorized, and who had that power. Again, the issues in the world concerned questions about the legal meaning of particular spaces and the rights of access and the rights of exclusion. Significant parts of the world of experience would be opened up or closed off to people according to how these answers were framed.

Speaking for a majority of eight, Justice Bradley participated in closing off large parts of the social world to people of color. He did this by the generation of key distinctions which constituted the categories of significance and then by locating the relevant rights and powers within—or outside of—those categories. As in the previous illustrations, some of these categories were themselves defined with reference to space. Bradley's decision in the *Civil Rights Cases* was a rendering of the legal meaning of the spaces in question—inns, theaters, places of public amusement—in the familiar terms of federalism, or the boundary between federal and state authority. What is of particular interest here, however, is the contrast between Bradley's revision of the legal landscape and that offered in dissent by Justice John Marshall Harlan and the different consequences that could have followed from Harlan's no less plausible rendering.

For Bradley the rights that had been asserted by Gee, Agee, Davis, Tyler, Robinson, and many others across the nation since the passage of the Civil Rights Act were not "civil" rights at all but merely "social" rights. That is, they were not the "fundamental rights which appertain to the essence of citizenship."[83] They were not rights that were inherent in membership in the nation. Moreover, the rights, whether civil or not, were not asserted to have been denied by the actors to whom the Fourteenth Amendment was directed, that is, by "states." "The individual invasion of individual rights" is all that was being complained of in these cases, and this was "not the subject matter of the amendment." "It [the Fourteenth Amendment] does not invest Congress with the power to legislate upon subjects which are within the domain of state legislation."[84] That amendment only prohibited certain forms of "state action" and Bradley could find no state action in the construction of racist geographies of exclusion. *If* state action could be found, then Congress might be authorized to enact "corrective" legislation—legislation that would undo the prohibited deed—but without this requisite state action, federal legislation such as that represented by the first two sections of the Civil Rights Act of 1875 was considered to be "direct and primary." "It steps into the domain of local jurisprudence and lays down rules for the conduct of individuals in society toward each other." Justice Bradley, regarding this invasion with alarm, asserted that "it is difficult to see where it is to stop."[85]

In Bradley's reading of the map of power, the problem in the world did not concern "individual invasion of individual rights" but the invasion of federal power into "the domain of state legislation." This invasion was manifested in legislation that was "primary and direct"—that is, operating directly on citizens—rather than "corrective" and addressed to states, state actors, and state action. The events in the world that triggered these legal disputes occurred in private spaces occupied by individuals who had—or did not have—"social" rights. These spaces could, perhaps, be reached by states but not by the federal government.

Justice Harlan's portrayal of the lines of power was significantly different. First, the right in question was not, as Bradley had claimed, "the right to associate with white people";[86] it was the right *not* to be discriminated against because of race. This was not a "social" right but a "civil or legal" right.[87] It was a right conferred by the Thirteenth Amendment and directly enforceable by the U. S. Congress. More important for Harlan, the legal spaces in question were not unambiguously "private." He distinguished inns, for example, from "private boarding houses" which would not be regulated by the Civil Rights Act. Inns, for Harlan, were "quasi-public" places. Railroads too were "public" in the sense that they "exercise public functions and wield power and authority under the state"; "the function performed [by railroads] is that of the state"; the railroad corporation was "a governmental agency, created primarily for public purposes and subject to be controlled for the public benefit"; the railroad itself was an "improved public highway."[88] Places of public amusement were also sufficiently state-like because municipal governments must license them and they, like inns, railroads, and grain elevators, were "clothed with a public purpose." "The public has rights in respect of such places"; they "are not a matter of purely private concern." In short, "in every material sense applicable to the practical enforcement of the Fourteenth Amendment, railroad corporations, innkeepers, and managers of places of public amusement are agents of the state."[89] Further, because "the right . . . of a colored citizen to use the accommodations of a public highway [i.e., a railroad] upon the same terms as are permitted to white citizens is no more a social right than his right . . . to use the public streets of a city or town, or a turnpike road or a public market," the denial of those rights by a corporation or individual clothed with state authority is an act within the authority of Congress to prohibit and act on directly.[90]

In the generation following the Civil War and emancipation, the legal landscape was the object of intensive restructuring. The fulcrum of this restructuring was the amended Constitution and its effects on the spatiality of federalism. How these effects were understood had important consequences for the exercise and experience of power on a face-to-face basis in real places—wherever rights were asserted or denied, protected or ignored. One feature of the legal landscape that survived its reconstruction was its ambiguity, and so its malleability. In the 1870s the dual spatiality of federalism was revived through the localization of civil rights and civil rights protection against Republican attempts to nationalize them. Proponents of this localization based their reading of the landscape on understandings of the dangers of federal "expansion" and "centralization," the obliteration of the boundary separating and defining the overlapping legal spaces of the states and the nation, and the invasion of the former by the latter. Successful resistance—based largely on assertions about the intentions of those who drafted and ratified the amendments—was a key geopolitical event of the era. So too was the spatialization of the public-private distinction through the invention and refinement of the state action doctrine. Where Harlan had believed that the federal government had as much authority to protect the rights of citizens in theaters, inns, saloons, trains, and "places of amusement" as it did if they were on streets and highways, the majority in the *Civil Rights Cases* portrayed protection in such places as invasive. The formal argument concerned where to draw the line between public and private.

Concluding Remarks

This chapter has surveyed the involvement of lawyers in the geopolitics of race and racism in the nineteenth century. Participants such as Ellis Loring, Benjamin Curtis, Lemuel Shaw, Reverdy Johnson, Montgomery Blair, Samuel Miller, John Campbell, R. H. Marr, and John Marshall Harlan examined the comings and goings of Med, Margaret Morgan, Edward Prigg, Harriet Scott, Bird Gee, and others and advanced conflicting interpretations of the legal landscape. They translated the complexities of concrete face-to-face conflicts into the terms of legal discourse. They debated topics such as the rules and exceptions to the granting of comity, the conditions and consequences of exclusive or concurrent jurisdiction over a disputed subject matter, and the meaning of the word *territories* in the Constitution. In engaging in these acts of translation, these participants were also engaging in acts of territoriality. In construing the legal landscape, they were constructing geographies of power. In each "case," however, there were at least two alternative and plausible readings. And while in a given case only one of these would be authorized as the true and correct interpretation, in any subsequent event this reading would be amenable to alternative *re*interpretations. In any event, the questionable would be declared obvious, the ambiguous clear, and the complex simple, but each declaration would generate its own questions, ambiguities and complexities — or, perhaps, tensions or contradictions. The practice of legal argument and judgment is perhaps most clearly seen as a type of (geo)political practice in the details of specific rhetorical performances and maneuvers through which distinctions are drawn or blurred or denied.

The Geopolitics of Jim Crow

In the decades following the *Civil Rights Cases*, the geopolitics of race became centered on segregation in U.S. cities. Despite profound changes in law, in race relations, and in urban form over the generations, many of us continue to live within geographies of race which had their initial formation a hundred years ago. In this chapter we look first at racial segregation in a rather general way that emphasizes both the inherent spatialization of inequality at the core of segregation and the political practices that contributed to its formation. Then we ask about the role of law in the process—or what I'll call the *de jurification* of racial segregation—and the consequences of de jurification for the geopolitical strategies of antisegregationists. From this rather general discussion we turn to an examination of the segregation ordinance movement, a grassroots social movement that promoted a kind of local apartheid in many cities in the early part of the century. The chapter ends with an account of how the geopolitics of race unfolded in Louisville, Kentucky. The events in Louisville were particularly significant, because it was the legal case that emerged from these that was argued before the U.S. Supreme Court. Chapter 5 will look at the arguments in that case in some detail. We begin, then, in Louisville.

On Segregation

In chapter 1 the connections between geographies of race and experience were illustrated by the following passage from Blyden Jackson's autobiographical essay, *The Waiting Years*. Returning to it now we can begin to explore the practices and events that contributed to the creation and molding of this specific landscape and others like it.

Through the veil I could perceive the forbidden city, the Louisville where white folks lived. It was the Louisville of downtown hotels, the lower floors of the big movie houses, the high schools I read about in the daily newspapers, the restricted haunts I sometimes passed, like white restaurants and country clubs, the other side of windows in banks, and of course, the inner sanctums of offices where I could go only as a humble client or a menial custodian. On my side of the veil everything was black: the homes, the people, the churches, the schools, the Negro Park with the Negro park police. . . . I knew that there were two Louisvilles and in America, two Americas. I knew, also, which of the Americas was mine.[1]

At this level of generality Jackson's Louisville is distinguishable only in name from Walter White's Atlanta, Thurgood Marshall's Baltimore, A. Phillip Randolph's Jacksonville, or even Chester Himes' Cleveland.[2] But of course these *were* different places, and these local geographies of race and racism contained their own specificities, having been shaped by the people who actually lived their lives within them. Still, the main features of Jackson's description would have been recognizable to nearly every black person living in urban areas of the United States throughout most of the century. These features were shaped by "the color line" that cut through all aspects of urban life in the South and North and that was predicated precisely on the denial of specificity. The color line—that controlling metaphor of not only segregation per se but other aspects of racial discrimination and white supremacist ideologies—was the product of innumerable acts of invention, revision, maintenance, and resistance. In this chapter I will examine some of these acts. My present purpose is to discuss some general issues concerning how segregation can be understood.

Segregation, like slavery, is an extremely complicated social and historical phenomenon that has involved the participation of millions of people over several generations. Segregation appears still more complex when we consider it in relation to other aspects of Jim Crow and white supremacy; to still other aspects of social power, for example, class and gender relations; and to other ideologies such as progressivism, black nationalism, and legalism. This complexity is significant for how the geopolitics of race unfolded in specific places such as Blyden Jackson's Louisville.

The term *segregation* is often used to signify the entirety of race-based proscriptions in the era of Jim Crow from the late nineteenth century to the 1960s. In this chapter I want to emphasize the spatial aspects of segregation. But this includes both the spatial forms and the spatial practices that produced these forms. Racial segregation necessarily presupposes racism and racial discrimination, but not all acts of racist discrimination require spatial segregation. Segregation, though, is necessarily *relational*. While one frequently finds reference to segregated institutions, by which is meant institutions for "one race," as in "segregated schools," or to acts of segregation, as in "black people were segregated on street cars," it is important to recognize that the two relevant categories of people were segregated from *each other*. Segregation was constructed in order to reinforce relations of racial domination and subordination.

My concern in this chapter is with the period 1890–1915, a span of years identified by Joel Williamson as having been dominated by racial radicals or fanatical white supremacists.[3] The geopolitical practices associated with segregation differed in crucial respects from those spatial practices that prevailed in the South before the Civil War. At that time white people and black people generally lived and worked in close contact. As historian C. Vann Woodward notes, "Interracial contact, unwelcome as it might be on both sides, was unavoidable" before emancipation.[4] In the period we are concerned with, though, something "revolutionary" seemed to be happening in U.S., or at least southern, race relations. And as we've seen in earlier chapters, a transformation in large-scale relations of power entails a transformation in how power is spatialized. Changes in race relations meant changes in the geographies of race and racism and changes in the geopolitics of race.

Although we are principally concerned with the spatial or geographical aspects of racial segregation, these cannot adequately be understood without reference to the multifaceted intensification of oppression that characterized this period, the nadir of African American history.[5] The first and in some respects most important move in what was a rising wave of racist proscriptions was the various successful attempts to disenfranchise black voters through a variety of subtle and not so subtle means. Williamson has called this process "the depoliticization of the Negro."[6] This move silenced the black voice in local and state politics throughout the South. There were, however, exceptions, such as Louisville and Baltimore. If the South was to remain a "white man's country," then the states—and localities— would have to be, exclusively and explicitly, white spaces of power. This depoliticization was accompanied by a rise in race-baiting by politicians and the escalation of race as an issue—for some as *the* issue—of public concern.

During this period, black people were subjected to an increase in various forms of grotesque violence. The fad of public lynchings of (mostly but not exclusively) black men included episodes such as the Waco, Texas, lynching of Jesse Washington, at which the spectators were estimated at ten thousand, and to which railroad companies hastily arranged special excursion trains.[7] Other lynchings took place in theaters to which tickets were sold. Often the death of the victim was preceded by torture and was followed by mutilation, with body parts cut away and taken as souvenirs of the great event. These horror shows were justified by the pretense of serving the cause of justice through visiting summary retribution on a deserving individual for some "unspeakable" crime. However, they occasionally took the form of a collective rampage against any and all blacks, as in the four-day Atlanta riot of 1906 and the Springfield, Illinois, riot of 1908.[8]

These kinds of events were at the outer reaches of the possible forms that race relations might take at the time. More common—indeed ubiquitous—were the innumerable daily affronts and humiliations that people suffered from the most casual contact with the white world. Readers of white newspapers were continually subjected to images of "the Negro" as criminal, as buffoon, and, increasingly, as retrogressing beast. Readers of black newspapers were treated to an unending catalog of horrors and slights from around the country.

Segregation, in the forms that it took in this period, was part of the spatial solution to various aspects of what was called the "Negro problem."[9] Below we will look more closely at what the problem may have been. It is useful, though, to keep in mind that creation of a "Negro problem" may have itself been the solution of sorts to various economic, political, and, according to Williamson, psychosexual problems that those who were most heavily involved may have been experiencing.[10] My goal here is simply the characterization of segregation at this time as a process of fanatical hyper-territoriality.

The spatiality of Jim Crow involved the assignment of legal meaning to determinable segments of the physical world. As indicated by Blyden Jackson, this meaning was often experienced as exclusion or denial. It presupposed the creation of more or less durable lines and spaces or the addition of an increment of meaning to existing lines and spaces. It entailed the assignment of consequences to the crossing of lines. It was constituted by ensembles of stationary space, such as rooms, toilets, buildings, parks, and cemeteries, and by movable spaces such as streetcars, trains, and later buses and airplanes. In some situations segregation was effected by duplication of functional spaces: schools, parks, cemeteries, bars, YMCAs, libraries, washrooms, phone booths, and elevators; in other situations, by subdivision or compartmentalization, as in waiting rooms, jails, theaters, some hospitals, streetcars, and so on. In many instances segregation meant the simple denial of facilities. Clothing stores, for example, usually had no dressing rooms for African American customers. To state the obvious, segregation was not only humiliating and inconvenient, it made daily life harder. But whether duplicates or subdivisions, facilities were nearly always patently unequal and the "colored" version obviously inferior in nearly every conceivable respect. Also, segregation entailed exclusion from the better "white" spaces. Exclusion and inferiority were integral to the entire system of radical segregation. Consider this more specific description of geographies of race and experience by Louisville high school teacher Lyman Johnson. Johnson here is recalling the city as it was for the generation following Blyden Jackson's:

> [In] Louisville the only park open to blacks was Chickasaw . . . it was a tiny little park. All the parks for white people—Iroquois, Cherokee, Seneca and Shawnee—were so spacious. Negros would drive by these parks and see how nice they were. . . . I'd drive out to Iroquois, stop my car near the tennis courts, and if I didn't see a policeman or a park guard I'd get out and walk around a little. If I stopped my car and a guard came up to me, my excuse was that I was just turning around. As long as our cars were moving we were not technically violating the law.[11]

This passage describes well the experience of differentiation and exclusion. It also conveys a critical awareness of the real power that backed up this differentiation and conditioned the meaning of the experience.

Note, though, that in this hyperterritorialized world white people were not necessarily excluded from black spaces. Black schools often had white teachers and administrators, white policemen could enter black bars, white jailers worked in black holding tanks, and white conductors assigned black passengers to the Jim Crow cars. Likewise, black people were not entirely excluded from "white only" spaces. Black porters worked the whole train, not just the Jim Crow car, and black servants were always allowed to accompany their employers. That is, where actual power relations were clearest, segregation was not required. Segregation, whether inferior duplication, compartmentalization, or exclusion, was used to clarify power relations and the dominance of whites in general over blacks in general. The world that Blyden Jackson and Lyman Johnson both remembered was seemingly constructed out of a concern for power for its own sake.

But of course, it was more complicated than that. As rigid as the color line may have been or however much clarity it may have conferred on lived-in landscapes, the spatiality of Jim Crow was still ambiguous. In fact, as John Cell writes, "The most impressive characteristic of segregation was a complex fabric of structural ambiguity." [12] According to Cell, "This state of ambiguity and contradiction was skillfully and very deliberately created. Confusion has been one of segregation's greatest strengths and achievements." [13] One source of the *structural* ambiguity or contradiction that Cell draws attention to was the apparent—to some—discrepancy between the meaning of Jim Crow and the meaning of U.S. law. "As long as the Fourteenth and Fifteenth Amendments remained on the books [and, one might add, the Thirteenth Amendment and the Civil Rights Act of 1866], the constitutional situation remained ambiguous. Based on that ambiguity the NAACP developed a strategy of challenging segregation in the courts, case by case." [14] That is, attorneys working with the NAACP were able, as part of their geopolitical strategy, to exploit elements of ambiguity and contradiction in the legal landscape. Before we examine how, it is necessary to look at the spatiality of Jim Crow as a specifically *legal* phenomenon. To do this we will ask: What difference did law make?

Understanding Jim Crow

Segregation has long been a topic of debate among historians of the South. Generally they have tried to explain the *origins* of segregation in order to better understand its relation to other dimensions of social, political, or economic change. We need not enter into this debate except to note some aspects of current interpretations that have a direct bearing on understandings of legal aspects of the geopolitics of race during this period.

The critical historiography of Jim Crow is considered to have been inaugurated by the publication of C. Vann Woodward's *Strange Career of Jim Crow* in 1955. Among the key arguments of that work was that

first, racial segregation in the South in the rigid and universal form it had taken by 1954 did not appear with the end of slavery, but toward the end of the century and later; and, second, that before it appeared in this form there occurred an era of experiment and variety in race relations of the South in which segregation was not the invariable rule.[15]

This is an argument about origins, emergence, change, and discontinuity in inherited geographies of race and racism. This claim has been challenged by a number of historians who have demonstrated that racial segregation as physical separation and exclusion predated the 1890s and, in some cases, predated emancipation. For example, segregation has been documented in the antebellum North and, to some extent, in newer cities of the South.[16] But of course in the nineteenth century few African Americans lived in these places. What matters to us is that, according to these other interpretations, the crucial change in the period should not be understood only in terms of a shifting spatiality of race relations, i.e., an increasingly rigid form of segregation. Rather, what was distinctive about the period was how geographies of race were being reinforced with formal laws.

Howard Rabinowitz, for example, notes that even in Woodward's interpretation, "the existence of a law enforcing segregation has always been a key variable in evaluating the nature of race relations" in the period.[17] In fact, as Woodward himself stated, the intended purpose of *The Strange Career of Jim Crow* was not only to illuminate the contours of historical geographical change but also to highlight the role that law had played in the process. The ideas that went into the book were developed to "overcome the prevailing impression—and in southern ideology, the firm conviction—that the subject [racial segregation] had no history [and] that changes in law . . . had been superficial and resulted in no real change in relations between the races."[18] Moreover, in demonstrating the comparative recency of segregation and particularly "the role of law in establishing and advancing it," Woodward sought in 1955 to "invite the hope that the evil [was] superficially rooted and [could] be easily uprooted by changes in the law."[19] What is of special interest to us, then, is the de jurification of white supremacy during this era.

The de jurification of white supremacy is the promulgation and proliferation of *laws*—statutes, ordinances, regulations, and court decisions—formally establishing and validating the hyperterritoriality of Jim Crow. Unlike Woodward, our concern is not the relative antiquity of segregation, but rather with the conditions and consequences of this de jurification. First, if, as seems clear, segregation had been part of the evolving spatiality of southern race relations all along, why did white supremacists begin to churn out laws in such a frenzy? There was, after all, a certain amount of work or effort involved in such activities. There was also more than a little resistance. Second, given this turn toward formal legal means to reinforce geographies of power, how did de jurification affect the geopolitics of race in subsequent years? We will look at these questions in turn.

One set of conditions for the de jurification of Jim Crow that is generally mentioned by historians was the relative absence of much northern or Republican or federal opposition to the steadily increasing oppression of black southerners. This, in combination with the relative disempowering of black men following disenfranchisement, simply meant that there was little in the way of formal political power that inhibited white supremacists from treating "the New Negro" pretty much as they pleased. This we might call the "Why not?" thesis. Also, the depression of the 1890s and the emergence of the Populists with their relatively biracial approach to the economic problems affecting southern agriculture are seen by some to have required the reassertion of race as a political issue in order to divide white and black farmers and ensure the dominance of race solidarity over class divisions.[20]

Another important consideration is that custom was seen by some whites to have been losing its effectiveness in keeping blacks in their hierarchical—and, in fact, literal—place(s).[21] Rabinowitz, offering what we might call the "generational" thesis, notes an increase in the assertion of rights among younger blacks in the 1890s. The generation of men and women coming into maturity in this era was the first never to have known slavery. This shift in rights consciousness was particularly striking in middle-class blacks who continued to seek access to amenities and who chafed under the unequal accommodations that were provided. It also manifested itself in increasingly aggressive responses to police brutality.[22] De jurification of racial codes of behavior, and more particularly formalization of racial segregation, has been seen as an indication of the weakening of racial hierarchy. In Cell's words, "The primary vertical lines of authority and deference characteristic of white supremacy were breaking down. . . . to meet this crisis the power of the state was invoked at an accelerated pace that sometimes left contemporaries on both sides of the color line gasping for breath."[23]

There was also a specific geography to the changing role of legal phenomena in race relations. The sites of the increasing assertiveness or "uppityness" were the rapidly growing cities of the region, especially the inland cities of the New South. According to this interpretation—an urbanization thesis shared by all participants of the debate—the anonymity and propinquity associated with city life lessened the effectiveness of the "vertical" controls that had worked to maintain the racial hierarchy in the countryside. This necessitated the imposition of "horizontal" or impersonal controls, that is, *laws*. "Precisely because urban blacks were more autonomous and less vulnerable [than were rural blacks] their place was circumscribed in more detail." Cell also notes that "city blacks were better educated, better organized and more 'uppity.' They therefore posed a much more substantial threat to white supremacy."[24]

These were, in very general terms, some of the conditions that one might point to in order to account for the de jurification of segregation in the period 1890–1915. I might also note that just as some aspects of the legal system of slavery were oriented more toward the disciplining of whites, so were some aspects of the legal system of Jim Crow. In fact, this element of intraracial control also reveals some of the weaknesses of the system. Dejurification effected a social redistribution of discretion among white people in that contacts, associations, and relations that had been permitted were now prohibited. Discretion—that is, "choice" or "power"—was taken away from white employers, merchants, landlords, realtors, public officials, and lovers, who were required to conform to the color line, and invested in others. For some white people, racial segregation exacted real and burdensome costs—material, psychological, and emotional. Some refused to conform. Still, it is important to recall that the color line had two sides.

Among the consequences of de jurification was that it brought the force of the state—or the threat of force—to bear on nearly every conceivable aspect of interracial relations. There were, potentially, legal consequences attached to almost any act concerning contact or relations between a black person and a white person. Much of this legal meaning was spatialized or hyperterritorialized in that there were legal consequences for crossing any of the color lines that ran through the southern landscape. Moreover, as a matter of practice de jurification put the force of the state into the hands of any white person who chose to exercise it. It deputized every streetcar operator, every shop clerk or nurse, every concerned citizen or librarian, and allowed or compelled them to draw and police the color line as they went through their daily lives.

Finally, and for our present purposes most significantly, de jurification of the segregation regime provided a more visible target of protest. In city after city it provided a focal point for mobilization and organization. It also heightened the perceived need for and visibility of legal action as a component of political—and geopolitical—strategy.

De jurification gave inherited geographies of race an expressly *legal* meaning. This was a kind of meaning that could be interpreted and assessed in the terms provided by constitutional law, property law, contract law, family law, labor law, the law of common carriers, and so on. Put another way, these elements of legal discourse were resources that could be used to challenge Jim Crow. Segregation laws not only regulated racial contact, they also regulated property and contract. Some claimed that they sometimes went so far as to "take" property and to unconstitutionally impair contracts. They reshaped the contours of social relations of power by redistributing rights and disabilities according to race. To the extent that these reconfigurations could be interpreted as requiring changes in property relations or in relations between the state and property owners or in the structure of federalism, they were open to the challenge that law could not accommodate segregation without itself losing integrity. Such claims were the basis for developing strategic legal arguments to be deployed in the geopolitics of race.

The Geopolitics of Antisegregation

Geographies of race were not only the products of white supremacists in city councils and state houses. They were also shaped in broad outline and in detail by the people who inhabited these geographies. In particular, they were shaped by the responses of black people to various dimensions of segregation. As these were complex geographies that had been shaped by millions of people, the responses were of course complicated. The transformations in the spatiality of race relations were mainly accomplished by people simply living their lives in the context of a changing social order. Black people continued to move into the cities of the South and, in increasing numbers, into those of the North as well. What they found there, of course, varied from place to place. In virtually all cities, residential segregation was becoming more pronounced, and the emergence of substantially all-black sections—cities within cities for some but not all purposes—marked a critical turning point in the historical geography of race.

Many people lived much of their lives "behind the veil." They found employment, amusement, and community there. Others ventured out into the white world for jobs during the day but returned at night.

The geopolitics of race in this period does not refer simply to the geopolitical activities of white and black people, or even of segregationists and antisegregationists. It also involved ideological contests among black leaders, both local leaders and those with regional or national reputations and influence. In the political history of race in the United States, the question "What is to be done?" has always generated a number of different, often contending, responses. There were in the period under discussion a range of ideologies that informed immediate and long-term (geo)political strategies. In very general terms, the most significant poles of this range of strategic positions were "accommodation" and "protest" (or, in Meier's analysis, "conservative" and "radical" used with the understanding that these terms have connotations that are very specific to the circumstances and contexts).[25] Our purpose here is to see how these contending ideologies yielded different strategies and how these strategies, in turn, were affected by the de jurification of Jim Crow.

Again, analytically it is hard to separate ideologies and strategies concerning segregation per se from those concerning other elements of racial repression and discrimination. Yet in broad terms it is clear that because the spatiality of race and racism was at the very heart of changes in race relations of the era, it was necessarily at the center of discussions and programs concerning what to do. The ideological positions of accommodation and protest had their spatial correlates in strategic assessments of the comparative merits of a form of measured separatism or integration. The thrust of these debates concerned the *spatial* conditions of liberation. The issue here amounted to whether the best approach to the "race problem" was to hold the line that had been drawn and stay within the spaces that were created, or to breach the line and fight against the confinement and the subordination that segregation entailed.

The conservative strategy was to "make an advantage out of disadvantage." Ideologically, it stressed economic measures of self-help and property accumulation, race pride and solidarity. Conservatives put an organizational emphasis on building institutions within black communities and between them, as with, for example, Booker Washington's National Negro Business League and other professional associations. In many respects, the accommodationism of Washington and others can be seen as a form of proto-separatism, albeit one born of expedience.[26] In holding the line and occupying the spaces so defined, conservatives worked out both an internal policy of uplift, pride, and solidarity and an external policy of conciliation, accommodation, and collaboration. Washington and his allies continually flattered southern whites, sometimes to the point of sycophancy. The corollary of this "foreign" policy stance of conciliation was that conservatives publicly denounced acts of protest and "agitation." Of significance for our understanding of strategies is that they explicitly downplayed the importance of rights, including voting rights and other civil rights. The spatial strategy of conservatives was to work with the given patterns of segregation, to accept segregation "realistically" as a fact of life, and to use it as a means of creating a base of power. Related to this was the discouragement of urbanization and migration. For Washington, the way up began and ended in the countryside of the southern states.

In contrast, radicals could see no advantage to be gained from the obvious disadvantages of segregation. They saw the rapid deterioration of the conditions of the vast majority of black people and had no faith in improvement in the long run. They believed that accommodating and conciliatory attitudes amounted to a voluntary renunciation of the gains made since the Civil War. Indeed, their assessment of the direction of change in the era and the deterioration of race relations led some to think that approaching conditions would be as bad as slavery had been. Rights, it seemed, were all they did have. Radicals, then, emphasized rights, both political and civil, and disparaged conservative ideologies of self-help. They recognized that the black world was embedded in the white world and that white people were not likely to allow a "separate equality."[27]

Of overriding importance to the politics of race in the twentieth century was the founding, in 1909, of the National Association for the Advancement for Colored People. This northern-based organization was established by radicals such as W. E. B. DuBois and leading white antiracists.[28] From the beginning the NAACP advocated a revival of "legalism" as a strategy for social change. It might be noted, though, that legal action as a component of political activity had not entirely disappeared. Perhaps the best-known instance in the era before the NAACP concerned the efforts of the New Orleans–based American Citizens' Equal Rights Association, which challenged the constitutionality of a Louisiana law mandating segregation in trains.[29] Their test case, *Plessy v. Ferguson*, was heard by the U.S. Supreme Court, which validated the principle of "separate but equal."[30]

Nevertheless, under the direction of the NAACP, legal action became more prominent. The viability of legal action was enhanced by the de jurification of racial proscriptions and especially by the emergence in 1910 of the segregation ordinance movement.

The Segregation Ordinance Movement

In the first decades of the twentieth century, black people as well as white continued to leave the countryside for the cities of the South.[31] While the black population of Louisville, for example, remained constant between 1900 and 1920, thus actually accounting for a slightly smaller percentage of the growing city, it had nearly doubled between 1880 and 1900. In other southern border cities, the reported increases in black residents in the first two decades of the century were striking: in St. Louis from 35,000 to 69,000; in Baltimore from 79,000 to 108,000; and from 22,000 to 54,000 in Richmond.[32] These increases should be understood as having occurred in the context of severe employment and housing discrimination. The very poor state of housing available to most blacks and the high population densities that resulted from problems of availability and affordability contributed to what many urban reformers of the day regarded as atrocious living conditions.

In 1910 white supremacists of various persuasions linked up with progressive urban reform activists and approached the "Negro problem" as a festering urban problem. This was a critical move in the geopolitics of race. Out of this convergence of interests came the residential segregation ordinance movement in various localities in both the upper and lower South.[33]

The segregation ordinance movement was a grassroots social movement whose participants hoped to impose what we would recognize as municipal apartheid on residential areas of U.S. cities. Their goal was to prevent black people from living in neighborhoods that they wanted to maintain as exclusive white spaces. As with any grassroots social movement, the keys to success were organization and mobilization. Groups were formed, meetings were held, allies were sought out, letters were written. Neighbors attempted to persuade neighbors to participate. As we saw in chapter 1 regarding the activities of W. D. Binford in Louisville, activists in the movement sought to shape understandings of the dynamics of race and space. As we also saw, and will see more clearly below, conceptions of law, of legal meaning, of rights, property, and constitutional federalism played a critical role in their activities.

The segregation ordinance movement appears to have begun with what was known as "the Baltimore idea" in 1910.[34] The events surrounding the invention, refinement, and opposition to this idea are particularly instructive for our understanding of the geopolitics of social life and, more specifically, to the geopolitics of race of the era.

An account of the geopolitics of race in Baltimore was published in *The Crisis*—the national magazine of the newly established NAACP—by W. Ashbie Hawkins.[35] Hawkins was a black attorney and officer of the Baltimore branch of the NAACP. In his view, the geography of race in Baltimore had been in a state of flux in the years immediately preceding passage of the segregation ordinance. Prior to the turn of the century, black people in Baltimore "had their homes, their churches, and what business places they possessed in the central, southern, and eastern sections of the city." In other sections—western, northern, and northwestern—there were black families, but these lived on narrow streets or in alleys. This, we might note, generally supports Woodward's view that racial residential segregation was not yet as "rigid" as it would become. Then came change. Construction of a railroad yard in southern Baltimore by the Baltimore and Ohio Railroad resulted in a large number of condemnations, while an "invasion" of Russians and other foreigners "forced" many blacks out of eastern Baltimore. At the same time, the development of cable cars allowed for the opening of suburbs. This led middle-class whites to move to the suburbs and, in Hawkins' words, "threw great blocks of handsome houses on the market." After some major black churches relocated in the northwest, middle-class blacks began to buy property in "the great northwest with its splendid houses and wide streets amid sanitary surroundings." Although this occasioned some friction, "after a short time the excitement wore off," and white people either moved away or "resign[ed] gracefully to their fate."[36]

Until 1910, Druid Hill Avenue was "the eastern boundary of [the black] territory." There was also a "tacit understanding that this section belonged to the Negro and that he was not to be further disturbed in his possession of the same." This line was crossed, however, in June 1910 when George Mc-Mechen, Hawkins' law partner and a graduate of Yale University, bought and moved into a house on McCullah Street, a block east of Druid Hill Avenue. White neighbors—in Hawkins' view mostly renters and "otherwise obscure personages"— held "indignation meetings" and gave newspaper interviews. They harassed and embarrassed the McMechens and, had there not been police protection, would physically have harmed the family.[37]

It was in the context of this chain of events that white attorney Milton Dashiell—who Hawkins referred to as a "rampant Negro hater"—"saw an opportunity for achieving a little popularity." Working with Councilmember George West, Dashiell proposed a city ordinance to prevent such transgressions. Dramatic hearings were held, and after a "long and tedious course through the city council" an "unskillfully drawn" ordinance was passed. This segregation ordinance was signed into law by progressive mayor Mahool. The initial version of the ordinance was quickly thrown out by the municipal court. But then "partisans . . . pushed further their war into Africa" and got a better lawyer to draw up a tighter ordinance. The new law, though, differed from the old chiefly in that it had "a large number of legal phrases thrown in to give it professional color and distinction, [but] while skillfully drawn it [was] meaningless and ineffective." Nonetheless, it too was passed into law by the city council.[38]

This sketch of the events in Baltimore is merely suggestive of the kinds of political actions that were involved in efforts to shape geographies of race in the Progressive Era. I'll return to some of these aspects below. Here I will simply note something of the wider influence these events had. "The Baltimore idea," as it became known, was well publicized and imitated in other cities. In April 1911, as the second Baltimore ordinance was being debated, the Richmond, Virginia, city council passed a similar law. In June, Norfolk enacted a municipal segregation law, as did Ashland, Virginia, in September. Moreover, these laws were being enforced. Over the next few years white citizens in other cities were agitating for similar solutions to the "Negro problem." Greenville, South Carolina, Greensboro and Winston-Salem, North Carolina, Atlanta, Georgia, and Louisville and Hopkinton, Kentucky, all enacted ordinances.[39] Though white residents of St. Louis had agitated for such a law as early as 1911, the city council there repeatedly refused to institute municipal apartheid.[40]

The crucial point here is that these segregation ordinances that were enacted in the different cities were products of political actions. This is the geopolitics of everyday life. The legal meaning that was crafted—whether skillfully or not—was the object of deliberate political projects. The inscription of that meaning on lived-in landscapes was the aim of grassroots, community-based political activists. Activists in the various cities with the assistance of lawyers, often city attorneys and public officials, drew lines, created spaces, and conditioned rights and social power according to the meaning assigned to these lines and spaces.

As was merely indicated with reference to events in Baltimore, these episodes were the result of actual individuals taking their time to work with others to shape events and bring about desired social change. Of particular significance in gaining an appreciation of the geopolitics of race in the period is recognizing the effort that went into organizing, mobilizing, and shaping understandings of events. Already mentioned were the "indignation meetings" and newspaper interviews given by Baltimore segregationists. As early as 1911, neighborhood property owners' associations in St. Louis had established "segregation committees."[41] Neighborhood groups then joined together to form the United Welfare Association, an organization that had officers and directed door-to-door canvassing as well as mailings and petitioning efforts. As in Baltimore, opposition to the segregation movement facilitated the founding of the local branch of the NAACP. The branch then organized a segregation and finance committee and a legal and publicity committee which became actively involved in the struggle.[42]

Within the local fields of conflict, all of the participants assumed that legal action—that is, litigation—would ultimately play a major role. W. D. Binford in Louisville mentioned the likelihood of this in his address to the realtors; W. Ashbie Hawkins anticipated litigation in his 1911 piece in *The Crisis*. Before he introduced the segregation ordinance to the city council, the sponsor of the Atlanta bill, Councilmember Claude Ashley, reported that he had been "informed by some of the leading constitutional lawyers in Atlanta that the ordinance will stand a test in the Supreme Court." He also added that "it has been adopted in Richmond, Virginia, and Baltimore, Maryland, and is working out admirably."[43] On the other hand, two days later, in response to black leaders who appeared before the police committee to protest the law on constitutional grounds, Ashley stated, "I don't care if all the courts in the United States declared the law to be invalid, I would still insist that the council give the people of the fourth ward the relief they are asking for."[44] In general, participants assumed that the geopolitical contests being waged on doorsteps, in church groups, at organizational meetings, and in newspapers—to say nothing of city council chambers and mayors' offices—would be transformed into narrower legal disputes. At some point the rhetoric of race and space would necessarily be translated into the available categories of legal discourse. In all cases, lawyers on each side were involved from the beginning in shaping how events unfolded. Of special significance was the role of the NAACP in coordinating the legal component of the fight against the segregation ordinance movement and in bringing the Louisville case to the Supreme Court. By way of examining the details of this transformation, I'll briefly sketch how the events in Louisville unfolded.

But first we should recognize the obvious fact that all of this activity demonstrates the critical awareness that people had of the importance of shifting geographies of race. Segregationists believed that their preferred arrangement would have beneficial effects. They believed that segregation was necessary and worth working for. This, of course, is not to excuse their actions, only to understand why segregation mattered so much to them. Antisegregationists were equally convinced of the disastrous consequences of the de jurification of racist exclusionary housing patterns. What was at issue, after all, was a fundamental dimension of experience: shelter. What motivated people was not abstractions like "property," or even "equality," but the concrete experience of "home."

The Segregation Ordinance Movement in Louisville

Louisville, like other border cities, was where North met South, and the quality of race relations there has always been distinctive. In the years before abolition it was a city with slaves within sight of freedom across the Ohio. During the war, Kentucky, a slave state, had remained in the Union. In fact, because the Emancipation Proclamation only applied to states in rebellion, slavery was only formally abolished upon ratification of the Thirteenth Amendment. In the years after the war and throughout most of the twentieth century, race relations in Louisville were determined by what historian George Wright has called "polite racism," which distinguished Louisville not only from other parts of the South but from other parts of Kentucky as well. "What existed in Louisville was racism in a polite form. It would remain polite as long as African Americans willingly accepted 'their place' which, of course, was at the bottom."[45]

In a similar vein Blyden Jackson writes, "In my Louisville, while it was understood that Negroes had a place and should be kept therein, it was also understood that Louisville was a better than average town where ugly, brutal, open racial friction was not an accepted thing. The local mores did not countenance the savagery of hicks."[46] Among the local ingredients that shaped the politics of race in Louisville in the early twentieth century were a strong paternalistic tradition of the white elite, a Republican Party that continued to be a viable institution after Reconstruction, and a strong core of conservative black leaders with close ties to white philanthropists. Unlike most cities further South, for example, blacks were not disenfranchised, and while there were separate school systems, streetcars were not *legally* segregated. On the occasions when a formal Jim Crow law was proposed, black people succeeded in defeating it.

The black community also contained strong institutions, churches, fraternities, and Central High School—of which Blyden Jackson has written, "My Louisville [that is, black Louisville] was a strong and rich community. I have never felt cheated because I grew up in it. It had one high school and I still wonder if any high school anywhere had a better faculty."[47]

Louisville also had a small black law school and medical college associated with the state university. There also existed a local black elite, styled "the four hundred," which consisted of professionals such as teachers, lawyers, doctors, journalists, ministers, postal employees, porters, waiters, and their families. According to Wright, at the turn of the century black people lived "throughout the city," although there were "clusters" of predominantly black neighborhoods. Soon, however, they were increasingly concentrated in the emerging ghetto known as Smoketown, which was also the center of the white-run vice district.[48]

While the segregation ordinance movements in Baltimore and Atlanta seem to have been triggered by specific transgressive events (for example, George McMechen's buying property east of Druid Hill Avenue in Baltimore), Louisville's ordinance appears to have been more proactive. Although W. D. Binford, in his address to the realtors, speaks of "Negro mercenaries" having invaded the "finest white squares" in Louisville, he speaks in generic terms. The first public record of a move toward formal municipal apartheid is an article in the *Louisville Times* of October 21, 1913, on the revised Baltimore ordinance enacted the month before.[49] The *Times* published the entire text of the Baltimore law. In an accompanying editorial, the paper says that the ordinance "will repay careful study." Asserting that "Louisville is essentially as Southern a city" as Baltimore, Richmond, Atlanta, and other places that had instituted segregation ordinances and that "the problem which confronted them confronts Louisville," the editorial ends by asking, "Does any valid reason exist why Louisville, through the General Council, should not take like action?"

Three weeks later W. D. Binford, an employee of the *Times*, addressed the Real Estate Exchange of Louisville, urging their support for the measure. Both the *Times* and the *Courier-Journal* printed Binford's address in full. As we saw in chapter 1, this address was a rhetorical mixture of Negrophobic white supremacy and the transparent paternalism of "conservative" racism. In one paragraph "the Negro" is a mercenary invader, in another "a brother." Again the *Times* editorialized on Binford's remarks: "The facts, as Mr. Binford sees them, are set forth dispassionately and there is no room for question that he sees them as they are." In the view of the *Times*, "The feeling between the races is excellent. There is room enough for both to continue to dwell peaceably and comfortably without the encroachment of one on territory heretofore exclusively occupied by the other." A segregation ordinance such as Baltimore's would, in fact, "safeguard against race prejudice," and it would clearly be better to deal with the problem now "when there is an absence of race prejudice."[50]

A month later, on December 16, 1913, an ordinance modeled on Baltimore's law—titled, "An ordinance to prevent conflict between the white and colored races in the city of Louisville"—was introduced in the lower house of Louisville's bicameral General Council. Again the *Times* printed the full text of the proposed ordinance and endorsed the idea, but also favored the proposal that an open meeting be held "at which members of both races shall be given the opportunity to be heard." In the meantime, the ordinance was to be submitted to the city attorney, Pendleton Beckley, to be assessed as to its constitutional validity.[51]

While those authorized to create formal legal meanings attended to the letter of the proposed law, members of the black community initiated the spirit of opposition. In the first week of January 1914, a mass meeting was held at Quinn Chapel–AME. The meeting was addressed by M. C. Mason of Cincinnati, an NAACP organizer. At this meeting Reverend William Steward was chosen to lead a delegation to speak with Mayor John Bushemeyer and City Attorney Beckley to convey the strong opposition that existed to the proposed restructuring of the local geography of race.[52] Steward was a letter carrier in a wealthy white neighborhood and had close ties to the white elite. He was the virtual superintendent of the black school system and controlled teaching appointments and other patronage positions. He also had a national reputation as vice president of Booker Washington's National Afro-American Council and as editor of *The American Baptist*. Steward represented the conservative elite of black Louisville.[53] The meeting between Steward and other black leaders with Bushemeyer and Beckley was described as a "lively discussion." The tangible result of the meeting was an agreement to hold a public hearing later in the spring, "the idea being to find out what elements originated the ordinance and what force or influence was back of it."[54]

This public hearing before the Revision Committee of the General Council was held on March 17, 1914. "Representatives" of both races were allowed to address the committee. Speaking for the black community were Reverend Steward, Reverend C. B. Allen, Reverend C. B. Parrish, and Albert Meyzeek. Parrish, a former slave, was principal of Eckstein Norton Institute, a black vocational school; he was also a liaison of sorts between the black community and official Louisville. According to historian George Wright, the conservative Parrish tended to "blame . . . blacks for most of their shortcomings." Meyzeek, a Canadian-born elementary school principal, had fewer ties to the local white elite and was more outspoken on racial issues than were the others.

The main lines of argument put forth at the hearing were that the segregation ordinance was unnecessary (there was no problem), humiliating, a burden to "uplift," and unconstitutional. Reverend Steward, in fact, claimed that similar ordinances had been judged in violation of the Constitution in other cities. Meyzeek complained of white-owned "palaces of sin" driving out the "better class of Negroes" from black neighborhoods. Significantly, J. D. Wright, the former president of the Real Estate Exchange of Louisville who had challenged Binford's interpretation of the issue six months earlier, appeared to speak against adoption of the measure, claiming that the phenomenon of black people moving into better neighborhoods was not the reason for declining property values in Louisville. A major theme of opponents of the proposed law was that de jurification of Jim Crow residential districts, far from preserving racial harmony in Louisville, would actually cause a deterioration in the quality of race relations.[55]

Among those speaking in favor of the ordinance was Patrick Savage, an attorney who claimed to represent five hundred white property owners. His principal points seemed to be that the unrestricted residential mobility of black people reduced property values in some neighborhoods up to 50 percent and that the law was clearly constitutional. One P. J. Dowling stressed the property angle but also, in the cryptic phrase of the *Courier-Journal*, "referred to the social question." In a pamphlet published a few years later, Reverend Parrish and Meyzeek recalled "a battle royal, pungent to the core, full of pith and point, yet with a vein of good feeling on both sides." The meeting closed with Reverend Parrish thanking the council for a "fine display of Christianity and Democracy."[56] The next day the *Times* published an article on the hearing under the headline "Segregation Displeasing to Negroes," while the *Courier-Journal* merely noted, "Sides Heard." Both papers also noted that there was opposition to the ordinance by some members of the council but the basis of that opposition was unclear.

In March and April mobilization against the ordinance continued. Reverend Parrish wrote a circular "with a special appeal to the best thought of the whites," printed three thousand copies, and distributed them throughout the city. Emissaries were sent to various influential white organizations. Edwina Thomas of the (white) Women's Club and several other prominent white citizens spoke against the bill with Mayor Bushemeyer, and delegates were sent to the Board of Trade and the (white) Ministers' Alliance seeking their support. May Child Nerney, secretary of the national office of the NAACP, was reported to have come to town and to have "made friends among white women."[57]

In late April, the ordinance was reported favorably out of the Revision Committee and introduced to the Board of Aldermen, the upper house of the General Council. Reverend Allen was again allowed to address the city officials and delivered "a thoughtful and conservative speech." Nonetheless, the proposed ordinance was passed unanimously. Reverend Parrish and Meyzeek regarded this "as a challenge."[58] On May 11, 1914, it was signed into law by Mayor Bushemeyer. In its final editorial on the topic the *Louisville Times*, which only seven months earlier had invented the movement, wrote, "By the provision of the ordinance the negro must keep within his present boundaries and the white man must respect the colored man's colony just as rigidly . . . with the authority of the law to back up enforcement, the line can now be drawn with precision."[59]

For their part, opponents declared, "Defeated, though undaunted, we sought the intervention of the Courts." And so throughout the summer and fall of 1914 more mass meetings were held; officers of the national office of the NAACP such as William Pickens, Joel Spingarn, L. Chapin

Brinsmade, and May Nerney traveled to Louisville to help organize a local branch and to galvanize opposition. Fund-raising efforts continued and attention shifted to crafting an effective legal strategy.[60]

The ordinance in its final form regulated "residences, places of abode and places of assembly" and made it unlawful for a person of one race to "move into," "occupy," "establish," or "maintain" a place on a block assigned to the other race. The "race" of a block was determined by the "race" of the majority of buildings on that block. A block was apparently to be either black or white but not both. The term *block* was given precise legal meaning, and rather detailed instructions were given for determining the boundaries and meanings of given blocks. There were also rather elaborate procedures for fixing the race of vacant blocks or blocks with only a few houses. Among these was the provision that developers of vacant or partially developed blocks had to declare the race for whom they intended to develop a block. A further provision gave the owners of other lots on the block the right to veto the proposed designation. An interesting twist here was that votes were to be weighted by the percentage of frontage feet of the block that an owner controlled. Thus a person who owned a hundred feet of frontage on the block had a vote that counted as five times that of someone who owned only twenty frontage feet. Also included in the ordinance were procedures for building inspectors to use in preparing and revising maps and, of course, penalties for noncompliance. These included fines of from five to fifty dollars for each offense, each day of continued noncompliance constituting a separate offense.

Setting Up the Facts

In October 1914, Charles Buchanan, a white realtor, agreed to sell a lot on the corner of Thirty-sixth Avenue and Pflanz Street to William Warley, a black postal employee who was also a founding member of the local branch of the NAACP. The lot was strategically located. Officially it was on a white block because eight of the ten lots on it were occupied by white people. But it was a corner lot and the houses across the street were occupied by black people. The contract that Buchanan and Warley signed contained an escape clause to the effect that Warley would not be obligated to pay unless he was allowed by law to occupy the property. Of course, he was prohibited from doing that by the segregation ordinance, so he invoked the escape clause of the contract, at which point Buchanan sued him in the Jefferson

County Circuit Court. Technically the suit was for "specific performance" of the terms of the agreement, that is, Buchanan was asking the court to enforce the contract. In order to do this, however, the court would have to invalidate the ordinance that Warley was using as a shield.[61]

The setup, then, was that Charles Buchanan, a white realtor, was challenging the constitutionality of the segregation ordinance while William Warley, a black political activist, was asserting the validity of the law. The facts in Louisville had been strategically crafted in order to fit within the legal arguments that were being developed by attorneys. As we will examine in some detail in chapter 5, the shape of the argument preceded the facts in the world which were to supposed to trigger the arguments.

The Fourteenth Amendment prohibits states from depriving citizens of property without due process of law and from denying citizens the equal protection of the law. Each of these—"states," "due process of law," and "equal protection"—presents plaintiffs with different interpretive and strategic opportunities and constraints. In this case it is clear that the NAACP's strategy was based on the assessment that any challenge to the segregation ordinance movement would more likely succeed on "due process" grounds than on "equal protection" grounds. Or, to put it baldly, the segregation movement would more likely be stopped if it were shown to compromise the property rights of whites than if it merely denied the civil rights of blacks.

Legal historian Benno Schmidt considers the strategy to have been risky because the "cuteness" of the setup ran the risk of alienating the intended audience, the justices of the Supreme Court. And indeed Justice Holmes found this cuteness to have bordered on collusion.[62] Nevertheless, for our present purposes it is enough to note that attorneys had taken control of the geopolitics of race in Louisville and that a case was being built that would facilitate the translation of the conflict into the categories of legal discourse. For this purpose William Warley was represented by Louisville's city attorneys Stuart Chevalier and Pendleton Beckley, while Buchanan was represented by Clayton Blakey of the Republican law firm of Blakey, Quin and Lewis. Blakey, of course, was aiming to lose—but for the right reasons—in the lower courts so that appeal could be made to higher courts. He succeeded in losing, and when the case reached the United States Supreme Court, Buchanan was represented both by Blakey and by Moorfield Storey, national president of the NAACP.

In Louisville, as elsewhere, actors were engaged in the geopolitics of race. The focus of their activities was a law or rules according to which the legal meaning of social relations of power would be inscribed on lived-in landscapes. The practices that constituted this phase of the geopolitical dispute were those related to persuasion. The sites of geopolitical practice included the places where meetings, rallies, face-to-face conversations, and hearings were held. After May 1914, opponents of the restructuring deliberately set about the task of transforming the conflict into a case. They created the facts that would best fit their legal interpretation. These acts were oriented toward the strategic—and specialized—translation of the local geopolitics of race into the terms of legal discourse. In subsequent phases the drawing and redrawing of lines were to be made on the map of meaning integral to legal discourse itself.

Concluding Remarks

Segregation is a word. It names the core feature of racial subordination in the twentieth century. As described by Blyden Jackson and Lyman Johnson, it names the spatiality of everyday life that was—and continues to be—a key part of how power actually works in the world. The geographies of power that were constructed in accordance with and in opposition to white supremacist ideologies did not simply appear or unfold. They were constructed and reconstructed, reinforced and modified by people. They were the products of deliberate actions. In this chapter we looked at the social-political-spatial phenomenon of racial segregation in general and in specific settings. The chain of events in Louisville comprised elements of the local geopolitics of race before being transformed into a narrow legal dispute. In the next chapter we take a close look at the specifically legal practices through which the meaning of segregation was given form.

5 The Reasonableness of Jim Crow Geographies

The geopolitics of race during the segregation era was principally about the inscription of the "color line" onto urban landscapes. But in translating the issues raised by segregation ordinances into the terms of legal discourse, another sort of line became more prominent. This was the metaphorical boundary that separates state power and property rights. In liberal legal and political thought, one of the principal reasons or justifications for organized government—i.e., the state—is the protection of property.[1] Political liberalism is conventionally regarded as a philosophy of "the limited state." This means that the coercive powers of organized government are supposed to be highly constrained. In chapter 1 we saw that a fundamental procedural constraint on the coercive power of the state is the rule of law idea itself. Another basic constraint is more directly and expressly concerned with property. States possess various powers that affect private property. Among these are the powers associated with the idea of eminent domain.[2] According to this notion, states can "take" property if, first, it is for the public good and, second, the owners are adequately compensated. States also possess a range of powers called police powers through which they can regulate how property is used.[3] In a very fundamental way, the concepts "state" and "property" are, in liberal thought, defined in terms of each other. The conceptual boundary between "the state"—which includes municipalities and other local governmental units—and "property" is often drawn with reference to the distinction between "taking" and "regulating."[4] "Taking," though, does not necessarily involve literal dispossession at all. Often it simply means regulating to such an extent that an owner is deprived of a specific right. The difference, then, is a matter of *degree*, that is, a question of where to draw the line.

Consider this illustration. Prior to the passage of a municipal ordinance, a property owner may have had a right to do something with her or his property—say, use it as a brickyard. As a result of a law restricting where brickyards may operate, the owner no longer "has" that right. Nothing is literally "gone." Still, the right is conceptualized as "gone" because of what the state did, so the state is understood to have "taken" it.[5] The idea that a restriction on one's actions constitutes the taking of property is grounded in other metaphors of how property itself is understood in liberal legal thought. "Property" in ordinary language usually connotes a *thing*, such as a parcel of real estate (Private Property: Keep Out). In legal discourse, though, property is not the thing itself but the rights a person has with respect to the thing in question.[6] Property is spoken of as "a bundle of rights."[7] The state, as we've seen, can diminish the various rights that are part of the bundle. When it does, it is common enough for disgruntled property owners to advance the legal argument that a given regulation "goes too far" and "crosses the line" by effectively "taking" a right. And to take a right in this way is to take property without paying just compensation. A common rejoinder to this argument is that the law in question is "well within the bounds of the police power." These, in fact, are the basic arguments put forward in legal disputes surrounding residential segregation ordinances.

The state and property are conceptualized as separate "spheres" or "domains." As one of the functions of organized government is the protection of property, one of the functions of law is to guard against the "invasion" of property by the state. The judiciary is supposed to prevent the political branches from "overstepping the boundaries" of legitimate power. But if the metaphorical boundary between the state and property—or what I will be calling the *metaphorical spatiality of liberalism*—is determined by the conceptual line distinguishing "taking" from "regulating," how is *this* line to be drawn? In the cases that came out of the segregation ordinance movement, the line between taking and regulating was drawn with reference to the concept "reasonable." Essentially if the law was deemed "reasonable," then it was merely a regulation; if it was "unreasonable," it would count as a taking. But this, of course, begs the question: how is the distinction between "reasonable" and "unreasonable" to be drawn? As you can see, such questions can yield an infinite regress like the endless "whys?" of a three-year-old. Practically speaking, in law as in the rest of life we only push so far. In *Buchanan v. Warley*[8] the foundation for answering all of these questions was provided by conceptions of race, or understandings of geographies of race.

What follows is a detailed examination of how the lines were drawn or how meaning was made through *Buchanan v. Warley*. In state courts segregation ordinances were assessed according to whether or not they represented an "invasive" taking of property. In federal courts this question of the metaphorical spatiality of liberalism was also framed in terms of the metaphorical spatiality of constitutional federalism that we examined in chapter 3. The question in this chapter is whether these laws deprived citizens of the United States of their property without due process of law in violation of the Fourteenth Amendment.

Legal arguments, as we discussed in chapter 1, can be seen as finely crafted maps of meaning. The meaning in question is the meaning of power. In argument, practitioners manipulate elements of the conceptual system of differentiation that is legal discourse in order to produce meaning. They refashion legal meaning in order to reshape the spatial systems of differentiation that are geographies of power. From our vantage point, the conceptual boundary that runs most starkly through the various renderings of the legal landscape is the one that marks the difference between Negro and white. It was a particularly vicious understanding of this distinction that segregationists used to revise lived-in landscapes.

Segregation Ordinances in State Courts

Before examining the specific moves that constituted the arguments and judgments of attorneys and judges in *Buchanan v. Warley*, I will survey very briefly the judicial treatment of other contemporary segregation ordinances in state courts. Here, in these other cases, legal interpretations of the formalization of residential segregation were invented, rehearsed, and revised in the context of actual arguments. From the fall of 1913, when the Maryland Supreme Court ruled on the Baltimore ordinance, to 1917, when the Atlanta law was assessed, each official rendering was grist for the interpretive contests of subsequent cases, just as they were taken account of by nonprofessional adversaries such as Binford and Steward.

State v. Gurry

As Baltimore was the birthplace of the municipal segregation ordinance movement, so was its law the first to receive judicial scrutiny. On October 7, 1913—two weeks before the *Louisville Times* publicized and endorsed "the Baltimore idea"—Justice Albert Constable, speaking for a unanimous Maryland Supreme Court, invalidated the Baltimore ordinance that had been enacted on May 15, 1911.[9] John Gurry had been indicted for buying property in a "white" block in Baltimore and was represented at the Criminal Court of Baltimore by W. Ashbie Hawkins. There the indictment was thrown out by Judge Thomas Elliot due to the vagueness and unenforceability of the segregation ordinance upon which the indictment was based. The state appealed the decision. Representing the state's position were Baltimore city attorney S. S. Field and Maryland attorney general Edgar Allen Poe. On appeal Hawkins was joined by C. Ames Brooks of the New York office of the NAACP.

After discussing various provisions of the ordinance, Justice Constable of the Maryland Court of Appeals framed the issue in terms of the "reasonableness" of a city's exercise of its police power. He staked out the conceptual territory by noting that "it is much easier to perceive and realize the existence and sources of [the police power] than to mark its boundaries or prescribe limits to its exercise." He then marked those boundaries with reference to the reasonableness of other laws mandating the spatial separation of races. Ultimately he placed the Baltimore law beyond the bounds of the reasonable because it "ignored the vested rights" of the property owners it would affect.[10] In making it unlawful for someone who owned a lot in the space designated for "the other race" to occupy that lot, the city engaged in "a practical confiscation of his property."[11] The race blocks created by the Baltimore ordinance of May 1911 were therefore found to be incompatible with Constable's reading of the spatiality of liberalism. In passing the law the state was considered to have invaded property. However, a month before *State v. Gurry* was handed down, the Baltimore City Council passed a revised segregation law that explicitly did not interfere with "vested rights." It was this improved segregation law that was endorsed by the *Louisville Times*.

State v. Darnell

In April 1914, a few weeks before the Louisville General Council passed its segregation law, the supreme court of North Carolina invalidated Winston-Salem's ordinance. A year earlier William Darnell and his family had moved into a house on Highland Avenue, which was in "white" territory in Winston-Salem. He was arrested and tried for violating the law.

Found guilty and fined by the municipal court, he appealed to the superior court of Forsyth County, where his conviction was affirmed. He appealed again to the state supreme court.[12] Arguing for the validity of the ordinance was the state attorney general and Gilbert T. Stephenson. Stephenson, a graduate of Harvard Law School, was the author of the scholarly treatise *Race Distinctions in American Law* as well as a series of more popular articles in the *South Atlantic Quarterly* and the progressive urban reform journal *National Municipal Review* which advocated urban racial segregation.[13] He was, perhaps, the leading legal authority on segregation ordinances. As had been the case in Maryland, the state based its argument on the reasonableness of the segregation.

In deciding *State v. Darnell*, Chief Justice Walter Clark showed no sympathy for the state's position. Comparing formal segregation to the formation of the Irish pale and the Jewish ghettos of Eastern Europe, he pronounced the legislation "revolutionary."[14] Echoing Justice John Marshall Harlan's "slippery slope" argument from the *Civil Rights Cases*, he saw no principled reason why the forced separation of black people and white people could be distinguished from the forced separation of, say, Democrats and Republicans, or Catholics and Protestants, or German and Irish. He also saw no way to distinguish urban from rural segregation. If city officials were allowed to carve a city into race districts, how could county commissioners be denied the same authority? What is reasonable in a city is no less reasonable in the countryside. Of special significance to subsequent debates was Clark's understanding of the effects of police power on property rights. One of the principal and essential rights in the bundle of rights that constitutes ownership is the right to dispose of one's property or to enter into transactional relations with a buyer or renter. In technical terms this is the jus disponendi, which was, in Clark's view, "one of the inalienable rights incident to the ownership of property which no statute will be construed as having power to take away."[15] In sum, Winston-Salem's segregation ordinance represented a revolutionary instance of state invasion that, if permitted, could have had radical consequences for the spatiality of social life.

Carey v. City of Atlanta

The next state ruling on segregation laws came in February 1915 when the Georgia Supreme Court rendered an interpretation of a 1913 Atlanta ordinance in the case of *Carey v. City of Atlanta*.[16] John Carey bought a house on a "mixed block" in Atlanta. He then sold it to another black person, who then rented it to a third. A peculiar feature of the Atlanta law allowed a majority of property owners on a block to vote on whether to accept or reject a neighbor. This provision was later amended to *require* the consent of adjacent owners. Neighboring property owners were given veto rights with respect to the occupancy of adjacent lots. In this case the neighbors vetoed the move and called the chief of police. The tenant was forced to move out, but the owner was then not allowed to move in.

Using a technique that would be employed to advantage by Moorfield Story before the U.S. Supreme Court in *Buchanan*, Georgia Supreme Court justice Samuel Atkinson set up a spatial hypothetical upon which to base his interpretation: three lots on a "mixed" block. The middle lot is vacant and for sale. On the left is a black neighbor who vetoes white occupancy; on the right, a white landowner who objects to living next to blacks. The spatial redistribution of rights effects a virtual stalemate in the world of the two races. In Atkinson's view, the result would constitute "in substance a taking of property itself." The Atlanta ordinance, then, was unconstitutional. Drawing on both *Gurry* and *Darnell*, however, Atkinson stressed that the law was unconstitutional on "due process" grounds and not because it denied anyone "equal protection."[17]

This, then, was the situation when *Buchanan* was making its way through the Kentucky courts. In three appellate decisions, segregation ordinances had been struck down. In all cases the ordinance in question had been invalidated principally for "property" reasons. That is, the ordinances were seen to have violated the property rights of participants in real estate markets. While the North Carolina court seemed to strike at the broad principles animating reconfiguration in the geography of race, the Baltimore and Atlanta ordinances had been faulted on rather narrow grounds. Indeed the defects of the Baltimore law were "remedied" a month before *Gurry* was even handed down. Of course, what had been decided in other states had no bearing on Kentucky law, but these three decisions were landmarks of sorts, which any subsequent argument had to take into account. Pro or con, they were grist for the interpretive mill. They had to be interpreted, distinguished, or extended as part of the legal interpretation of geographies of race elsewhere. In particular they served as reference points in the discursive constitution of "reasonable."

Buchanan v. Warley

When *Buchanan v. Warley* was heard by the Kentucky Court of Appeals, it was on appeal from the Jefferson County Circuit Court, which had found "for" Warley by not invalidating the Louisville ordinance.[18] The case was disposed of at the same time as *Harris v. City of Louisville*, which concerned the arrest of Arthur Harris for violating the segregation law. Justice J. B. Hannah affirmed the lower court decisions, which, of course, is what the opponents to segregation had hoped, since they wanted to be able to bring the case to the U.S. Supreme Court.

Hannah's opinion began with the recognition of the problems "caused by close association of races under congested conditions found in modern municipalities." He then addressed the decisions rendered in *Gurry, Darnell*, and *Carey*. The ordinances that were examined in *Gurry* (Baltimore) and *Carey* (Atlanta) contained "defects" that Louisville's ordinance did not contain. The Louisville law protected vested rights and did not delegate state authority to individuals. These cases could therefore be clearly distinguished from the case at hand. The more sweeping objections of the North Carolina court were dismissed as "time worn sophistr[ies]." Hannah also accused Justice Clark of having closed his "mind to the gravity of the race problem as it exists in our country to-day, and especially to those phases of it most intimately concerned with congested municipal conditions."[19]

As these earlier cases provided but little guidance, Hannah turned afresh to the question of property rights and their relation to state police power, or, in our terms, the spatiality of liberalism. Interestingly, he acknowledged that the boundary between state and property was historically contingent and shifting. In Progressive Era fashion, he wrote, "The advance of civilization, and the consequent extension of governmental activities . . . has resulted in a gradual lessening of the dominion of the individual over private property and a corresponding strengthening of the regulative power of the state in respect thereof." "To-day all private property," he continued, "is held subject to an unchallenged right and power of the state." In concluding, he dismissively declared, "So much for the jus disponendi."[20]

In a like manner he disposed of any federal constitutional objections to the city's exercise of police power. "No extended discussion [was] necessary to establish that reasonable restraints on the use of private property are not subversive of the constitutional limitations." Indeed those "constitutional guarantees [concerning due process] [were] not absolute guarantees but [were] subordinate to the paramount right of government to impose reasonable restraints . . . where expedient."[21]

But was the segregation ordinance "reasonable" after all? In Hannah's view it was. Recognizing "the peril to race integrity induced by mere propinquity," and the fact that "under the congested conditions of modern municipal life there would be practically as much, if not a greater degree of, association among children of white and colored inhabitants when living side by side than there would be in mixed schools under the direct observation of teachers," such an ordinance was more than merely reasonable.[22] Invoking the segregationists' version of the "slippery slope" argument, Hannah quoted from an 1867 Pennsylvania case that said, "The natural separation of the races is . . . an undeniable fact, and all social organizations which lead to their amalgamation are repugnant to the law of nature. From social amalgamation it is but a step to illicit intercourse, and but another to intermarriage."[23] In a final paragraph devoted to a discussion of the beneficial consequences of segregation, Justice Hannah endorsed Booker Washington's program of uplift and racial solidarity. He castigated those middle-class blacks who would, by moving into other (white) neighborhoods, "abandon their less fortunate fellows and be false to the duties and responsibilities laid upon them by virtue of their own success." In Hannah's view, the absence of strict segregation was bound to impede "the uplift of the colored race." On the other hand, "municipal segregation will indirectly enforce their [successful black people's] acceptance of those responsibilities and coerce their performance of the duties thereby imposed, and thus," he concluded his assessment of the shifting legal geography of race in Louisville, "in the end, it will justify that enlightened civic spirit by which it is demanded."[24]

The Louisville ordinance—and the geography of race that it was designed to engender or maintain—was the first to be legitimated by an appellate court. The law and the legal meaning of space it effected were the result of refinements of earlier ordinances enacted elsewhere. In September 1915 the segregation ordinances of Richmond and Ashland, Virginia, were given the approval of the Virginia Supreme Court in *Hopkins v. Richmond*,[25] and while *Buchanan* was being adjudicated in the U.S. Supreme Court, an amended Atlanta law passed muster with the Georgia Supreme Court in *Harden v. Atlanta*.[26] In each of these cases Justice Hannah's rendering of the legal landscape was cited. The Atlanta law was considered to have been "a reproduction of that which was adopted in the city of Louis-ville, Ky.; and which was upheld as constitutional in an able opinion by Hannah, J."[27]

Segregation Ordinances in the Supreme Court: Orientations

Each of the cases surveyed is illustrative of the transformation of social-political conflicts over the spatiality of social life into narrower legal dis-putes and the translation of these disputes into the terms of legal discourse such as the limits of police power, the significance of the jus disponendi, the meaning of due process, and so on. Each case was an event that was brought into being by participants in local geopolitical struggles in order to further their objectives of shaping inherited geographies of power. As a compo-nent of geopolitical strategy, litigation may be oriented toward engaging one set of state actors, the judiciary, in order to reinforce or challenge oth-ers—in these cases, city councils. In appealing a state supreme court deci-sion to the U.S. Supreme Court, the plaintiffs were also attempting to bring federal interpretive authority to bear on state authority. To constitu-tionalize in this sense is to invoke conceptions of federalism in order to an-swer questions concerning the power of the state to modify property rela-tions. If the city council—as an arm of the state—was found not to have had the authority to so reconfigure the legal landscape, it would be because it violated principals of federalism.

It was the job of attorneys for Buchanan to first call the revised legal landscape into question; to exploit elements of ambiguity, complexity, and instability inherent in that landscape; and to then clarify, simplify, and sta-bilize their preferred meaning. The focus in this section shifts now to specific rhetorical or interpretive performances of attorneys for and against racial segregation, and to an analysis of specific rhetorical moves.

After the Kentucky Supreme Court ruled "for" Warley in 1915, the case was appealed to the U.S. Supreme Court, which agreed to hear arguments in April 1916. This, of course, changed the dynamics of the process con-siderably. The stakes were raised, to say the least. While Clayton Blakey continued to represent Charles Buchanan, the Court also allowed the em-inent Moorfield Storey, president of the NAACP, to present arguments for the plaintiff, Buchanan. Oral arguments were first heard in 1916 before eight justices, Justice William Day being ill. The case was scheduled for reargument a year later before a full court on which Louisville native Louis Brandeis had replaced Charles Hughes.[28] In 1916 Storey, who was assisted by John Davis, and Blakey filed separate briefs, but in 1917 they filed a supplemental brief jointly. Warley was again represented by Louisville city attorneys Pendleton Beckley and Stuart Chevalier. In 1916 these briefs were also supplemented by extensive amici curiae briefs by the participants in the local geopolitical conflicts in Baltimore, Richmond, and St. Louis.[29]

Attorneys for the plaintiff (now the appellant) wanted the Supreme Court to rule that the segregation ordinances—and, of course, the spatial patterns they mandated—were in conflict with the Constitution, while attorneys for the defendant wanted a ruling that recognized and legitimized municipal authority to condition property relations on race. The plaintiff's attorneys asked that the Kentucky decision be reversed, the defendant's attorneys that it be affirmed.

Strategic Maneuvers: Opening Positions

In the following sections I will present a rather detailed analysis of the key moves made by attorneys in their strategic attempts to rhetorically restructure geographies of race. I will focus on three central legal-geographic questions to which participants advanced conflicting but plausible answers. The first of these concerned the boundary between the categories "state" and "property" as located with reference to understandings of "the limits of police power." The categorical boundary that determined this limit was that which distinguished "reasonable" from "unreasonable" or "arbitrary." The legal arguments presented are, in fact, extended discourses on the concept "reasonable" in U.S. law. Different lines of argumentation were directed toward giving content to the concept "reasonable." Attorneys sought to ground the difference between "reasonable" and "unreasonable" with reference to two legal-geographic sources of meaning: the legal history of locational restrictions (proto-zoning and other instances of racial separation deemed "reasonable") and an understanding of how geographies of race do—or should—work. These three questions—(1) the spatiality of liberalism and the limits of police power; (2) the legal history of locational restrictions; and (3) the spatial dynamics of social life—will be treated in turn to bring out the *differences* in legal-spatial interpretation. But note: each question begs the next, so that the metaphorical boundary between state and property according to which the map of liberalism is constructed was considered to *depend on* the limits of police power, which, in turn, depended on conceptions of "reasonable." These, in turn, depended, first, on how courts had assessed "reasonableness" in prior cases, and second, on how participants understood the dynamic spatiality of social life. This last mentioned was of central importance, but it in turn depended on how power itself was conceptualized in argument.

Before presenting a more detailed analysis of the arguments, I will briefly describe key elements of the more general rhetorical strategies that shaped the principal arguments.[30] Again, in 1916 there was a rough distribution of interpretive labor for Storey and Blakey, with Moorfield Storey concentrating somewhat more on constitutional questions and Clayton Blakey concentrating more on the issue of police power. In 1917 their arguments were joined and strengthened.

A striking feature of all the plaintiff's briefs (one by Storey and Davis, 1916; one by Blakey, 1916; one by Storey and Blakey, 1917) is the overt appeals to a pragmatic reading of law and the legal landscape. Pragmatism, in this context, refers to a style of argument that emphasizes claims about "facts" or real world "consequences." Rhetorically, pragmatic arguments are often used to characterize one's opponent as being concerned only with "words" or abstractions. Strategically, Storey and Blakey's pragmatic arguments were deployed, in part, to give the Court reasons or justifications for intervening. Theirs was a conservative pragmatism that demanded attention to the effects of such a radical invasion of property as was represented by the segregation ordinances. Storey, quoting from Justice Holmes' dissenting opinion in an earlier case, implored the Court to "look beyond the mere letter of the law."[31] "The law," he argued, "will not allow the right of property to be invaded under the guise of a police regulation for the preservation of health when it is manifest that such is not the object and purpose of the regulation."[32] The *real* purpose of such an ordinance, according to Storey, could be determined by its "natural effects" and not its proclaimed objective. The Louisville segregation law was not really "an ordinance to prevent conflict and ill feeling" as its title announced, but an act to "establish a Ghetto for the colored people of Louisville."[33] The Court, urged Storey, must "look through the words to the facts."[34]

The City of Louisville's rhetorical position was rooted in the notion of legislative deference. This is the idea that each branch of government is supreme in its own sphere, and that unless abuse of authority is incontrovertible, courts should give the benefit of all doubts to the legislative branch before invalidating a law. In the view of Chevalier and Beckley, the Court should not invalidate a police regulation unless "it *clearly* violates the

Constitution"[35] or "unmistakably and palpably is in excess of legislative power."[36] The Court should assume that the Louisville City Council had all of the relevant information and that its members acted in good faith. In answer to the plaintiff's consequentialist pragmatism, Chevalier and Beckley urged that the Court accept that the stated purpose of the law truly expressed the city council's intentions. "Constitutionality can't depend upon the preponderance of evidence in a particular case but upon the language of the law itself," they claimed.[37]

Chevalier and Beckley also countered the plaintiff's position with their own pragmatic arguments. "The field . . . within which the police power may be exercised," they asserted, "is not to be ascertained by mere abstract, philosophic speculation or prophesy," as Storey was attempting to do, but with reference to facts and to the *actual* effects.[38] In their view, the "admirable effects" of the ordinances enacted in Baltimore and Richmond clinched the argument. But in any event, if there was a doubt about the effects—and there was at least that—the judiciary should not interfere. Citing the Court in an earlier case, they wrote: "[A]s to the extent legislation should interfere in affairs[,] political philosophers have disputed and will always dispute. It is not in our province to engage on either side nor to pronounce anticipatory judgments."[39] While Storey and Blakey's consequentialist pragmatism was oriented toward justifying federal judicial intervention in the local geopolitics of Louisville, Chevalier and Beckley's rhetoric of legislative deference was aimed at justifying the denial of intervention.

One other significant element of the contending arguments was the principal stories about race that lawyers told in order to lend an imperative air to the different understandings. As will be discussed in more detail below, Storey and Blakey put forward a highly paternalistic view of the history of U.S. race relations. Under the subtitle *What America Owes the Negro*, Blakey likened "the Negro" to a child and "the dominant race" to an adult. The Negro, he wrote, "must be encouraged to aspire!" and assume his responsibilities. "For the Negro the white man presents an enviable high example whom he wishes to imitate with the hope of equaling," but "segregated as a contamination, obliged to sink and creep, his legitimate longing to acquit himself in all men's sight [would be] forever annihilated."[40]

The principal story about race in the defendant's briefs was presented under the heading "Amalgamation or Separation." Here Chevalier and Beckley suggested that the municipal segregation ordinance was a *response* to the emergence of the NAACP and its alleged program advocating intermarriage. Contrary to the plaintiff's claims, Chevalier and Beckley asserted that there *was* a "negro problem" in America and that there were only two solutions to that problem. Moreover, these solutions were mutually exclusive: *either* the NAACP's proposal for "amalgamation" *or* complete separation. *Amalgamation* was a white supremacist term for "race mixing" or interracial sexual relations. In other settings a word frequently encountered was "mongrelization." The only thing wrong with segregation ordinances such as Louisville's was that they were "not sweeping enough."[41] I'll argue below that these rhetorical supplements or stories illustrate the complex interplay of conceptions of race with conceptions of class and sexuality in arguments aimed at restructuring geographies of power. I'll return to these themes below; the point here is simply to note some of the critical differences in the rhetorical strategies of the attorneys for and against formal segregation.

Drawing the Lines I: Rendering the Spatiality of Liberalism

Of the three legal-spatial questions addressed by the attorneys in *Buchanan*, the first, focusing on the metaphorical spatiality of liberalism, was both the most abstract and, in a formal sense, the most central. The basic legal issue, after all, was the City of Louisville's power to modify property rights in the ways stipulated by the segregation ordinance. As I noted above, in the terms of legal discourse this boundary is located with reference to conceptions of the state's police power.

Plaintiff's Rendering

Storey and Blakey made somewhat different moves in their attempts to show that in passing the ordinance the city council "went too far."[42] Blakey set up a rather narrow range for the exercise of police power. The subject matter of the ordinance was asserted to be "outside the province of the police power."[43] Drawing on J. S. Mill's *On Liberty*, he argued that the "police power has limitations," and that "police regulations must confine themselves to prohibiting acts harmful to the community generally."[44] He then asserted that the city "overstepped the bounds set by the Constitution" by legislating not for the community at large but for the benefit of certain of its [white] citizens.[45]

The strategy, of course, was to construct the category "police power" or, rather, "legitimate exercises of police power" in such a way that the acts to be categorized—passage of the ordinance—would fall on the other side of the categorical boundary in the category "not legitimate." "Police power is broad," he said, quoting the Supreme Court's decision in an earlier case, ". . . but it cannot be given the wide scope that is here asserted for it. . . ."[46] It follows that if the city council did not have the power to create race blocks, to assign *that* meaning to lines and spaces, then those lines and spaces simply did not have that legal meaning. Here Blakey was engaged in an act of countercategorization in an effort to deny the legal meaning inscribed on the landscape by the city council.

Moorfield Storey took a different approach. The limit of police power was, in his view, determined by the reasonableness of its exercise and, as we saw above, reasonableness, in turn, is to be determined by consequences or effects. And the effect of this ordinance was the destruction of rights. In carving out race blocks, the city was "invading" and "taking the essence" of property.[47] Where Blakey began his legal line-drawing with a rather constrained category of "police power," Storey began with the image of a fixed, inviolate core of property. But the result was the same: the segregationists had gone too far and crossed the conceptual line from legitimate to illegitimate state action, from the regulation to the taking of property. In crossing that conceptual boundary they exceeded their authority.

Defendant's Rendering

In their defense of the race block as a legitimate legal space, city attorneys Chevalier and Beckley asserted an expansive, open-ended version of state power to "regulate" property against the dangers of disorder. The bounds of "reasonable" were likewise widely spaced. The import of their overall strategy of legislative deference was to remind the Court that their power to invalidate ordinances was reserved for cases which were clearly and without a doubt unreasonable. It would seem that the fact of there being an argument at all and the fact that the Kentucky court had considered the ordinance to be reasonable were sufficient for the Court to confirm their view. Relying on the maxim "sic utero tuo ut non alienum laedus" (roughly, one may not use property in such a way as to injure another), they argued that property had always been subject to various limitations.[48] In fact, because "ultimate title to real estate rested in the State," they contended that "the highest possible title [was] but a right to its use, subject to such conditions as the State, its ultimate owner, may see fit . . . to impose."[49] This, then, was a strongly state-centric view of the spatiality of liberalism. The boundary between state and property was determined by reference to "reasonableness," but "reasonableness" was measured from the state's perspective. Significantly, the attorneys acknowledged that the boundary was historical and was shifting as state power expanded. Quoting extensively from Judge Hannah's reading of the legal landscape, Chevalier and Beckley asserted that the "jus disponendi"—that allegedly essential feature of property that Storey claimed had been destroyed by the state's invasions—had "little place in modern jurisprudence" and must give way to "advancing civilization."[50]

We have in these narratives contending and incompatible renderings of the legal landscape focusing on the spatiality of liberalism. These discrepant interpretations of the conceptual boundaries between "state" and "property," and between subsidiary or satellite concepts such as "regulation" and "taking," "reasonable" and "unreasonable," and so on, were oriented toward conferring legal meaning on actual landscapes. These participants in the geopolitics of race set up the boundaries of relevant categories and fit selected features of the world inside or outside of the categorical lines. They drew maps of power and argued that the world did or did not, should or should not, correspond to those maps. Each version had enough plausibility to be persuasive. Legal argument, though, is considered to be more than an endless exchange of "'tis and 'tain't." Participants in legal argument must give *reasons* justifying where lines are drawn. In their attempts to clarify, simplify, and give order to ambiguous geographies of power, attorneys must convincingly *demonstrate* that the lines are—or ought to be—where they say they are. The conceptual map had to be not simply serviceable but *true*. Within the practice of legal argument, the principal way of establishing the accuracy of conceptual maps of power is to compare them to a select set of previously authorized renderings of the "same" legal territory. This brings us to the second major legal spatial question debated by the attorneys: the legal history of locational restrictions and racial separation.

Drawing the Lines II: Following the Lines Laid Down

The first question addressed the conceptual map of relative power in the most abstract terms. It concerned the limits of collective or state power to constrain individual discretion with respect to property. This boundary fixing took place on a zero-sum field of power—that is, any "gain" for the state was seen to entail a "loss" for property and vice versa. The second question more specifically addressed the relative power to restructure the *spatiality* of social life. The objective of this line of argument for Chevalier and Beckley was to create the legal categories of "reasonable locational restrictions" and "reasonable racial separations" and to locate the segregation ordinances within these preexisting legal categories. These categories were established by precedent and the doctrines enunciated in previous rulings. The ordinances were asserted to be like those which the Court had previously authorized and unlike those which the Court had invalidated. The plaintiff's attorneys, of course, drew different lines, cited different precedents, and distinguished between *Buchanan* and other cases.

Defendant's Rendering

Chevalier and Beckley presented a three-step argument in support of municipal authority to restructure geographies of race. First, they presented a finer-scale analysis of the recent legal history of the reasonableness or unreasonableness of police power in general. A key legal landmark here was, of course, the *Slaughter House* decision upholding the reasonableness of the New Orleans' law that regulated butchers.[51] They also noted that the Supreme Court had authorized literacy tests and property taxes in voting cases as well as prohibitions on the manufacture of alcohol. These various exercises of police power were all "reasonable."

Significantly, both cases they used to fix the category of "unreasonable" dealt with racial segregation. In *Soon Hing v. Crowley*,[52] the prohibition of Chinese laundries in wooden buildings "within certain designated limits" of the city of San Francisco, was deemed unreasonable by the Supreme Court. Chevalier and Beckley noted that unlike that law, the Louisville ordinance did not *impose* boundaries. Rather, they claimed that the resultant spaces were being worked out gradually simply by regulating real estate transactions.[53]

Yick Wo v. Hopkins also involved restrictions on Chinese laundries in San Francisco.[54] The Court in *Yick Wo* found the ordinance unreasonable because it was applied "arbitrarily." The law under discussion in *Buchanan*, however, was asserted by the city attorneys to be "reasoned," "fair," and "good."[55] There was nothing "arbitrary" about it. Here the meaning of "reasonable"—and so the limit of police power—was dependent on the meaning of "arbitrary." If the law was "reasoned" it could not be but "reasonable."

The second step in the defense of the reasonableness of the segregation ordinance was to conceive of it as a kind of zoning regulation that simply concerned where obnoxious activities could or could not take place. Again, *Slaughter House* was seen to be on point here in that it regulated the *location* of butchering. Chevalier and Beckley also cited recent Court rulings upholding the reasonableness of municipal restrictions on the location of brickyards[56] and livery stables,[57] as well as numerous state court decisions concerning laundries, lumberyards, garages, and billboards.[58] Of particular interest for us is the case of *L'Hote v. New Orleans*, which defined the spatial limits within which prostitutes might be permitted to work.[59] In that case the Supreme Court ruled that "if the power to prescribe territorial limits exist[s]," then the court could not second-guess the legislators who drew the lines. The Court there said that "some must suffer by the establishment of any territorial boundary."[60]

This argument was intended to demonstrate that it was within the authority of cities to protect the "amenities of civilization" by placing restrictions on the (private) location of obnoxious entities. The (at this point merely implicit) categorization, of course, was that black people were like slaughterhouses, brickyards, livery stables, and prostitutes in some significant respect and that the feature they shared rendered efforts to restrict their location "reasonable." The role that *L'Hote* played in the argument was to justify such spatial arrangements even if some innocents might suffer.

Of course, the legal classification of black people with obnoxious occupations was not a wild leap for Chevalier and Beckley. They had ample legal precedential material from which to build their categories. The existence of this material shaped the central tasks of attorneys on both sides. Racial segregation had, of course, been upheld by the Supreme Court in a number of previous cases, most notably, *Plessy v. Ferguson*.[61] The job of Chevalier and Beckley was simply to demonstrate that residential segregation was in *principle* no different than segregation in other aspects of social life, or, if it was different, that these differences made it *more* reasonable or *more* legitimate. Their task was to expand the legal category of valid segregation to include residences and places of assembly. The principal task of Storey and Blakey was to demonstrate that there was all the difference in the world between the other judicially sustained instances and this one.

The next step in defense of the reasonableness of racial residential segregation drew on the legal history of the reasonableness standard as developed in a line of earlier segregation cases. Of central importance in this regard was the portrayal of racial segregation as "natural," and therefore the portrayal of the "opposite" of segregation as unnatural. I'll return to this theme below. It is sufficient to note here that something that is considered natural might more easily be seen as reasonable than something that is construed as being contrary to the law of nature. Chevalier and Beckley stated flatly that there was "no legal or practical distinction between this form of segregation, and the several other forms which have been upheld by this court."[62] What was deemed reasonable in those circumstances was reasonable here as well. There was "nothing new in the present ordinance, nothing which has not been repeatedly and universally recognized as valid by all the courts before which the questions have arisen."[63]

They supported these claims with long quotes from a number of earlier cases. In all of these cases, what was being justified was the principle of racial segregation as it applied to trains and schools. But while, in Chevalier and Beckley's view, residential segregation could not be distinguished in a legal sense from these other cases, there were, after all, practical differences that they considered significant between homes or neighborhoods on the one hand and schools and trains on the other hand.

In the first place, to the extent that the reasonableness of racial separation on train cars and in schools was based on the effect it had in preventing conflict or promoting racial purity, then residential segregation was clearly *more* reasonable than even these other situations. In a passage lifted from (but not attributed to) Judge Hannah's lower court ruling, Chevalier and Beckley asked:

> [I]f there is danger of conflict and of peril to the preservation of the purity of the race, where there is merely the brief and temporary and almost casual association in the schools and in the vehicles of public travel, how much greater must be this same danger where the relationship is the fixed and permanent and uninterrupted one of immediate neighbors on the same block; the negro with his family living side by side with the white man's family, day after day and year after year.[64]

A second important practical difference between segregated railroad cars and segregated neighborhoods was that with respect to the latter there was neither a requirement nor a possibility of "equality." Chevalier and Beckley accused the plaintiff of failing to distinguish "between those conditions or advantages which the law, because of the public nature of the employment, compels to be furnished to all alike, as in the case of common carriers and innkeepers, and those advantages which the individual must achieve for himself . . . as in the case of churches, clubs, homes, private schools, etc."[65] This odd deployment of the public-private distinction was intended to uncouple "separate" from "equal." The idea was to validate the act of separation while dispensing with even the formal pretense of equality. They emphasized the "inequalities arising from matters with which the law has no concern, such as geographic location," and asserted that "geographical inequalities incident to such a law afforded no ground of complaint."[66]

Plaintiff's Rendering

The plaintiff drew different lines. First, as mentioned, Storey and Blakey's arguments proceeded from a much more restricted view of police power in general. Blakey argued that police power had well-defined limits, while Storey argued that the reasonableness standard that marked those limits was to be determined with reference to "likely" or "natural" effects or consequences of the ordinance in question.[67] Neither attorney addressed at all the proto-zoning locational decisions used by the defendant. For them residential segregation was not simply a matter of restricting the location of some obnoxious activity. However, the issue of prior Court validation of Jim Crow legislation in other cases presented a problem that could not so easily be avoided. Nevertheless, it's striking that Storey did just that, not even mentioning *Plessy* in his 1915 brief.

The plaintiff distinguished residential segregation from separate-coach laws on three grounds. First, in language reminiscent of Harlan's dissent in the *Civil Rights Cases*, trains were categorized as "quasi-public" and so the appropriate objects of regulation in a way that homes were not.[68] "The distinction is apparent," wrote Blakey. "[I]n one case the legislature is dealing with quasi-public property; in the other it is dealing with private property and private rights."[69] Second, extending the Court's reasoning in an earlier case in which it required equal accommodations in segregated sleeper cars, both Storey and Blakey argued that segregation could *only* be permitted if what was segregated could be equalized.[70] Because the uniqueness of lots and neighborhoods made them inherently unequalizable, they could not be subject to segregation. Or, to put it another way, the impossibility of meeting the requirement of equality did not justify the uncoupling of "separate" from "equal" as the defendant claimed; rather it prohibited this *conceptual* separation.

The third ground on which the plaintiff tried to distinguish residential segregation from segregation on trains was that the latter did not "deprive any citizen of his property" while the former did. Indeed, as we saw above, the plaintiff claimed that residential segregation ordinances destroyed the very essence of property. As for the relevance of cases upholding racial segregation in schools, the plaintiff considered that they had no bearing whatsoever on the present case.

Participants in these legal arguments were working with received legal categories in the form of precedents or prior judgments as they tried to give legal meaning to the geographies of race in Louisville. In their attempts they deployed different tactical maneuvers. The defendant stressed the similarity of events in Louisville to other events that had been given judicial recognition. The plaintiff emphasized crucial differences that would require different treatment. Working within a broad conception of police power, the defendant argued for a simple extension or application of existing doctrines dealing with locational restrictions and racial segregation. There was, after all, "nothing new" here. In categorizing black people as "like" other obnoxious entities and homes as "like" trains and schools, Chevalier and Beckley dismissed the very question of the scope of municipal authority as having already been decided. The plaintiff worked with a narrower conception of police power and drew categorical lines differently. Storey and Blakey dismissed the lines of cases concerning locational restrictions and schools, and distinguished homes from trains, on property grounds. The differences between "quasi-public" and "private," between competing conceptions of equalizability, and between regulating and destroying property made all the difference in the world. These rhetorical maneuvers were part of divergent accounts of the legal concept "reasonable" as it had previously been crafted by the Court. It was the meaning of this legal concept that was to fix the boundary between "state" and "property." But ultimately reference to inherited legal categories would not be enough. In order to justify claims of similarity and difference (and in terms of legal history, continuity or discontinuity), reference would necessarily be made to the world.

Drawing the Lines III: Legal Reasoning and (as) Geographical Argument

In this section we will look at conflicting claims about geographical phenomena—or how geographies work—that were put forth in order to support the more abstract arguments examined so far. Opposing attorneys in *Buchanan* advanced different narratives or stories of geographical change and the social consequences of change. These geographical stories were aimed at establishing the categories "reasonable" and "unreasonable" and at placing the ordinance in the preferred category. But note that these accounts of geographical processes were highly speculative, even figurative or imaginary. There were very few references to *actual* places. These renderings reflected deeply ideological understandings of social space. Moreover, in these conflicting accounts we can see—more clearly than in the other, more abstract arguments—contrasting ideologies of race held by white people. These renderings expressed competing ideologies of race and space that were competing *for* authoritative validation by the Supreme Court.

Defendant's Rendering

Chevalier and Beckley grounded their interpretations of geography and geographic change on a highly naturalistic account of the spatial dynamics of race relations. The basic mechanism that guided the process was rooted in biological instincts of apparently divine origin. "Segregation," according to the Louisville city attorneys, "has existed naturally wherever the whites and negroes have lived in the same community."[71] In their version of reality, "a natural distinction exist[ed] between the races which was not created," nor could it be "abrogated by law."[72] Indeed, the law simply recognized "those social barriers which nature itself has long ago erected between the white and colored races."[73] Drawing extensively on what they called a "profoundly philosophical" opinion of a justice of the Kentucky Supreme Court, they located the precise mechanism which produced segregation:

> [T]here exists in each race a homogenesis by which it will perpetually reproduce itself, if unadulterated. Its instinct is gregarious. As a check there is another, an antipathy to other races, which some call race prejudice. This is nature's guard to prevent amalgamation of the races. A disregard of this antipathy to the point of mating between the races is unnatural and begets a resentment in the normal mind.[74]

As amalgamation is "contrary to the law of the races" and "repugnant to the law of nature," segregation, racism, and racist violence against transgressions are all, so to speak, naturalized. These social barriers are spatialized—under normal conditions—as distinct racial localities within a larger community.[75] In terms of spatial process, this is how it was imagined to work: "The law of nature or of races which influences the white man to retire from the negro will also compel the constant widening of the borders of the negro sections."[76] The result would be that, contrary to plaintiff's fears, black people would not be confined to a small portion of the city.

What Chevalier and Beckley were describing was the usual or normal process. But these were not usual or normal times. Segregation per se was not an issue. It was no more a legal question than would be the blueness of the sky. The issue concerned problems that resulted as this normal process worked out under "modern conditions of municipal congestion." In an effort to demonstrate the gravity of the problem and the relative reasonableness of the solution, Chevalier and Beckley in effect told two stories of geographical change. In their portrayal of the problem they told a story of how changes in the geography of race in Louisville, if unregulated, would have disastrous consequences. In contrast, the reasonableness of the spatial solution was demonstrated by the many good consequences of regulating the natural process of segregation. Basically these are stories of projected consequences of social geographical change with and without state intervention.

The root of the problem as told by the city attorneys was the "invasion" of white neighborhoods by Negroes. The invasion itself was caused by those Negroes who wanted to "gratify their new-born social aspirations" and who sought "social equality" with whites.[77] As this was unnatural, it was also impossible. Given the natural antipathy that exists between the races, one of two consequences would necessarily follow. *Either* the Negro "must be induced to move again, either through persuasion or compulsion" *or* the block would have to be "turned over to the negroes."[78] While this might be considered to be part of the "usual" process, difficulties arise under modern conditions of urban congestion which render the processes haphazard, uncertain, and unstable. What was required was order, certainty, and stability. The problems of uncertainty and instability were grave enough in themselves but, unregulated, there were still more alarming consequences to be feared. Somewhat paradoxically, these problems were "conflict"— perhaps leading to bloodshed—and "amalgamation" and the dangers to race purity that result from "mere propinquity." Still other undesirable consequences were extortion by realtors, severe depreciation of property values, and "hard feelings" between the races.[79]

The reasonableness of the ordinance could also be gauged against the negative geographical consequences of black geographical mobility more generally. The defendant's attorneys asserted, for example, that "the morals of the negro" were not contingent on geographical location. "We all know," they said, "that the shiftless, the improvident, the ignorant, and the criminal carry their moral and economic condition wherever they go." They asked disingenuously, "[O]n what [grounds] then do [Negroes] assert the privilege of spreading that blight to white sections of the city?" Asserting that "people make the slums, not the slums, people," the attorneys for the city suggested that black people should be "content to live among their own people and endeavor to make their own parts of town attractive and liveable."[80]

Racial equality was "a foolish dream." The "inordinant social aspirations" of "a few negroes" and their insistence on living "in social intimacy with the whites" and on "social commingling" caused too many problems and required governmental intervention. Geographical change without the ordinance was fraught with "danger," "evil," "peril," "uncertainty," "insecurity," "violence," and declining property values. It would only be reasonable to create spatial conditions conducive to "harmony," "peace," "security," "friendship," "thrift," "racial purity," "progress," and stable property values. The segregation ordinance would foster these laudable goals.

The reasonableness of the proposed spatial reconfiguration was also to be assessed relative to other ways of solving the problem or other methods of achieving the same end. Throughout the briefs, Chevalier and Beckley continually alluded to "friction" and "conflict," to bloodshed and riots "provoked by negroes moving into . . . white sections"; to the possibility that racial problems might be "settled by the sheer force of superiority of number or physical power."[81] Drawing on the same "profoundly philosophical" discussion which posited the homogenetic theory of racial purity, they wrote that

> in a less civilized society the stronger would probably annihilate the weaker race. Humane civilization is endeavoring to fulfill nature's edict as to the preservation of race identity in a different way. Instead of exterminating the other, it is attempted to so regulate their necessary intercourse as to preserve each in its integrity.[82]

What could be more reasonable? All that would be required is the maintenance of existing spatial arrangements. "All we ask through this law is that whites be left in peaceful . . . enjoyment of those sections which they have already in a sense preempted for their homes, leaving negroes to the similar enjoyment of those sections which they have also chosen for their residence."[83]

Yet another measure of reasonableness was seen in the fact that in simply regulating "that natural and normal segregation which has always existed," the procedures of the ordinance would work gently and gradually over time. It would merely "prevent a few of each race from overstepping the racial barriers which Providence and not human law has erected." It would act "only within what may be termed the 'twilight zone' . . . where the conflicts would most likely arise."[84] Not simply working *with* nature, the law itself was "an outgrowth of an instinctive race consciousness" and "but the formal recognition of the color line as a social fact, and of the necessity of establishing metes and bounds for the protection of the worthy and well disposed of each race against the aggression of the undesirable and selfish of the other." "It is far better for all concerned that the respective bounds of the two races be definitely and clearly defined by law than to leave the matter . . . to the uncertain outcome of conflict."[85]

Peace, certainty, and security for whites and safety for blacks were not the only positive fruits of the de jurification of the geography of Jim Crow. Black people could also expect several other advantages to follow from the spatial reorganization of Louisville. Chevalier and Beckley stated that the law might "encourage the negroes who now flock to the towns, where they often degenerate, to remain in the country where they prosper and improve morally and physically . . . and where their wisest leader has always advised them to remain."[86] At the same time, "by bringing [black people] together as a race there will be supplied a new incentive to have them improve their condition." Endorsing Judge Hannah's views on the spatial conditions of racial solidarity and uplift, the defendant's attorneys stated that enforced segregation and concentration would indirectly compel these more fortunate members of the race "to accept their responsibilities for their less fortunate fellows" and "coerce their performance of the duties thereby imposed."[87] At the very least, if enforced confinement and forcibly limited mobility "did nothing more . . . than to shatter the negro's foolish dream of social equality with whites, and thereby open up greater opportunities for his industrial improvement, the wisdom of [the ordinance's] passage would be more than justified."[88]

Plaintiff's Rendering

Against Chevalier and Beckley's naturalistic or homogenetic interpretation of the processes responsible for racial segregation, Storey and Blakey presented a version that emphasized the normal or expected and beneficial process of class differentiation. This story of geographical change was couched in strong environmentalist terms. Environmentalism in this sense refers to understandings of society that assume a rather strong, even deterministic, influence of social environments such as slums on the development of group characteristics and individual traits. Consistent with the consequentialist thrust of their general argument, their reading here focused on the disastrous effects that the ordinance would have in frustrating or inhibiting the normal process of *class* segregation and in confining black people to a ghetto. Their interpretations, like the defendant's, can be seen as a story of comparative social geographical change: one trajectory without state intervention, the other with it. Likewise, the difference between the versions constituted the difference between "reasonable" and "unreasonable."

The basic mechanism that drove geographical change in the plaintiff's version was that ineluctable something known as "uplift." This was a process which entailed the attenuation of some differences between some black people and "the white man," and the heightened differentiation *among* members of the black community. This process would also have a normal or expected spatial expression. According to a pseudohistorical account offered by Blakey:

> [A] large majority of the colored inhabitants of the City of Louisville [once occupied] undesirable portions of the city, but . . . the better element among the colored inhabitants of the City of Louisville, as they became more prosperous, better citizens and more able to have better homes and reside in better localities have gradually removed to more desirable territory for residence sites in the city, and in this way the city has extended its boundaries, unused or partially used localities have become settled by the better class and more prosperous colored inhabitants, and the localities so settled by these more prosperous and better element of the colored inhabitants have become more valuable as residence sites than when same were unused or only partly occupied by white people.[89]

Note that the principal figure in this account is not "the [generic] negro" but "the colored inhabitants of the City of Louisville" and specifically
its "better element." The outward push was driven by the social process of
class differentiation. The spatial expression, then, is part of the *solution* to
some aspects of the race problem more generally. That is, what the defendant portrayed as "the problem,"—black people buying property in white
neighborhoods—the plaintiff regarded as a solution to a more significant
problem. In Blakey's more dramatic and environmentalist rendition, black
people, after the abolition of slavery, had been "herded into those quarters
of the city where the scum and off-scouring of the land plied their nefari-
ous callings." Because "the negro" was "naturally imitative," he "sprouted
an ambition to pattern after the white man." Then

> there sprang up in his soul a desire to escape from the slums and to give
> his children the advantage of environment which had been denied him.
> Gradually the better element acquired homes in better localities, until
> finally it was no unusual thing for each locality to number among its res-
> idents many negroes whose lines were as exemplary and whose homes
> were as respectable as those of his white brothers.[90]

This was good, normal, and reasonable. It also denied the naturalness of
racial segregation asserted by the defendant and suggested that, were the
normal process of class differentiation to proceed without interference,
inherited geographies of race would gradually give way to more normal
geographies of class.

The positive good that resulted from this process was best seen in contrast to the disastrous consequences of artificially inhibiting it. Enforcement of the segregation law would prevent "the better and more prosperous element of the colored inhabitants from obtaining residences in a
better locality" and "confine those members of the colored race who are
anxious to improve their condition to undesirable quarters of the city."
There their children would be "constantly thrown in touch and intimate
association with the degraded and vicious elements of the city" and contaminated by "the vicious negroes who predominate in the territory."[91]

In the 1917 supplementary brief, Storey and Blakey presented figures to
substantiate these claims. They said that "the classification of territory
made by the ordinance" would confine 20 percent of the city's population
to about 12 percent of its area, that 63 percent of the "houses of ill-repute"
were "within the territory allotted to negroes," that "saloons are far more

numerous in this region than in the white territory, and that the negroes [would] thus [be] compelled to live in a region where criminals and vicious people congregate." "Is it not natural," they asked, "that the better class of negroes would . . . wish to escape from such surroundings?"[92]

Moreover, laws such as the segregation ordinance were seen to reduce black people "through being . . . bound in effect to the soil in the designated localities, to a condition not far removed from slavery."[93] Indeed, they "compel them to reside in a very small area and . . . differ only in degree from imprisonment."[94] In so confining black people to an unhealthy and crowded ghetto, the law "represses ambition and self respect" at a time when the Negro "must be encouraged to aspire!" "Thrown contemptuously back upon himself, segregated as a contamination, obliged to slink and creep, his legitimate longing to "acquit himself in all men's sight as a man" [will be] forever annihilated." "If the negro is made a pariah he will assume a pariah's disqualifications."[95]

Storey and Blakey also countered the defendant's arguments regarding the "perils of proximity" and "evils of propinquity" by noting that the law allows people of different races to live back-to-back but not side-to-side. "The front of the house may be closed," they quipped, "but the rear stands invitingly open."[96] The law also made exceptions to allow black people to live in alleys behind the houses of white people, and, in fact, to allow members of different races to "live under the same roof as master and servant, a relation which has never assured race purity."[97] The evils of propinquity, then, were clearly not what motivated the law, because such evils, if they had existed, would still exist. Shifting their focus to more metaphorical boundaries, Storey and Blakey recalled the defendant's claim that the law would only "prevent a few of each race from overstepping the racial barriers which Providence and not human law has erected." "Had Providence in fact erected such a barrier," they reasoned, "it would have been impassable and no human law would have been needed." In fact, "it is because no divine barrier exists that they seek to establish one by human legislation."[98] From all of this it was clear to the plaintiff's attorneys that where relations of power were relatively clear and unambiguous, existing spatial arrangements could be maintained, but where power relations were unclear or ambiguous, that social space would be reorganized "to place the negro citizens of Louisville in as inferior a position as possible," and establish "a permanent superiority for the white race."[99]

Participants in the legal facet of the geopolitics of race offered contending interpretations of the dynamics of geographical change in efforts to ground *assessments* of geographical change. They presented competing *theories* of geography in efforts to guide actual spatial practices. The immediate objective was to give content to the category "reasonable," and to mark the line between "reasonable" and "unreasonable." It was with reference to this categorical distinction that all other legal questions in the case were to be answered. The reasonableness of participants' version of geographical change would determine, it seemed, the reasonableness (or unreasonableness) of the ordinance, of the lower court decision upholding the ordinance, and of federal judicial intervention into local geopolitical contests.

The defendant's reading of the landscape related shifting geographies of race to dangerous stories of sexuality and violence. The figure that lurked just beyond the frame of the narrative was the Negro-beast rapist who would transgress the natural or divine boundaries which separated races. Recall that at this time a mere glance at a white women would be sufficient justification for the lynching of a black man.

The plaintiff's reading subordinated geographies of race to the normal geographic expression of class formation and differentiation. These processes would tend toward racial equalization and the revision of historical problems associated with race distinctions. In the defendant's story, the ordinance would preserve and protect the natural and pure spatiality of race and sex; in the plaintiff's story, it would artificially freeze an inherited spatiality that facilitated the perpetuation of racial subordination.

Other key categories that were deployed in attempts to give meaning to these geographical stories were the natural and normal, the evil and dangerous, the certain and secure, the peaceful, the violent, the vicious, the prosperous, the pure, the contaminated. Notions such as these gave meaning to the geographical narratives. Upon the plausibility of these stories legal arguments were based. Upon the plausibility of these arguments legal meaning—the meaning of power—would be inscribed on lived-in landscapes. Each move and countermove, each distinction and its paired denial, constituted a strategic manipulation of inherited categories in the service of the geopolitics of race. This is how meaning is made; this is how geographies are made.

The Authoritative Rendering of the Legal Landscape

Arguments by attorneys in *Buchanan v. Warley*, including those submitted by friends of the court, were quite lengthy. The attorneys wanted to touch all bases and to leave no possible approach untried. In contrast, the opinion delivered on November 5, 1917, for a unanimous Court by Justice William Day was brief and made little reference to most of the arguments put forward by counsel. Actually, it seems that the issues involved were relatively simple and the correct interpretation rather obvious.

After acknowledging that the police power is very broad and that its exercise, "is not to be interfered with by courts where it is within the scope of legislative authority," Day then recognized that, "broad as it is," it cannot run "counter to the limitations of the federal Constitution."[100] The issue here was one of marking the line between the state and federal spaces that constituted the metaphorical spatiality of federalism. The location of this boundary had priority in Day's narrative because the arguments addressed to the justices as federal officers were framed in terms of the federal Constitution. Whether the action of the state in the form of Louisville's General Council's passage of the segregation ordinance did, in fact, run counter to constitutional limitations was the next question. This was answered with reference to the metaphorical spatiality of liberalism.

Again noting that "dominion over property springing from ownership is not absolute and unqualified," and that "the disposition and use of property may be controlled in the exercise of the police power" Day stressed that "property is more than the mere thing which a person owns. It is elementary that it includes the right to acquire, use, and dispose of it. The Constitution protects these essential attributes of property."[101] In drawing the principal lines this way rather than some other way, Justice Day found that the Reconstruction amendments "did not deal with the social rights of men, but with those fundamental rights in property [of] citizens of every race and color." More specifically, he said that, "the Fourteenth Amendment of the Constitution prevent[s] state interference with property rights."[102] In his view, "the right which the ordinance annulled was the civil right of a white man to dispose of his property if he saw fit to do so to a person of color and of a colored person to make such a disposition to a white person." The crucial point was that "this attempt to prevent the alienation of the property in question to a person of color was not a legitimate exercise of the police power of the state."[103] The Constitution puts limits on the police power, and "these limitations are exceeded in laws and ordinances of the character now before us."[104] Simple as that.

The opinion of the Kentucky Supreme Court was reversed, the "ordinance to prevent conflict and ill feeling between the white and colored races in the city of Louisville" was invalidated, the contract entered into by

Charles Buchanan and William Warley concerning the lot on the corner of Thirty-sixth Avenue and Pflanz was deemed enforceable, and race blocks as legal spaces in Louisville and elsewhere were formally obliterated—their legal meaning found to be incompatible with the Court's understanding of "property," "state," and "federalism." According to the Supreme Court, the map of power represented by these key terms could not be so drastically redrawn. It was this meaning—the meaning of the "essential attributes of property," of "fundamental rights of citizens," of "limits on police power" and of "the supreme law of the land"—that was provisionally inscribed on the landscape. Because the ordinance did not simply "regulate" property but "took" it without due process of law, it could not stand.

In passing, Day mentioned that the locational restriction or proto-zoning cases with which the defendant had tried to classify racial segregation did not "touch [the case] at bar." [105] He distinguished *Buchanan* from *Plessy* on the grounds offered by Storey and Blakey, that is, that laws mandating racial segregation on trains allowed for the possibility of equal treatment and did not "take" property. Day also recognized that there was "a serious and difficult problem arising from a feeling of race hostility which the law is powerless to control," [106] but ultimately race had nothing to do with it. *Buchanan* was decided as a property case on due process grounds, and geographies of race were shaped according to understandings of what the metaphorical spatiality of liberalism could and could not accommodate.

Concluding Remarks

Legal reasoning is a social practice. A legal argument is a piece of work. Each instance of drawing distinctions, of categorizing or of supplementing the bare bones of formal argument with stories about how the world is or should be, exemplifies an important kind of (geo)political maneuver. This, as I've said, is how meaning is made, but the meaning in question is the meaning of power. Cases such as *Buchanan* also raise questions about the power of meaning—or, better, the socially conferred power to *create* meaning. In studying struggles over legal meaning we might ask: Who has the opportunity to speak and whose voice is excluded? It is not an incidental fact that all of the arguments examined so far were made *by* white men *to* other white men. Among those permitted to speak, whose version of reality will be recognized as "true" and whose rendering of the legal landscape will, for whatever reasons, be found wanting by the authorities? In asking such questions, are we not asking about how the power to create meaning is distributed?

Buchanan v. Warley is often cited as one of the most significant early victories of the NAACP. And its landmark status should not be underestimated. As we will see, though, the consequences for subsequent rounds in the geopolitics of race were more ambiguous. Invalidating a local segregation ordinance by no means entailed the dismantling of racial residential segregation. In the following years and over the following generations, racial segregation in U.S. cities generally became more and more entrenched. But the geographies of race and racism over the next fifty years or so had a different legal foundation and so required different legal strategies.

6 Restrictive Space and the Doctrine of Changed Conditions

In this chapter we return to a consideration of the situation of Clara Mays, whom we encountered in chapter 1. In October 1945, Mays, an employee of the federal government, along with her three sisters, six nieces, and a nephew, were found to be in contempt of court for refusing to leave their home on First Street NW in Washington, D.C. The previous January, the Federal Court of Appeals for the District of Columbia had affirmed a lower court ruling which ordered them out of their home at the urging of their neighbor William T. Burgess. Burgess, like Mays, had come into possession of property that was within the territory described by a racially restrictive covenant which had been drawn up in 1925. The covenant stipulated that none of the lots within the territory were to be sold to or occupied by "any person or persons of the Negro race or blood" for twenty-one years.[1] The Mayses were black. The covenant was to expire in ten months. The covenant also gave Burgess, along with every other white person who owned property in the covenanted tract, the right to enforce the agreement. Burgess exercised his right and sought an injunction through the courts.

Part of the reason that the courts enforced the contract and ordered the Mayses to leave their home was that the neighborhood was considered by judges to be part of a "solidly white community." This interpretation was made despite the findings that black people lived on the same street one block away, that black people lived on the same block on the next street over and that immediately around the corner were a number of integrated row houses. Because this was considered a solidly white community by the courts, the "doctrine of changed conditions" that the defendants had offered as a justification for the denial of the injunction was deemed inapplicable. That is, because the courts found that "conditions" in the neighborhood had not changed since the covenant was drawn up in 1925, the state was justified in using force to remove the Mayses from their home.[2] Justice Henry Edgerton of the Court of Appeals dissented. He had a different interpretation of the historical geography of race in the North Capitol neighborhood of Washington, D.C. He also had a different understanding of what counted as "conditions" and as "change," as well as different ideas about where in the world to look for these "changed conditions."

Later in this chapter I'll examine more closely the conflicting interpretations of doctrine and geography that characterized the arguments in *Mays v. Burgess*.[3] Here I'll simply note that the experiences of the Mayses and thousands of others in the period 1917 to 1948 demonstrate that while white supremacists were rebuffed in *Buchanan v. Warley*,[4] they nevertheless succeeded in constructing their desired geographies of race in U.S. cities. But in the generation following *Buchanan* there was a significant shift in how the geopolitics of race was conducted. During the era of segregation ordinances, conflicts were fought out city by city. Now they were conducted neighborhood by neighborhood, block by block, and lot by lot. This shift was related to the change in the legal basis of segregation and exclusion—from city ordinances to private contracts and deed restrictions. The source of legal meaning that supported these geographies of race was not the "unreasonable" actions of city officials but the "reasonable" actions of developers, conveyancers, and neighbors. In this era segregationists used racially restrictive covenants to create complex legal spaces from which black people such as the Mays family were excluded, and within which certain rights were distributed among white property owners to ensure compliance.

In this chapter we examine the role of legal reasoning in interpretations of the geographical conditions upon which the validity of restrictive covenants depended. We will also look at conceptions of space that were integral to these judgments. My principal focus is on the doctrine of changed conditions as it was used as a defense in *Mays v. Burgess*[5] and other cases. We will explore two particularly geographic aspects of doctrinal interpretation: conflicting views of the spatiality of rules of doctrinal applicability and the ways in which conflicts were played out in a series of cases involving one neighborhood in Washington, D.C.

Note that the focus of our analysis also shifts in this chapter. In chapter 3 we looked at a number of cases and issues over a long period of time in order to understand change in the nineteenth century. In chapter 5 we examined a number of arguments in a single case. In the present chapter we study the politics of legal reasoning with respect to a single doctrine as it played out in a number of cases.

The period of study is the twenty-two years between 1926 and 1948. In 1926 the Supreme Court declared that it did not have the jurisdiction to hear an appeal of the Washington, D.C., restrictive covenant case of *Corrigan v. Buckley*.[6] This, as will be discussed below, had the effect of eliminating most of the arguments against the enforcement of restrictive covenants except those relying on the doctrine of changed conditions. In 1948 the Supreme Court ruled in *Shelley v. Kraemer*[7] that judicial enforcement of covenants constituted a type of "state action" in violation of the Fourteenth Amendment's equal protection clause. In the legal history of the geopolitics of race, we might call the period under discussion "the era of changed conditions." As in other chapters, introductory sections will provide context for the cases.

Post-*Buchanan* Moves

The Supreme Court's unanimous opinion in *Buchanan v. Warley* was considered a victory by opponents of racial segregation. And while to some extent this view was justifiable, it should be recognized that in the best of times a victory such as that would have directly benefited very few black people. Moreover, the early decades of the twentieth century were by no means the best of times. Positive assessments of *Buchanan* must be grounded in consideration of the horrific consequences had the case gone the other way. To the extent that success in *Buchanan*—even if merely symbolic— demonstrated the value of organized opposition to Jim Crow, facilitated the emergence of the NAACP as a significant national force, and consolidated the turn away from accommodationism, antisegregationists may have had reason to be hopeful. A defeat in this case might easily have demonstrated to local community leaders the futility of "legalism" and "protest" and could have caused the withering of the nascent civil rights organization. Also, *Buchanan* has been seen as an articulation by the Court of the "limits" of police power in the regulation of race relations—a formal acknowledgment that the regime of Jim Crow even *had* limits.[8] Given the context of antiblack violence, it is only too plausible that a victory for segregationists in Louisville, Baltimore, Atlanta, and Richmond might well have sanctioned the establishment of what was in effect apartheid in cities throughout the nation and in rural areas as well.[9] As it was, cities contin-

ued to pass and enforce segregation ordinances for another generation. A
1925 New Orleans residential segregation law, having been struck down
by the parish district court, was actually upheld by the Louisiana State
Supreme Court, even though the judges admitted that it could not easily
be distinguished from *Buchanan*.[10] It was subsequently invalidated by the
U.S. Supreme Court on the strength of *Buchanan*, as was a 1930 Richmond
ordinance.[11] As late as 1940 a Winston-Salem segregation law was the subject of litigation in the North Carolina Supreme Court.[12] Had the U.S.
Supreme Court given the go-ahead to formal segregation in *Buchanan*, the
geographies of race created by the following generation might well have
been more vicious than they were. This, perhaps, is the best that can be
said. As a practical matter, whatever possible or speculative positive consequences *Buchanan* may have had, on the ground these were effectively
negated by the proliferation of restrictive covenants.

Restrictive covenants will be discussed in their own terms below. Considered as instruments of geopolitical action, it is important to note that
they were far easier to use than were city ordinances. Instead of dealing
with hearings and the sometimes messy, complicated, or drawn-out procedures of local municipal government, property owners had only to agree
among themselves to effect the same end: exclusion of black people from
"white communities." In fact, individual owners or developers could simply
enter restrictions on deeds and bind subsequent owners to their terms,
thereby single-handedly closing off whole neighborhoods. Exclusion quite
literally came with the territory.[13]

Covenants were easy to establish. They proliferated. Large areas of
cities might be covered by them, so that the housing stock available to black
families might be less than it would have been under a formal segregation
regime. It has been estimated, for example, that up to 80 percent of Chicago was covenanted.[14] Most important from a segregationist's point of
view was that covenants were effective. As contracts their terms were enforceable by courts, which is to say that the same force that would have
backed up segregation ordinances was available to back up exclusionary
contracts. As geopolitical tools of exclusion—and expulsion—restrictive
covenants worked quite well for more than thirty years.

These geopolitical moves were occurring at the same time as—and to
some extent in reaction to—the most dramatic demographic transformation in the geography of race since emancipation. As was mentioned in the
previous chapter, the segregation ordinance movement itself has been seen
as a reaction to the rising number of black people moving to the cities in

the early years of the century. During and after the First World War (and continuing for the next fifty years), millions of people participated in what has become known as the Great Black Migration.[15] In general terms the Great Migration refers to the large-scale movements of African Americans from both the countryside to the cities and from the South to the North. Numerically and geopolitically, its most significant component was the rapid rise of the black population in northern cities. Thus, between 1910 and 1920 nearly half a million black people moved north; in the following decade the figure was 750,000, and in the next ten years nearly 400,000 more relocated to the cities of the North. Most of these people moved to just a handful of cities.[16] And while these numbers are suggestive of general trends, their real significance is to be seen in the specific localities concerned and in the biographies of the participants. Numerous black community studies that explore the local racial histories of U.S. cities show the dynamics of place creation in very different contexts.[17] These studies also show the ways in which the people in these places fought against forms of oppression that also had their own local specificities. One factor, however, that was common to the politics of race in all localities and which contributed to the creation of the (generic) ghetto as a distinctive kind of place was the deployment of restrictive covenants by segregationists.

Restrictive Covenants as Geopolitical Resources

A restrictive covenant (or equitable servitude) is an agreement between or among property owners that obligates them to restrict the uses to which the real property covered in the contract will be put. It creates legal relations. Such an agreement also creates a legal space that serves as a referent for legal meaning. To create such a space is to engage in the practice of territoriality. Like any other legal space, the meaning so contained is amenable to interpretation and vulnerable to conflicting interpretations. This ambiguity or indeterminacy is a function not only of the language of the contract itself (i.e., the legal instrument through which the space is created) but also of the legal doctrines that are used to guide interpretations.[18]

These agreements may be between owners of adjoining or neighboring lots or between successive owners of the same lot. The restriction may be affixed to the deed, acceptance of which implies consent to be bound by the restriction. Or it may result from efforts of property owners to enlist neighbors to sign a contract which binds the owners to restrict their property in the stipulated way. Ownership of property in a restricted territory also adds to the owner's "bundle of rights." Specifically, all of the owners have the right to sue for damages in the event that any of them violates the agreement. Covenants may run for a definite period of time—say twenty-one, fifty, or ninety-nine years—or in some jurisdictions they may be perpetual. Whatever the duration, anyone who comes into possession of a restricted lot is considered to be bound by the restrictions.

Historically, restrictive covenants have been used to prohibit a wide range of actions or uses from the territories covered. Their use has represented a kind of private zoning. They may, for example, forbid commercial activity, the sale of alcoholic beverages, manufacturing, the keeping of animals, and so on. Before racially restrictive covenants became popular, perhaps the most common uses to which they were put concerned the prohibition of commerce in residential areas and the establishment of building or frontage restrictions. These last were thought to be most relevant to the adjudication of racial disputes.

Typically there were two matters for which restrictive covenants were brought before the bench. First, an owner or a group of owners might request that a judge declare a covenant void. That is, they might seek judicial cancellation of the restriction in order to remove a "cloud" from the title. Or holders of one or more of the restricted lots might bring suit against other parties who were alleged to have broken the agreement. That is, plaintiffs in such cases would charge that the defendants had caused the restricted property to be used in precisely the prohibited manner. The objective sought would be judicial enforcement of the agreement in the form of an injunction against the restricted use. Typically, then, the plaintiffs in these cases were in favor of maintaining segregation and the defendants were, for various reasons, against restrictions.

In the case of racially restrictive covenants, a white property owner anywhere in a restricted tract might want to either prevent another white owner from completing a sale (or rental) to a "non-Caucasian" or, if the sale had been completed, to remove the offending non-Caucasian from the property that had been purchased—and from the neighborhood. This often meant forfeiture of the property. In some cases blacks were also fined or, if they refused to move from their homes, jailed.[19]

A Strand of History

The earliest reported case involving a racially restrictive covenant was *Gondolfo v. Hartman*, decided in 1892. This case concerned property in Ventura, California, that contained a deed restriction prohibiting the use or occupancy of the property by "a Chinaman or Chinamen."[20] This restriction was found by federal district judge Erskine Ross to be in violation of the Fourteenth Amendment. However, while *Gondolfo* seems to have been regularly raised as a precedent by opponents of segregation, in most judicial opinions it was either dismissed as a "stray case" or was simply ignored.

After a series of unsuccessful efforts in state courts, the NAACP brought the case of *Corrigan v. Buckley* to the U.S. Supreme Court.[21] This case was both odd and significant, though precisely what it accomplished became a matter of conflicting interpretation. The definitive legal interpretation of *Corrigan* by a subsequent Supreme Court in *Shelley v. Kraemer* was that it accomplished nothing.[22] However, as a sociolegal "fact" it was quite consequential.

The *Corrigan* case concerned a racially restrictive covenant in Washington, D.C. Under then existing rules, the U.S. Supreme Court also functioned as a court of last resort for the District of Columbia. That is, cases could be brought to the Court on appeal if the appellant considered the case to involve a constitutional question. The Court dismissed the case "for want of jurisdiction," which, in effect, implied that there were no constitutional questions involved.

Judicial pronouncements are a kind of "speech act." That is, not only do they *say* something, but, as we've seen, in authoritatively saying they also *do* something.[23] Something happens. For example, in the act of making authoritative pronouncements judges create law and precedent, they make winners and losers. They open up or close off avenues for subsequent argument. Some judicial speech acts are relatively unambiguous in what they do or are intended to do, such as sentencing someone to die. Others are far less clear and more open to subsequent (conflicting) interpretation. The Court in *Corrigan*, by officially saying nothing, was construed by subsequent state courts as having effectively said it all. In restrictive covenant cases for the next twenty-two years, state and inferior federal courts consistently asserted that the Court had established the constitutional validity of restrictive covenants.[24] In such cases there is no fact of the matter. However, for the practical political purposes of transforming geographies of race, the argument that restrictive covenants were in violation of the Constitution was closed off for a generation.

One of the consequences of the *Buchanan* litigation was the transformation of a local dispute into one with potentially national significance. This transformation should be seen in and of itself as a geopolitical move to the extent that participants tried to resituate events within a more extensive spatial frame of reference. As a result of that case, formal segregation ordinances were prohibited throughout the United States, not just in Louisville. Similarly, one of the spatial consequences of *Corrigan* was that restrictive covenants were legitimated everywhere in the country. This meant that the NAACP campaign against residential segregation was effectively restricted to state courts (and to the U.S. District Court in the District of Columbia). This led to a radical fragmentation of the campaign. From here it appeared that any victories would, at best, be restricted to the space of individual states.

Typically in post-*Corrigan* racially restrictive covenant cases, four logically independent lines of argument about restrictive covenants were advanced by opponents of segregation (usually defendants). They maintained

1. that enforcement of restrictive covenants was *unconstitutional* after all;

2. failing that, that they were *contrary to the public policy* of the state;

3. failing that, that they represented an illegitimate *restraint on alienation* contrary to the common law of the state; or

4. failing that, that enforcement should be denied because of *changed conditions*.[25]

I would like to emphasize that each of these arguments, if accepted, would have had a different range of possible *spatial* consequences. In general, we might assume that opponents of segregation were trying to eliminate restrictive covenants over the widest possible areas. But as a result of interpretations of *Corrigan*, the first and most spatially expansive of the four arguments—their unconstitutionality—was closed off. Similarly, until near the end of this period, the second argument—that restrictive covenants were contrary to public policy—was also summarily rejected in the absence of explicit legislative or executive statements against them. Moreover while some jurisdictions *did* accept the third argument—that restrictions on ownership by non-Caucasians represented an unreasonable restraint on alienation because they restricted the number of potential buyers for white sellers—this victory was effectively nullified by the creation of a distinction between "own" and "occupy." According to this legal distinction, while covenants cannot be used to restrict the class of people who may *own* (buy) property, they may restrict the class of people who may *use* it. Therefore, in some jurisdictions such as California, non-Caucasians were allowed to buy property in restricted tracts but they were not allowed to live or make their homes there.

In virtually all of the cases reported between *Corrigan* in 1926 and *Shelley* in 1948, the only defense argument that was considered by judges was the fourth, that expressed in the doctrine of changed conditions. A more detailed analysis of the application of this doctrine will be presented below. For our immediate purposes, however, I would like to emphasize that of the four defense arguments typically advanced against racially restrictive covenants, this was by far the one with the most restricted *spatial* scope. Unlike arguments regarding constitutionality, public policy, and restraint on alienation which, had they been accepted in full, might have had consequences beyond the immediate case and over very large areas, findings of changed conditions were necessarily place-particular and explicitly *not* generalizable to other cases. As such, this defense was sometimes successfully employed to let individual parties (often white sellers) off the hook. It was virtually useless in advancing the wider geopolitical aims of the NAACP. Seen as a geopolitical maneuver, closing off all arguments save that of changed conditions, then, can be seen in and of itself as effecting a spatial strategy of containment.

Inside the Doctrine

The doctrine of changed conditions is a set of principles that allows a court in equity (see below) to decline to enforce a contract if, in the judge's opinion, conditions have changed in such a way that enforcing the terms of the contract would do more harm than good *to the parties involved in the contract*. The variant known as "changed conditions in the neighborhood" arises specifically in cases dealing with restrictive covenants.[26] In these cases it is not simply that one or more parties to the agreement find themselves in unforeseen situations, it is that the world itself—or a small but significant portion of it—has undergone relevant change. Moreover, it is a change that the defendants are deemed not to have been instrumental in bringing about.

For example, consider a covenant among home owners not to use their property for commercial purposes. Consider next that at some time subsequent to the agreement but prior to its expiration, a liquor store and a barbershop are opened up in the vicinity. Next, a mortician buys one of the restricted lots. The contract prevents him establishing a funeral home on the premises. If he attempted to do so and if this attempt were legally challenged, it is likely that he would assert a defense of changed conditions. That is, his attorney would claim that as a result of the opening of the liquor store and barbershop, conditions in the world had changed to such an extent that the purpose of the contract had been defeated. Enforcement of the contract would therefore be inequitable. Whether the claim would be accepted by a judge is of course another matter.

"Equity" in the Anglo American legal tradition is supplemental to "law," strictly speaking. It is "justice administered according to fairness."[27] As such, the *application* of an equitable doctrine is case-specific and necessarily context-dependent. Unlike, for example, constitutional or statutory interpretation, a ruling in one case is considered to have no bearing on other cases. However, the *rules* of application are derived from and contribute to common law and so, to that extent, a ruling in one case may be interpreted as being relevant, though not controlling, in other cases. In the words of California Supreme Court justice B. Rey Schauer, "[S]ubject to certain broad principles each case of this character must be determined upon the facts peculiar to it."[28]

Assessment of doctrinal applicability is a form of categorical interpretation. That is, the immediate objective is to fit a set of facts—whether social facts or internal doctrinal facts—into a preexisting categorical scheme. Frequently this is a dichotomous scheme. The conceptual mechanics of interpretation can be structured by responses to questions that may, or perhaps must, be answerable with a yes or a no. In the following section we examine some of the questions that were required in interpreting the applicability of the doctrine in a series of cases. More important, we examine the categorical scheme which compelled the sense that just these questions and not others ones were required and that just these answers counted as appropriate responses. We also examine the way in which the categorical scheme was mapped to the world so as to yield the appropriate answers.

The Mechanics of Doctrinal Application

Raising the defense of changed conditions requires a finding of fact. It requires judges to answer questions like: What is this place like? How has it changed (or not changed)? What explains the change? Only by providing answers to questions like these can it be determined whether the doctrine applies to a case or whether an injunction should be issued. Raising the defense, then, requires a historical geographic interpretation. Like all such interpretations, it requires an implicit theory by which relevant facts can be distinguished from irrelevant facts. Based on these distinctions, claims of causation and *responsibility* can be justified.

At first glance, application of the doctrine of changed conditions to racially restrictive covenant cases seems to have been a relatively straightforward affair. And no doubt it was considered to be so by those whose job it was to apply it. All that seems to have been required was a certain amount of evidence concerning what conditions had been at a particular time in the past (say, at the time a covenant was established) and evidence concerning conditions at some subsequent period (say, at the time of the alleged breach). One simply had to compare the two pictures: if they were sufficiently different, the purpose of the covenant had been defeated and therefore enforcement rendered inequitable; if they were sufficiently similar, the restriction could still have been enforced. The idea, I think, is that it was *obvious*.

It also seemed fairly clear to many observers that a restrictive covenant was a restrictive covenant, whether it applied to kinds of buildings, the uses to which they were put, or who could own them. The same principles of interpretation were employed in any case. The principle seemed to have been this: just look. Indeed, judges in these cases often said things like "[A] glance at the neighborhood shows . . ."[29] or "[A] mere glance at the present situation demonstrates. . . ."[30]

However, interpretation also required some specification of what counted as "conditions" and what counted as "change." Significantly, the task was made easier because what specifically the judge had to look for was stipulated in the contract. In the case of racial covenants, the condition was blackness. Just as a neighborhood was obviously—empirically—commercial or residential, so was a neighborhood clearly either Negro or Caucasian. Similarly, what counted as "change" was also implied by the contract. Change meant changing from white to black.

The obvious point here is that categorization of similarity or difference—and, hence, change—was contingent on the unquestioned categorical scheme of Negro and Caucasian as *mutually exclusive attributes of definable areas*. There is no notice taken of the fact of integration or of mixed neighborhoods. There is, however, discussion concerning precisely how many Negroes it takes to make a district "definitely colored."[31] Phrased somewhat differently, judicial interpretation of changed conditions took racial segregation as a given, as something that goes without saying. Given the belief in the essential immutability of what was considered to be a fact, moral, political, and legal questions concerned only the form that it would take.

Two points need to be stressed here. First, in determining the applicability of the doctrine of changed conditions, judges assumed as given and immutable precisely that which, in the larger social-political conflict of which the cases were part, was being challenged: racial segregation. The finding of fact that was required by raising the defense of changed conditions, therefore, only admitted of two possible facts: either the neighborhood in question was "definitely colored" or it remained "solidly white." The facts had to fit the categorical scheme.

Second, this assumption involved a spatialization of social life that drew attention away from human beings and focused instead on imagined "territories" and "boundaries." This geopolitical language is explicit in some cases or implicit in the geopolitical metaphors of "Negro penetration," "invasion," or "infiltration" to be found in virtually all of the cases of this period. Sometimes, as in *Fairchild v. Raines*[32] and *Lettreau v. Ellis*,[33] judges focused on the territories. Sometimes the emphasis was on the boundary *(Clark v. Vaughn)*[34] and whether it was a "dividing line" and a "complete barrier" *(Grady v. Garland)*[35] or, perhaps, "an unnatural barrier" as in *Hundley v. Gorewitz*[36] and *Gospel Spreading Association v. Bennetts.*[37]

In actual practice then, judicial interpretation of geographies of race involved three steps:

1. Indicating the relative location of black and white territories

2. Indicating precisely where the boundary that defined and separated these territories was located

3. Assessing the stability of the boundary

This last point was crucial, for if the boundary was found to be moving, the doctrine might be applied. It seems then that the validity of the contract was dependent on the stability of the boundary. These territories and boundaries were thought to *exist*, as things, apart from interpretation. In interpreting changed conditions in terms of a dichotomous categorical scheme, and given the belief in the existence of white and black zones separated by a boundary, a central geographical question became "Has the boundary moved?" Questions like "Has it disappeared?" or even "What boundary?" simply made no sense. To question the existence of the line was to question the zones, and therefore to question the immutability of segregation.

Thus the categorical scheme of black and white was read onto the physical world. If racial segregation was a given, immutable fact, the political or moral question that animated assessments became "Should the Negro districts be allowed to expand or not?" "The choice," wrote California Supreme Court justice Roger Traynor in *Fairchild v. Raines*, "lies between the continuation of such conditions [inadequate housing] and expansion of urban negro districts."[38] The mechanics of the doctrine of changed conditions worked in such a way that the answer turned on whether or not—as an empirical fact—the Negro districts had already expanded. This is what changed conditions meant.

As we've seen, in an adversarial legal system there will be conflicting interpretations of doctrine, of precedent, of the meaning of legal instruments, of rules, of standards, of history, of mental states, and so on. In cases that require geographical interpretation—especially those in which the outcome turns on a geographical interpretation—we should also expect *conflicting* construals of social geographies. Where defendants purport to see change, plaintiffs are likely to deny that change has occurred. However, judges also disagree among themselves and present their own conflicting interpretations. This can most clearly be seen in dissenting opinions and in appellate decisions which reverse lower court rulings (thereby correcting the geographical interpretations of other judges).

Indeed, not only do we find conflicting interpretations of geographies, but we find disagreement over the *spatial* technique employed in assessing the meaning of race boundaries. We find disagreement over specifically *where* one looks for the changed conditions. I mentioned above that the validity of the contract depended on the stability of the boundary. However, some judges operated under the assumption that the conditionality was precisely the reverse: that the stability of the boundary depended on the validity of the contract. Moreover, which view the judge took was related to *where* he looked for the changed conditions, on where, exactly, "the Negroes" were located. This in turn depended on the spatial technique employed in finding them.

Judicial Construal of Space

In this section we examine variation in judicial techniques of spatial analysis. More specifically, we look at judicial discretion in the spatial scope of change, and therefore of relevance. The root question here was whether judicial scrutiny should be confined to the covenanted tract itself or whether it should embrace the neighborhood or "surrounding territory." Clearly, if judges only looked for changed conditions inside the restricted space that was created by segregationists, they were less likely to find them than if they expanded their view to include the wider area within which the space itself was located. I will refer to the technique of restricting attention to changes inside the tract itself as *localization*, and the more embracing technique that considers changed conditions outside of the tract—e.g., the neighborhood, the wider community and so on—as *regionalization*.

With respect to variation and discretion of technique, I should mention that, first (for the above stated reason), decisions—outcomes—turned on the spatial technique employed by the majority. That is, while the outcome was based on the applicability of the doctrine of changed conditions, assessment of the applicability of the doctrine depended on the spatial technique that was used. Second, both appellate reversals of lower court rulings and appellate dissents were often explicitly based on disagreements over the appropriate spatial scope of reference and relevance. Third, variations and inconsistencies in techniques generated controversy in contemporaneous legal scholarly commentary. It was, it seems, a big deal.[39] I will here survey three cases to show how these techniques were applied and challenged.

Clark v. Vaughn

One of the earliest changed conditions cases, *Clark v. Vaughn*, included a strong dissent that directly attacked the majority's strategy of regionalization.[40] This case involved a restrictive covenant regime in Kansas City, Kansas. In 1923 a covenant had been established that was to be in force for 15 years. Among the parties to the contract were Grace Clark and the parents of Ethel and D. W. Vaughn. In 1927 the Vaughns agreed to sell their lot to William Boone. Boone, a black man, took possession of the property and Clark sued. The trial judge refused to issue an injunction and Clark appealed to the Kansas Supreme Court. While I have no evidence of direct involvement by the NAACP in this case, it is significant that the Vaughns and Boone were represented by different attorneys.

The specific lots in question were spatially separated from the remainder of the tract by Quindaro Boulevard. Kansas Supreme Court justice William Hutchison found the relative location of the lots to be a material fact. In his discussion of changed conditions he stressed, among other things, the fact that two formerly Caucasian churches in the neighborhood had been "sold to and are now used by Negroes,"[41] and that attendance and employment in the neighborhood "school for whites" had been rapidly decreasing. Hutchison then set the boundary of the races down the middle of Quindaro Boulevard and held that conditions south of the boulevard had changed to such an extent that prohibiting the white defendants from selling to blacks "practically confiscates their property" and only "serves as a protection to the property of the plaintiff in the solid district north of the boulevard."[42] Thus, "general encroachment . . . in the immediate vicinity of defendants' property" and "unequal reciprocal protection [due to the directionality of the moving boundary] would make the enforcement of the covenant under the changed conditions very burdensome and inequitable to these [white] defendants."[43] The trial judge's interpretation that conditions around Quindaro Boulevard had changed was therefore affirmed and William Boone was allowed to keep his home.

In dissent, Justice William Jochems acknowledged that the boundary was moving. That was precisely why the contract should be enforced. Moreover, he also recognized that the specific lots in question were spatially separate. That was precisely why they should *not* be legally severed. In localizing the space of change and relevance—i.e., confining it to the space specified in the contract—Jochems noted that there was nothing the covenantors could do to "prevent colored people from acquiring all the property around them right up to the boundary of the properties involved in the contract."[44] He concluded that "the fact that colored people were moving in the direction of the property must have been the moving cause of the contract. What these people who entered into the contract had in mind," he wrote, "was not to prevent colored people from surrounding them, but to prevent the restricted property from being used or occupied by people of that race."

An important fact for Jochems was that the changes were "not such as occurred in the use of the property embraced in the contract. They [were] changes occurring on property outside of the contract over which the parties had no control." Thus, to refuse to enforce the terms of the contract was to unjustly subvert the will of those who created the space. More strategically, Jochems noted that the "[d]efendants' property, although lying across the street from the remainder of the property involved in the contract, served as a buffer for plaintiff's property. It kept Negroes just that much further away from plaintiff's property." Jochems was also impatient with what he viewed as the expedience of those who would obliterate the restriction. "It may well be argued," he wrote, "that the contract was of greater advantage to plaintiffs than to defendants, but if defendants made an improvident contract that is no reason why they should be relieved from it." [45]

In this case the legal-spatial severance of William Boone's home from the remainder of the restricted tract and the redrawing of the boundary down the middle of Quindaro Boulevard was rhetorically portrayed as the result of neutral observation. From our vantage point it should be viewed as active participation in the geopolitics of race. It should be stressed, however, that had Jochems succeeded in persuading a majority to see things his way, it would also have been participation posing as mere observation. Further, the categorical scheme used to interpret and inscribe the legal, social relational meaning of this part of the world would have been the same: Negro-Caucasian.

Grady v. Garland

A more explicit discussion of the spatial scope and focus of changed conditions is to be seen in *Grady v. Garland*, in which plaintiffs sought removal of restrictions on property located in Washington, D.C.[46] In *Grady*, owners of six of the eight restricted lots in the space wanted to extinguish the *perpetual* restrictions because of changed conditions. Garland, owner of one of the remaining two lots, requested a dismissal. The lower court granted the request and Grady appealed to the U.S. Court of Appeals for the District of Columbia. Associate Justice Josiah Van Orsdel localized the dispute and held that as no change had occurred within the restricted tract, then no change had occurred of which the court should take notice. First he set the boundary separating the white neighborhood from the black down the middle of First Street. Then he asserted that "the restriction is for the property to which it applies and is not affected by similar conditions which may arise in adjoining property. The object of the restriction here was to prevent the invasion of the restricted property by colored people, not the invasion of property surrounding it." [47]

Placing a high value on the sense of security of those who had come to rely on the contract and stressing the protective value of the tract to the white neighborhood to the east, Van Orsdel wrote, "A mere glance at the present situation demonstrates the protection which the restriction is to the [plaintiffs] Murgia and Garland. It furnishes a complete barrier against the eastward movement of colored population into the restricted area—a dividing line." Note that for Van Orsdel the beneficiaries of the restriction are not simply the named parties but all of the white residents of the neighborhood to the east. Thus the stability of the boundary was seen to depend on the validity of the contract. And this, in spite of the fact that a majority of the signers of the contract wanted to abolish the restricted tract. Van Orsdel went on to denounce the strategy of regionalization and denied the relevance of changes outside the tract by noting that "all that would be necessary to defeat such a covenant would be the settlement of a few colored families in the immediate vicinity of the restricted area." Interestingly, he relied almost entirely on precedents from commercial or building restriction cases which had nothing to do with race.[48]

Associate Justice Harold Stephens directed his dissent squarely to the scope and focus question. He noted the "well-established rule" that "changes within or without an area covered by restrictive covenants" should be considered in assessing the applicability of the doctrine. Localizing the spatial frame of reference and relevance was "necessarily predicated upon the proposition that a person seeking to remove a covenant must show that he has breached it himself and that the person for whose benefit the covenant runs has ignored that breach. I find nothing in the authorities warranting this." Finally, citing and relying on the *Clark* decision, Stephens also argued that cases concerning building restrictions and commercial uses had "no relation to covenants against colored occupancy."[49]

In this case we again find conflicting interpretations of the spatiality of a rule and conflicting interpretations of context. Van Orsdel was not simply recognizing or finding a dividing line; he and the concurring justices were *inventing* that line. Again, consider the alternative. Had Stephens been writing for the majority, the line would not have been found "at a mere glance." It would not have been "found" at all.

Fairchild v. Raines

A 1944 case from Southern California, an area where restrictive covenants flourished, provides additional insight into these judicial spatial strategies.

This case, *Fairchild v. Raines*, dealt with a definable subdivision, the Palisades, in Pasadena.[50] Only thirty-five (or possibly only twenty-three) of its sixty-nine lots were covered by the restriction, and these thirty-five lots were not contiguous. Plaintiffs sought to enjoin Helen and Ross Raines from using, occupying, or residing in the house they had purchased without actual knowledge of the restriction.

The trial court ruled for the plaintiffs and the Raineses appealed. Judge Marshall McComb, writing for the California Court of Appeals, affirmed. McComb found that the doctrine of changed conditions was inapplicable because "there had been no change in Negro occupancy as to any of the lots described in the agreement above set forth except in the single instant of lot 43 which is the subject of the present controversy."[51] Because California was one of the jurisdictions in which the own/occupy distinction was held to exist, the Raineses were not ordered to forfeit their property. They were, however, ordered to leave their home and wait six years for the restriction to expire before moving back in.

The Raineses appealed to the California Supreme Court (at which point, we might note, they were rhetorically transformed from "Negroes" into "colored Americans").[52] The Los Angeles branch of the NAACP filed an amicus brief on their behalf and segregationists also had their friends of the court file briefs. The state supreme court reversed the lower courts' rulings by finding, first, that conditions *had* changed; second, that the trial court had erred in failing to make findings of fact resolving the issues raised by the defense of changed conditions; and, third, that this failure was the direct result of confining analysis to the lots described in the contract. That is, the basis of the reversal was Judge McComb's inappropriate localization.

Justice B. Rey Schauer began his analysis by stating that "the number and relative locations of the lots covered and not covered by the agreement are material."[53] Quoting from testimony of neighborhood residents that some parcels in the neighborhood had "become substantially surrounded . . . on three sides by negroes," he found that that part of Pasadena was now "more suitable for Negroes than for white people." Granting that "the precise purpose of the covenants is to avert changes in the restricted territory, not in the surrounding neighborhood" and, further, "that there had been no change in 'Negro or non-Caucasian occupancy' of the lots *included in the agreement* until the occupancy by defendants Raines of lot 43," Schauer determined that these facts, while important, were "not necessarily controlling here."[54] He then addressed the question of scope and focus directly:

[I]n an area as small as that involved in this case . . . *and where the restricted lots do not form a single contiguous group*, it would not seem essential that the occupancy of any of such restricted lots themselves should have undergone the critical change if it has occurred in the very neighborhood of which they are a contiguous part geographically, and apparently in social aspects.

More to the point, he wrote, echoing Stephens' dissent in *Grady*, "[I]t is obvious that a change in the race character in the neighborhood, without violation of the covenants of the agreement, could only occur through a change in the occupancy of neighboring lots *not* included in the agreement."[55]

While Schauer did not cite *Clark v. Vaughn*, he did distinguish *Fairchild* from *Grady v. Garland*. He did this by citing the "complete barrier . . . dividing line" passage quoted above. Schauer found that "in the cases before us there is no 'complete barrier,'" and further that "not only the 'surrounding neighborhood' but the very tract and block of which the restricted areas are a part have been invaded." In sum, "since the lots covered are not a contiguous group and do not constitute a complete barrier or dividing line," then the plaintiffs do not have an absolute right to the injunction.[56]

In a concurring opinion, Justice Traynor agreed that the trial court had failed to provide an "adequate basis" for determining changed conditions. However, he devoted the bulk of his opinion to a discussion of policy questions and the desirability of expansion of "negro districts."

In this case we see the California Supreme Court erasing the space which the district court had participated in constructing. We see differences in interpretation concerning both doctrine and geography, and what one has to do with the other. We see conflicting geographies of judgment both in the sense of conceptions of spatiality that inform judicial interpretation, and in the sense of the geographies of power and experience that are produced by these interpretations. It should also be noted that while contemporary observers might applaud the reversal of the district court's ruling, both Schauer and Traynor were still using the same categorical scheme of Negro/Caucasian and were still participating in the mapping of racism onto the landscape of Southern California.

In this section we saw how judges could manipulate the spatiality of a rule in order to "find" change or in order to virtually ensure that the relevant "conditions" would not be found. We saw how claims about the spatiality of a rule justified interpretations about places, and hence justified the geopolitical consequences of these interpretations. We also looked at other elements of spatiality and spatial strategy to be seen in legal argument. We saw how attorneys presented different lines of argument, each of which would have had a different range of spatial consequences had it been accepted, and how judges rejected all but the most spatially restrictive of the four lines of argument commonly advanced. These can all be seen as spatial maneuvers within an on-going geopolitics of race and racism. Legal interpretation, in these cases, was simply one form of political action. The point of these actions was to shape actual geographies of power. One way or another they were consequential. Real people were forced to leave their homes, were excluded or expelled from large sections of cities, were compelled to pay costs or damages or they were not. Judicial interpretations of the relations between geographies and social life were not idle speculations.

One point to bring out here is that while interpreters purported to be passively observing empirical geographies of race from a distance, so to speak ("a mere glance . . ." etc.) they can more accurately be described as active participants in the construction and revision of geographies of racism. Regardless of whether judges chose to reinforce (as in *Grady*), modify (as in *Clark*), or erase (as in *Fairchild*) the racist spaces created by the covenantors, regardless of whether they chose to contain or expand "Negro districts," they acted from within the worlds they were describing and not from some neutral position "outside." From this perspective there is no point "outside" of social life, of history, or of geography from which judges can gaze at society.

Judicial Construction of Place

In this section we examine ways in which the spatial strategies of localization and regionalization were deployed by judges in a series of cases that concerned changed conditions in one neighborhood of Washington, D. C., in the period 1937–1947. Two cases served as interpretive baselines. The first, *Grady v. Garland*, the 1937 case which we discussed above, was a chronological base against which change could be measured.[57] The second, *Hundley v. Gorewitz*, though involving another nearby neighborhood, served as a doctrinal baseline.[58] In that case, judges fashioned a theory of urban geographical transformation that was referred to in subsequent cases as "the Hundley rule." This rule allowed judges to infer the direction and magnitude of prospective change and to thereby justify the strategic moves of localization and regionalization. The arguments about the dynamics of urban geographical change were similar in many respects to the "theories" of geographical process offered by attorneys in *Buchanan*. As before, most of these cases were characterized by conflicting interpretations of geography, of change, and, ultimately, of what should count as "conditions."

It is significant that between the earliest case (*Grady*) and the last (*Hurd v. Hodge*)[59] restrictive covenants had become an intensely and explicitly political issue in the District of Columbia.[60] Later cases were organized by the National Legal Committee of the NAACP and argued by its chairperson and Howard Law School dean, Charles Houston Jr.[61] Also, the last of these cases, *Hurd v. Hodge*, was heard by the U.S. Supreme Court at the same time and to the same effect as *Shelley v. Kraemer*.[62]

Clement Vose's 1959 study, *Caucasians Only: The Supreme Court, the NAACP, and the Restrictive Covenant Cases*, discusses the details of the local geopolitics of race in Washington, St. Louis, and Detroit in this period. Especially important to events under discussion here were the roles of attorney Henry Gilligan, who represented segregationists in many cases, and Raphael Urciolo, a lawyer and realtor who testified that if he "had a choice between selling to a colored man or a foreigner and another—I would prefer to sell to the colored man because he has so much harder time getting a house than the other person."[63] Gilligan was also the attorney for the North Capitol Citizen's Association, one of approximately seventy such associations operating in Washington at the time. Local lawyers like Gilligan and Urciolo were key players in the geopolitics of race.

The Baselines

Grady involved a tract on First Street NW and S Street in the North Capitol neighborhood of Washington, not far from Howard University. In *Grady*, the majority of the U.S. Circuit Court of Appeals for the District of Columbia localized the referent of change to the restricted tract. Reversing the lower court's ruling, they found that the restriction "furnished a complete barrier against the eastward movement of colored population into the restricted area—a dividing line."[64] As we saw, changes elsewhere on First Street which Justice Stephens regarded as significant were dismissed as irrelevant by the majority.

The location of the tract examined five years later in *Hundley v. Gorewitz* was about a mile north of the First Street area that was the topic of dispute in *Grady* and later cases. Frederick and Mary Hundley were represented by Charles Houston, while Rebecca Gorewitz's attorney was Henry Gilligan. In *Hundley*, conditions in the neighborhood were found to have changed significantly enough to warrant its recategorization from "caucasian" to "negro" and to justify extinguishing the covenant. What is of interest to us is *how* this determination was made. Chief Judge Lawrence Groner, who had been in the majority in *Grady*, based his assessment of changed conditions on a general understanding of urban geographical processes. His reading of the landscape was presented in two parts. First, he offered a theoretical account of the "natural growth of a city" and then he applied this account to the case at hand:

[1]
. . . in the natural growth of a city, property originally constructed for residential purposes is abandoned for homes of more modern construction in more desirable locations, for a serious decline in values would follow unless the way was open either for use of the property for business purposes or for the housing needs of a lower income class.

[2]
And it [the exception to the rule of enforcement] is also applicable where removals are caused by constant penetration into white neighborhoods of colored persons. For in such a case to enforce the restriction would be to create an unnatural barrier to civic development and thereby establish a virtually uninhabited section of the city.[65]

What is significant here is not simply the use of the terms "natural" and "unnatural." More telling are the assumptions regarding processes and causation with respect to what the world is like and how it works. If we examine this brief passage more closely, we can see that there are two different models of causation presented. In the first model (presented in passage 1, above), abandonment *precedes* and allows for expansion of the Negro (or lower-class or commercial) district. This explains "changed conditions" and justifies a recategorization of the area. We might call this the "individual choice" model of urban transformation, because the underlying mechanism of urban change is to be seen in the choices of individual property owners to abandon their homes for something better. In the second model (presented in passage 2, above), expansion of inner zones induces "penetration" and flight and change. This is more of a metabolic model, the focus of analysis here being the city as a kind of organism. In this model, growth is assumed to be an inexorable property of cities. Note, though, that in the individual choice model individuals are white and choice is a white prerogative. In *both* models black people are assimilated to the environment, that is, to "conditions."

Moreover, there are two mechanisms that underlie these models of change. The first, as mentioned, is a kind of private ordering whereby social changes are understood primarily as the aggregate of private decisions. Again, this is framed within a sharp black-and-white scheme. The second mechanism relies on a deeper naturalization of value, in which value is determined by the environmental variables such as proximity to the city center and propinquity of other groups. In this model it is presupposed *both* that a change in value leads to a change in color (white → black) *and* a change in color leads to a change in value (high → low). This highly naturalistic account of the processes that drive urban geographical transformations establishes an intimate link between these processes and resultant urban form. As we saw in the arguments presented in *Buchanan v. Warley*, if the process is natural, then the form—racial segregation—cannot be less so. And if the form is natural, then its legitimacy is not to be lightly questioned and intervention is to be discouraged. In such a world the law should work with and not against nature. In situations that were seen to correspond to this model, this meant that a court in equity ought not to interfere with the natural process of sorting by artificially maintaining the line.

Moving to a specific application of this theory in the case at hand, Groner found that south of the tract "some half dozen or so city blocks are predominantly Negro" and that north on 13th Street, "the intersecting streets are solidly Negro." Indeed, "a glance at the neighborhood shows a definite trend." That is to say, the boundary which separates and defines Negro and Caucasian territories had moved. This transformed the restricted tract into an "unnatural barrier." Indeed, a material fact was that a Negro had purchased property "almost directly across the street" from the plaintiff. "And this," wrote Groner, "was just the beginning. . . . The trend is unmistakable, its effect is apparent."[66]

This result could only have been achieved by regionalizing the spatial scope of reference and relevance. According to Groner, "[T]he obvious purpose [of the covenant] was to keep the neighborhood white."[67] In contrast to *Grady*, there was no attempt to limit the scope of analysis to the tract or confine interpretation to the contract. It is perhaps worth noting that the other judges who heard this case were future U.S. Supreme Court justices: Wiley Rutledge, who in a brief concurring opinion expressly reserved judgment as to the validity of covenants in any circumstances, and Fred Vinson, who was to write the unanimous opinion invalidating restrictive covenants in *Shelley v. Kraemer*.

The Hundley rule, as developed by Justice Groner, seemed to permit judges to regionalize the spatial scope of reference beyond the restricted tract if imminent change in conditions could be inferred from knowledge of general processes. If one could identify an "unmistakable" or "definite trend," then one would be justified in removing the "unnatural barrier" which the restricted tract represented. Employment of the Hundley rule shifted attention to these vectors of change. If we imagine that Groner invented the rule in order to provide an objective basis for assessing the applicability of the doctrine of changed conditions, we have to wonder how he intended to ground the applicability of the rule itself. After all, one would have to regionalize first—that is, take into account changes beyond the borders of the restricted tract—in order to test the applicability of the rule.

Mays v. Burgess

Two years later, back on First Street where the dividing line had been discovered in *Grady*, Justice Groner, writing for the majority, again had an opportunity to display his analytic skills. This case, *Mays v. Burgess* (I),[68] concerned the fate of Clara Mays and her family. Again the court was the U.S. Circuit Court of Appeals for the District of Columbia and again Gilligan argued for the segregationists. Among Mays' attorneys was William Hastie, who was soon to be appointed governor of the Virgin Islands and who would also become the first black federal appeals court judge. Mays had purchased property on First Street between W and Adams. William Burgess and other white neighbors sought an injunction against her ownership or occupancy of the property. That is, they requested the court to order her and her family evicted. Groner quoted the passage from *Hundley* cited above in order to distinguish the facts presented in *Mays*.

After summarily dismissing other defenses, he wrote that "the only question now open for discussion is whether, under the rule announced in *Hundley v. Gorewitz* . . . the purpose of the restrictive covenant has failed by

reason of a change in the character of the neighborhood." Then, by way of
answering his question, he continued, "[A]pplying the rule to the facts in
this case, it is easily seen from the trial court's finding of fact that no such
change or transformation of the property has occurred." Reading the facts
in *Mays* in terms of the Hundley rule, Justice Groner noted that "all of the
adjacent area for 6 blocks on First Street is covered by similar covenants
and . . . occupied exclusively by persons of the white race." "Indeed," he
continued, "there is no colored occupancy on First Street from T Street
north to the Soldiers' Home grounds, nor on or to the east of First Street."
Then, reaching the boundary, he recognized that "in blocks to the west of
First Street for several blocks, although separated by an alley, there has
been extensive colored penetration. And it may well be that in a short time
this penetration will reach the territory we are discussing." In sum, there
may have been a "trend," but it seems to have fallen short of the "definite"
or "unmistakable" standards developed in *Hundley*. "For the present it is
enough to say that First Street, between U and Adams, and the neighboring properties eastward are an unbroken white community of nearly a
thousand homes under restrictive agreements, most of which are still in
effect."[69]

Note that the alley indicated by Groner ran directly behind the lot in
question. Tracing the boundary, it seems that it ran down the middle of the
alley between First and Second Streets which defined the western edge of
the tract. To the west: "extensive colored penetration." To the east: "an unbroken white community."

Though the covenant that was the subject of litigation had, at the time of
the ruling, a year and seven months before it expired, that covering the 2100
block (immediately south) had expired two months before the decision.

Associate Judge Henry Edgerton, a self-conscious liberal, in dissent, interpreted the social geography of the North Capitol neighborhood somewhat
differently.[70] Edgerton did not see the alley as the impenetrable wall that
Groner considered it to be. For him "most, if not all, of the property immediately west of this block, and for a considerable distance beyond, is occupied by Negroes." In the block immediately south, "colored people have
begun to buy homes." Moreover, he stated, "[T]he property in this block is
more valuable to colored purchasers than to white purchasers." In a phrase,
"[T]he 'trend' in the neighborhood is toward colored ownership and occupancy." Directly quoting Groner he continued, "[A]s we said in *Hundley v.*

Gorewitz, 'the trend is unmistakable, its effect apparent.'" For Judge Edgerton, the Hundley rule and the doctrine of changed conditions were both applicable to this block of First Street. They therefore provided a defense against putting the Mayses out of their home.[71]

Significantly, just as Groner had attempted to localize the spatial referent of change from the neighborhood to the tract, Edgerton countered with the opposite move of regionalization. Moving from consideration of changed conditions in the neighborhood to broader arguments about public policy, Edgerton stated that the rule in *Corrigan* establishing the validity of covenants in Washington "would not cover this case even if general conditions in the District of Columbia had remained the same. I think that it is quite inapplicable today because general conditions [in the city as a whole] have not remained the same." Here he changed not only the spatial scope of change as authorized by the Hundley rule but, more important, he changed what counted as conditions. "The conditions in which many of the 187,000 Negroes of the District of Columbia have long been obliged to live are now worse than ever." For Edgerton, then, the appropriate space of reference was the District of Columbia housing market. And the referent of "conditions" was not blackness—as given by the contract—but the quality of housing and living space. We will see below how he was to develop this geopolitical maneuver in a subsequent case. Nonetheless, in spite of Edgerton's more radical interpretation of changed conditions, Mays was given sixty days to "remove herself and all of her personal effects from the premises."[72]

The same day that *Mays* was decided, the court also handed down a decision in the case of *Gospel Spreading Association v. Bennetts.*[73] This case involved, in Judge Groner's words, "land located in the same general neighborhood in Washington City" as that examined in *Mays*. Indeed, it was at First and U Streets, two blocks south of the Mayses' house. Again quoting extensively from his *Hundley* opinion regarding "unnatural barriers," Groner found this area to have been transformed by "constant penetration by colored persons" into a "definitely colored section." Therefore Groner reversed the lower court's decision and corrected the trial judge's errant geography. He knew a Negro district when he saw one. "The plain meaning of this," he wrote, "is that U Street on which this property fronts, is a wholly colored neighborhood." In this case Judge Edgerton concurred in the result.

In January 1945, then, it seemed that Clara Mays and her family were out of bounds and therefore out of house and home but the Gospel Spreading Association was in. However, in October 1945 Mays was again back before the same U.S. Circuit Court of Appeals. Because she had, in Groner's words, "refused and neglected to comply with the judgement of the District Court," the Burgesses filed a motion to have her adjudged in contempt.[74] This was done and Mays appealed. Her defense was hardship (it had been literally impossible for her to find another home) and, again, changed conditions. That is, the conditions in the neighborhood were said to have changed *since* she had last appeared before the court of appeals (four black families had moved into the neighborhood). By this time the covenant had less than ten months to run.

Groner, however, stuck to the narrow question of contempt. He did not address the hardship defense at all. His response to the changed conditions argument was simply that "the infiltration of four colored families" was not enough to bring the facts of the case within the scope of the Hundley rule or to recategorize the neighborhood. The home that Mays had bought remained an integral part of the "solidly white community." The boundary remained in the alley. Accordingly, the lower court's judgment of contempt was affirmed and Mays' appeal was dismissed with costs.

Edgerton, again in dissent, made much of the "new facts." The covenant on the 2100 block had expired and four colored families had moved onto the adjoining block. This showed, he stated, that "the trend" was "definitely colored." It was therefore "necessary for the District Court to reconsider in the light of these new facts the applicability of the Hundley rule to the case."[75] Taking notice of the fact that less than ten months remained on the covenant and that it was therefore only a matter of time before the change would be complete, Edgerton thought that "proximity in time of colored occupancy may have as much bearing [on assessing the applicability of the Hundley rule] as proximity in space." That is, notice should be taken of the *rapidity* with which "conditions" were changing.

Edgerton also addressed the defense of hardship with a lengthy discussion of what Clara Mays and her family—now including six nieces and a nephew recently discharged from the armed forces—had personally had to endure as a result of both segregation and her suits. For example, referring to the effects on the experiential geographies of members of the Mays family, he wrote:

[T]he only place available for occupancy that has come to her attention is in Maryland, about eight miles from the District boundary, which location is too far from the city for defendants Mays and her sister (who works at night) to travel to and from their employment, there being no public transportation at the hour of night when her sister finishes work.[76]

Finally, raising the principle that equity will not enforce a contract in which the benefits do not outweigh the burdens, Edgerton said that "the restrictive promises of a defendant's predecessors are not to be enforced in disregard of the principle that no injunction should cause extreme hardship to the defendant without commensurate benefit to the plaintiff. Equity is not indifferent to human suffering."[77]

One and a half years later, the U.S. Court of Appeals for the District of Columbia heard the case of *Hurd v. Hodge*[78] which would eventually reach the Supreme Court as a companion case to *Shelley v. Kraemer*. The tract in question in *Hurd* was around the corner from the tract involved in *Mays*, not far from Howard University on the 100 block of Bryant Street. The area was west of First Street, that is, in the area categorized by Groner in the first *Mays* case as "colored." In fact eleven of the thirty-one lots on the block had been "continually occupied by Negroes for 20 years." In this case the covenant created a *perpetual* restriction. Again the attorneys of record were Charles Houston and Henry Gilligan.

Judge Bennett Clark, who had replaced Groner as master geographer of the court of appeals, dealt with the constitutional questions by giving the usual wave to *Corrigan v. Buckley*. He also paid scant attention to the changed conditions argument. Instead, he simply noted that "*Mays v. Burgess* involved the same area as that considered in the instant case and is controlling here."[79] That is, conditions on Bryant Street were found not to have changed in 1947 because conditions around the corner on First Street were found not to have changed in 1945. In fact, they were found not to have changed on the 2200 block of First Street in 1945 because "the infiltration of four colored families" on the 2100 block of First Street was insufficient to justify application of the Hundley rule. It is important to note here that by the time *Hurd v. Hodge* was argued, all of the covenants on First Street including the one at issue in *Mays* had expired. Apparently what was good enough for Groner in 1945 was good enough for Clark in 1947.

Yet again in dissent, Judge Edgerton abandoned a contract interpretation of covenants entirely and relegated discussion of the doctrine of changed conditions to a footnote.[80] Instead, he advanced strong arguments against judicial enforcement of racially restrictive covenants on constitutional, restraint on alienation, and public policy grounds. Edgerton said that these issues had never been addressed by the Supreme Court and that these arguments had never, in fact, been closed off. "The erroneous impression" that they *had* been resulted "from a misinterpretation of *Corrigan v. Buckley.*"[81] Whether or not conditions had changed was therefore irrelevant. However, Edgerton—in his argument from public policy—*did* situate his arguments in terms of changed conditions of a different sort. And the spatial scope of these changes embraced, successively, the neighborhood, the city, the nation, and the globe.

The expanding geographical locus of "changed conditions" is reflected in the rhetorical structure of Edgerton's argument that the enforcement of racially restrictive covenants is contrary to public policy. First, beginning with the local housing market, he noted that "the shortage of decent housing, or any housing for Negroes" in the District was "particularly acute" and that the situation was worsening. Citing studies made in the thirties and since the end of the war, he claimed that black people in the nation's capital were "largely confined to wretched quarters in overcrowded ghettoes." He then asserted that these conditions—which were in part caused by the proliferation of restrictive covenants—were in turn responsible for dramatic racial disparities in death rates, particularly deaths related to tuberculosis and childbirth. The causal chain here runs from restrictive covenants to appalling housing conditions to disease and death. Nothing which contributed to such a state of affairs could possibly be consistent with the public policy of a democracy.[82]

But this situation was not simply a matter of local concern. It existed "in thousands of American communities" and was a national problem. Edgerton here relied heavily on Gunnar Myrdal's recently published *An American Dilemma: The Negro Problem and American Democracy* and numerous other studies in order to nationalize the referent of "changed conditions." He referred to statistics concerning housing conditions for black people in Detroit, Norfolk, Savannah, and elsewhere and found that nationally "congestion in Negro neighborhoods has reached a new high and it is extracting unheard of economic and social costs."[83] The problem and its costs were national in scope and enforcement of covenants contributed to their exacerbation. But there was more. Events on First Street and elsewhere in the North Capitol neighborhood—as in Detroit, St. Louis, Los Angeles, and other U.S. cities—were seen to have international consequences which were contrary to national interests. In making this rhetorical move, Judge Edgerton tried to globalize the spatial referent of "changed conditions."

Ratification of the Charter of the United Nations, which sought to promote "respect for human rights . . . without distinction as to race," was taken to be indicative of U.S. policy on the matter. Edgerton even cited a Canadian case that had reached the same conclusion with regard to racial covenants. More pragmatically, he developed the argument that official support for racism in America was contrary to the nation's emerging interests in a postwar and postcolonial world. "American desire for international goodwill and co-operation cannot be neglected in any consideration of the policy of preventing men from buying homes because they are Negroes. . . . In Western Europe, to say nothing of other parts of the world, the position of Negroes is widely advertised and widely resented."[84] Then, after mentioning remarks made by General Eisenhower on the "enlightened self-interest" of being fair, he quoted at length from a recent address by President Truman:

> We are living in a time of profound and swiftly moving change. We see colonial peoples moving towards independence. . . . We, as Americans, will want to supply guidance and help when we can. One way in which we can help is to set an example of a nation in which people of different backgrounds and different origins work peacefully alongside one another. . . . More and more we are learning, and in no small measure through the medium of the press, how closely our democracy is under observation. We are learning what loud echoes both our successes and our failures have in every corner of the world. That is one of the pressing reasons why we cannot afford failures. When we fail to live together in peace, that failure touches not us, as Americans, alone, but the cause of democracy itself.[85]

Edgerton then added that "suits like these, and the ghetto system they enforce, are among our conspicuous failures to live together in peace." The world had changed. Public policy had changed. The court of appeals should change its assessment of "changed conditions." Recall that these remarks were included in an interpretation of the validity of a contract between neighbors. Edgerton's rhetorical strategy in *Hurd* was to situate disagreements about the validity of such contracts in the context of changed conditions at local, national, and international scales of reference. In doing so, he consistently kept the focus on *racism* as the problem and on judicial enforcement of covenants as not simply an incidental part of that problem but as a necessary component of the geopolitics of race. Within the constraints on interpretation imposed by the conventions of legal practice, the radicalness of Edgerton's move should not be underestimated. In a sense, he tried to turn the map of legal discourse inside out.

In these five cases, we examined judicial participation in the creation of the geography of race in one neighborhood in Washington, D.C., during a ten-year period. Of fundamental importance to this activity was application of the Hundley rule and the geographical interpretation that it required. If the color line ran through the alley between First and Second Streets and then ran down the middle of U Street, it was because the court said it did. If the court found that the "infiltration" of four colored families into the solidly white community on the other side of the line did not mean that the boundary had moved, then it hadn't moved. If it found that the expiration of covenants in the surrounding territory did not constitute changed conditions sufficient to deny enforcement of perpetual restrictions, then it didn't.

Among the more important of the changed local conditions, however, were the political changes that occurred between the time of *Grady* and *Hurd*. These changes are perhaps best symbolized by the reaction to the refusal of the Daughters of the American Revolution in 1939 to allow Marian Anderson to sing at Constitution Hall. Local historian Constance Green has written that "the furor aroused in the city and throughout the country exceeded any outburst of indignation within the memory of Washington's oldest inhabitants." Anderson subsequently sang before seventy-five thousand people at the Lincoln Memorial after the intervention of Secretary of the Interior Harold Ickes—an event that Green called "a turning point . . . in Washington Negroes' seventy-year-old fight against discrimination."[86]

The changed political conditions were also potently demonstrated by A. Philip Randolph's threat to march on the Capitol with fifty thousand blacks in July 1941. The changed conditions were also manifest in stepped-up demands by Washingtonians for home rule, organized opposition to all forms of segregation, and increasingly organized white reaction to this opposition.[87]

In this period from *Grady* to *Hurd*, we see the metamorphosis of judicial disagreement from the rather legalistic question of the appropriate scope and focus of change which marked Justice Stephen's dissent in *Grady* to the increasingly impassioned dissents of Henry Edgerton in both *Mays* cases and in *Hurd*. We also see the increasing rigidity of the judicial supporters of restrictive covenants. With respect to the politics of localization versus regionalization, we see not only inconsistency of application within successive opinions of a single judge but, in *Hurd*, we see the referent of change being another time and another "place."

Under these changed political circumstances, conflicting interpretations could not be contained within narrow doctrinal boundaries. What was obvious in *Grady* became increasingly and aggressively questioned. The key interpretive move was Edgerton's reinterpretation of *Corrigan* and his erasure of the limits it had imposed on defense arguments. In opening up what had seemingly been closed off, he allowed himself to take into account changed conditions where he found them. But while he situated the events in successively more extensive contexts, the most important consequences were felt by those who would or would not be expelled from their homes and neighborhoods.

Concluding Remarks

In the generation following *Buchanan v. Warley*, an era characterized by a dramatic increase in the number of African Americans living in northern cities, restrictive covenants became a significant tool for constructing geographies of race and racism. While it is safe to say that most of these racist contracts were not contested, our study of those that were challenged reveals key moves in the geopolitics of race in the mid-twentieth century. In drafting and signing contracts, people like William Burgess, Grace Clark, and Rebecca Gorewitz created legal spaces of racial exclusion. In sending threatening letters and otherwise harassing transgressors, attorneys like Henry Gilligan effectively policed the color line. In bringing suit against violators, they invoked the violence of the state to reinforce the intentions of segregationists. They kept the "white territories" of United States cities solid and pure. In crafting arguments that the racialized meaning inscribed on urban landscapes was incompatible with the Constitution or with public policy, attorneys like Charles Houston and William Hastie tried to erase the color line and thereby increase the quantity and quality of housing that was available to African American families.

In this chapter our focus was on the role played by judges and the practice of doctrinal interpretation during the era of "changed conditions." We explored in some detail how meaning was made, how lines were drawn, and how geographies of power were constructed. There were, speaking generally, three key legal-spatial interpretive moves which strongly influenced the shape that geographies of race and racism were given. The first was the elimination of all but the most spatially restrictive arguments against the validity of the covenants. The second involved struggles over the meaning of the color line in the practice of interpretation itself. These conflicts concerned whether judges could look for changes outside of the restricted space or whether judicial scrutiny had to be confined by the spaces that were created by segregationists. The third move concerned the uses made of theories of urban geographical change in order to assess the applicability of a secondary rule which, in turn, was used to assess the applicability of the doctrine of changed conditions.

We might well ask, did any of this matter? If our frame of reference is the parameters of a given case—say *Mays v. Burgess*—I think that it is safe to say that it mattered to the actual people involved. If we adopt a broader frame of reference—say the geopolitics of race in the twentieth century— it seems likely that had racially restrictive covenants been declared unconstitutional in *Corrigan v. Buckley*, then the geographies of race and racism of the era would have been different. Specifically *how* different is hard to say. In any case, between the broad sweep of historical possibility and the details of specific events, it's also hard to say what "matters" means. For our objective of understanding the practice of legal reasoning and the geopolitics of race, it seems to have mattered to judges that the outcomes of these games involving the interpretation of "changed conditions" provided sufficient justification to deny housing to people and to exclude people from all parts of a city outside of recognized "negro districts." In the next chapter we will look at some of these questions in the broader context of the historical geopolitics of race treated in this book.

7 Epilogue

In 1948 the U.S. Supreme Court endorsed Judge Henry Edgerton's understanding of the legality of racially restrictive covenants. In a unanimous opinion, the Court reversed the U.S. Circuit Court of Appeals for the District of Columbia ruling in *Hurd v. Hodge*[1] and the Missouri Supreme Court's similar ruling in *Shelley v. Kraemer*.[2] The gist of the opinion was that judicial enforcement of the racist contracts counted as "state action" and therefore violated constitutional rights of equal protection. Restrictive covenants were thereby invalidated as legal techniques for shaping geographies of race and racism. This legal victory by antisegregationists was followed by others, most famously *Brown v. Topeka Board of Education*[3] in 1954. Quite soon after, in 1955, the Montgomery, Alabama, bus boycott that brought Dr. Martin Luther King to international prominence exploded into public consciousness and altered racial politics forever. The Montgomery boycott is conventionally understood to be the beginning of the Civil Rights Movement. By the same conventions, the Civil Rights Movement is understood to have come to fruition in the civil rights acts of the 1960s and to have ended with the murder of Dr. King in 1968. However we bracket historical events, it is clear that from *Brown* onward a significant proportion of the struggle for racial equality took place in the courts. By the end of the 1960s, there had been profound changes in racial politics in the United States, profound changes in U.S. law, and profound changes in the role that law played in racial politics. Among the countless signs and indices of these social transformations was the appointment in 1967 of Thurgood Marshall to the U.S. Supreme Court. It is safe to say that a decade earlier the idea of an African American Supreme Court justice would have been unimaginable to most Americans.

These changes, though, were more than matched by radical transformations in urban form that were occurring at the same time. In a sense, geographical change was a step ahead of legal change. The complex set of processes referred to by the term *suburbanization* resulted in the massive expansion in the physical size of U.S. settlements—now known not simply as "cities" but as "metropolitan areas." From 1950 to 1970—that is, precisely coinciding with the Civil Rights movement—millions of Americans moved out of cities into new houses in new developments that were seemingly built overnight. These new urban geographies were held together by the proliferation of privately owned automobiles and publicly constructed freeways. The spatiality of this world was centered on the ideal of the single-family detached dwelling situated on a large lot. The cumulative effect of all of this was that a given number of households occupied a much larger area than the same number of households would occupy in the "crowded" cities. Then, as people relocated, so did services and eventually workplaces. In a generation, the worlds of experience—and the experience of space—for many Americans had radically changed.

Like many of the other changes we examined in this book, suburbanization has been a highly racialized process. Of the millions of Americans who participated in the creation of these new worlds, very few were African Americans. The techniques of exclusion exercised by developers, bankers, realtors, landlords, planners, and federal, state, and local officials were— and remain—highly effective in maintaining the (metaphorical) whiteness of suburban landscapes.[4] Other spatial processes such as urban renewal, the siting of (segregated) public housing, and the disinvestment in large parts of older cities played an important part. As a result, contemporary geographies of race and racism are characterized by a degree of separation between races—measured in physical terms—that would have been unimaginable to the architects of the municipal segregation ordinances of the early part of the century. We have created a world (or set of worlds) in which many people simply have no experience at all with people of a different racial identity beyond explicit relations of authority. The geographies that we have created reflect and perpetuate the ideologies of race that we have inherited. Much has changed through the generations, but highly racialized landscapes, spaces, and places remain central to U.S. social life and continue to shape social and self consciousness.

Another book could be written on the role that law, legal action, legal argument, and legal reasoning have played in these more recent rounds of racial geopolitics. There have been thousands of cases concerning housing discrimination, public housing siting and assignment, urban renewal, exclusionary zoning, school segregation, and, perhaps the most volatile issue, busing as a means of achieving desegregation. Through all of the changes, through all of the struggles, through all of the arguments and rulings, the geopolitics of race has been a constant theme in U.S. social history.

Recognition of this seeming permanence has led many observers, black and white, to question the effectiveness of legal action as a means of achieving social change in connection with race. One argument is that litigation simply does not deliver the goods.[5] Deeper critiques suggest that trying to change the world with legal argument does, on balance, more harm than good for subordinated peoples. Because legal action as a tactic has historically been associated with integrationism as an ideal, it is not surprising that a recognition of the limits of law is sometimes associated with a revival of forms of separatism.[6] Of course, another constant in the geopolitics of race over the generations has been the diversity of views concerning what is desirable and possible. At this point in our history, there seems to be nothing resembling a common vision of what kind of world we want—or even who we are. What is so striking when we look at the geopolitics of race as a long process is how much effort has gone into the project of perpetuating racial subordination and preserving white privilege. We have transformed the world without letting go of the color line.

This has been a study of boundaries: how they are made, how they are challenged, and how they matter. As we have seen, boundaries are not the seemingly inert lines depicted on maps. They *mean*. In the first instance they are the signatures of difference inscribed on the physical world. In the events we examined, the meaning of difference was the meaning of race itself. In these cases the focus of argument was the spatialization of difference. The cases illustrate the creation and contestation of racial hierarchy according to ruling understandings of difference. Social space was constructed in order to stabilize the inherent instability of race.

But to say that boundaries mean is to recognize also that they require interpretation in order to exist at all. Interpretation and judgment are social activities. As we saw, to the extent that the meanings of race and of law are complex, ambiguous, multiple, and shifting, then the meanings attached to lines and spaces or to what it means to cross a line may be open to divergent interpretations. In litigation we encounter these contending renderings. In this book we studied the social practice of drawing lines in the world and between people. Our principal focus, though, has been on the way we draw conceptual distinctions in order to create and challenge meaning.

Finally, it is crucial to recognize that we are not talking about the politics of interpretation in quite the same way as the term may be encountered in literary criticism or in other consciously interpretive endeavors. Even acknowledging the ways in which these kinds of activities may be complicit with power, legal interpretation is, after all, distinctive. In litigation the question at the end of the day is, Which interpretation of a text, of difference, of geography, of history, will be validated by law or the state or the concentrated force of organized government? The question is, Which argument, which interpretation, among available alternatives, will be sufficient to validate the use or withholding of violence or the threat of violence? Which rendering of reality will provide the foundation for the distribution of violence in a given case, or over longer spans of time as geographies of power are reconfigured?

The everyday experiential geographies of those of us who inhabit a "thoroughly racialized world"[7] are more or less marked by violence and brutality. Part of how racism works is to effect an uneven social distribution of violence, whether against or through law. Part of how geographies of race and racism work is to effect an uneven *spatial* distribution of violence. Part of how law works is to effect a spatialization of violence by authorizing acts of exclusion, expulsion, and confinement—or *not*. Stated simply as a cultural fact about how we do things here, a portion of this distribution is a product of legal argument. It is a function of where lines are drawn. In these contexts power is focused on the control of meaning. Power is manifested in the socially conferred capacity to limit ambiguity in the name of the law, in the name of reason. Some of the historical figures encountered in this book, such as Henry Edgerton, were, I believe, very much aware of this. They knew that in the act of judgment they could expand or contract the limits of justice. But neither power nor judgment is the monopoly of judges or other government officials or lawyers. They have not imposed geographies of race on us. We all have contributed to building our world simply by living our lives. We are all, in different ways, responsible for envisioning, constructing, and bequeathing geographies more conducive to social justice than those we have inherited.

Notes

Chapter 1

1. *Commonwealth v. Aves*, 18 Pick. 193 (1836).
2. C. Vose, *Caucasians Only: The Supreme Court, the NAACP, and the Restrictive Covenant Cases* (1959).
3. *Mays v. Burgess*, 147 F.2d 869 (1944).
4. See, generally, D. Bell, *Race, Racism, and American Law* (1992); J. Greenberg, *Crusaders in the Courts* (1994); L. Miller, *The Petitioners* (1966); M. Tushnet, *Making Civil Rights Law* (1994).
5. D. Massey and N. Denton, *American Apartheid* (1993); G. Tobin, ed., *Divided Neighbors: Changing Patterns of Racial Segregation* (1987).
6. A. Singh, J. Skerrett, and R. Hogan, eds., *Memory, Narrative, and Identity* (1994); R. Josselson and A. Lieblich, eds., The *Narrative Study of Lives* (1993).
7. See, for example, R. Pitten, "Negotiating Boundaries: A Perspective from Nigeria," in *Setting Boundaries: The Anthropology of Spatial and Social Organization*, ed. D. Pellow (1996); L. Prussin, *African Nomadic Architecture: Space, Place, and Gender* (1995); A. Robben, "Habits of the Home: Spatial Hegemony and the Structuration of House and Society in Brazil," *American Anthropologist* 91 (1989): 570.
8. The literature on the relationships between space and social relational power has grown quite large in recent years within academic geography as well as in other disciplines. Among the works that have been important in shaping my understanding of the topic are N. Blomley, *Law, Space, and Geographies of Power* (1994); A. Pred, *Making Histories and Constructing Human Geographies: The Local Transformation of Practice, Power Relations, and Consciousness* (1990); E. Soja, *Postmodern Geographies* (1990); M. Foucault, "Space, Knowledge and Power," in *The Foucault Reader*, ed. P. Rabinow (1984); M. Foucault, *Power/Knowledge: Selected Interviews and Other Writings, 1972–1977* (1980); J. Wolch and M. Dear, eds., *The Power of Geography: How Territory Shapes Social Life* (1989); J. Agnew and J. Duncan, eds., *The Power of Place: Bringing Together Geographical and Sociological Imaginations* (1989). See sources mentioned in note 13 below.

9. B. Jackson, *The Waiting Years: Essays on American Negro Literature* (1976), p. 3.

10. R. Sack, *Human Territoriality* (1986).

11. The various literatures on the *concept* of property, to say nothing of the countless doctrines, rules, facts, and experiences of property, are inexhaustible. For a sense of the complexity alluded to, consult C. Macpherson, ed., *Property: Mainstream and Critical Positions* (1978); A. Parel and T. Flanagan, eds., *Theories of Property: Aristotle to the Present* (1979); J. Pennock and J. Chapman, eds., *Property* (1980); M. Radin, *Reinterpreting Property* (1993); C. Rose, *Property and Persuasion: Essays on the History, Theory, and Rhetoric of Ownership* (1994); A. Ryan, *Property and Political Theory* (1984); J. Cribbet, "Concepts in Transition: The Search for a New Definition of Property," *University of Illinois Law Review* 1986 (1986): 1; M. Cohen, "Property and Sovereignty," *Cornell Law Quarterly* 13 (1926): 8.

12. G. Rose, *Feminism and Geography: The Limits of Geographical Knowledge* (1993).

13. M. Castells, "Crisis, Planning, and the Quality of Life: Managing the New Historical Relationships between Space and Society," *Society and Space* 1 (1983): 3; D. Massey and J. Allen, eds., *Geography Matters!* (1984); D. Gregory and J. Urry, eds., *Social Relations and Spatial Structures* (1985), especially, E. Soja, "The Spatiality of Social Life: Towards a Transformative Retheorization"; H. Lefebvre, *The Production of Space* (1991); and sources mentioned in notes 8 and 10 above.

14. Pred, *Making Histories*; Lefebvre, *Production of Space*; Soja, "Spatiality."

15. See Soja, "Spatiality." The ideas expressed by these terms are perhaps most fully developed in the work of the feminist geographers; see especially G. Rose, *Feminism and Geography.*

16. N. Bartley, *The Rise of Massive Resistance: Race and Politics in the South during the 1950s* (1969).

17. T. Barnes and J. Duncan, eds., *Writing Worlds: Discourse, Text, and Metaphor in the Representation of Landscape* (1992); J. Duncan and D. Ley, eds., *Place/Culture/Representation* (1993); D. Cosgrove and S. Daniels, eds., *The Iconography of Landscape: Essays on the Symbolic Representation, Design, and Use of Past Environments* (1988); J. Duncan and N. Duncan, "(Re)reading the Landscape," *Environment and Planning (D)* 6 (1988): 117.

18. On colonization and emigration, see H. Bell, "The Negro Emigration Movement, 1849–1859," *Phylon* 20 (1957): 132; W. Boyd, "Negro Colonization in the Reconstruction Era," *Georgia Historical Quarterly* 15 (1956): 360; P. Staudenraus, *The African Colonization Movement, 1816–1865* (1961). On nationalism, see A. Herod, *Afro-American Nationalism: An Annotated Bibliography of Militant Separatist and Nationalist Literature* (1986); B. McAdoo, *Pre–Civil War Black Nationalism* (1983); W. Moses, *The Golden Age of Black Nationalism, 1850–1925* (1978). On community control, see A. Altshuler, *Community Control: The Black Demand for Participation in Large American Cities* (1970).

19. W. Cohen, *At Freedom's Edge: Black Mobility and the Southern White Quest for Racial Control* (1991).

20. D. Goldberg, *Racist Culture: Philosophy and the Politics of Meaning* (1993); M. Omi and H. Winant, *Racial Formation in the United States: From the 1960s to the 1990s* (1994).

21. T. Morrison, *Playing in the Dark: Whiteness and the Literary Imagination* (1992).

22. H. Koning, *The Conquest of America: How the Indian Nations Lost Their Continent* (1993).

23. B. Fields, "Slavery, Race, and Ideology in the United States of America," *New Left Review* 181 (1990): 95.

24. G. Wright, *Life behind a Veil: Blacks in Louisville, Kentucky, 1865–1930* (1985); *Louisville Courier-Journal*, November 15, 1913.

25. *Louisville Courier-Journal*, November 15, 1913.

26. R. Rice, "Residential Segregation by Law, 1910–1917," *Journal of Southern History* 34 (1968): 179 ; B. Schmidt, "Principle and Prejudice: The Supreme Court and Race in the Progressive Era. Part 1: The Heyday of Jim Crow," *Columbia Law Review* 82 (1982): 444.

27. *Louisville Courier-Journal*, November 15, 1913.

28. The spatiality of federalism is treated more fully in chapter 3. See also Blomley, *Law, Space*.

29. P. Williams, *The Alchemy of Race and Rights* (1991); P. Gabel, "The Phenomenology of Rights—Consciousness and the Pact of the Withdrawn Selves," *Texas Law Review* 62 (1984): 1563.

30. For illustrations on squatting, see J. Abu-Lughod et al., eds., *From Urban Village to East Village: The Battle for New York's Lower East Side* (1994). On sit-ins see M. Wolff, *Lunch at the Five and Ten: The Greensboro Sit-ins* (1970); M. Oppenheimer, *The Sit-in Movement of 1960* (1989). On the Anti-Apartheid movement, J. Lazerson, *Against the Tide: Whites in the Struggle against Apartheid* (1990); D. Mermelstein, ed., *The Anti-Apartheid Reader* (1977). On the Sanctuary movement, see B. Coatin, *The Culture of Protest: Religious Activism and the U.S. Sanctuary Movement* (1993).

31. S. Merry, *Getting Justice and Getting Even: Legal Consciousness among Working-Class Americans* (1990); A. Sarat and T. Kearns, eds., *Law in Everyday Life* (1993).

32. G. Stephenson, *Race Distinctions in American Law* (1911).

33. See chapter 5.

34. See Greenberg, *Crusaders*; L. Miller, *Petitioners*; Tushnet, *Civil Rights*; M. Tushnet, *The NAACP's Legal Strategy against Segregated Education, 1925–1950* (1987); R. Kluger, *Simple Justice: The History of* Brown v. Board of Education *and Black America's Struggle for Equality* (1976); S. Wasby, *Race Relations Litigation in an Age of Complexity* (1995); G. Rosenberg, *The Hollow Hope: Can Courts Bring about Social Change?* (1991). For other contexts, see L. Medcalf, *Law and Identity: Lawyers, Native Americans, and Legal Practice* (1978); B. Marquez, *LULAC: The Evolution of a Mexican American Political Organization* (1993); G. Lopez, *Rebellious Lawyering* (1993); M. Davis, *Brutal Need: Lawyers and the Welfare Rights Movement, 1960–1973* (1993). On public interest law, see N. Aron, *Liberty and Justice for All: Public Interest Law in the 1980s and Beyond* (1989).

35. W. Felstiner, R. Abel, and A. Sarat, "The Emergence and Transformation of Disputes: Naming, Blaming, Claiming . . . ," *Law and Society Review* 15 (1981): 631; L. Mather and B. Yngvesson, "Language, Audience, and the Transformation of Disputes," *Law and Society Review* 15 (1981): 775.

36. R. Gordon, "New Developments in Legal Theory," in *The Politics of Law*, ed. D. Kairys (1990); J. Schlegel, "Notes toward an Intimate, Opinionated, and Affectionate History of the Conference on Critical Legal Studies," *Stanford Law Review* 36 (1984): 391; M. Tushnet, "CLS: A Political History," *Yale Law Journal* 100 (1991): 1515; S. Burton, "Reaffirming Legal Reasoning: The Challenge from the Left," *Journal of Legal Education* 36 (1980): 358; A. Altman, *Critical Legal Studies: A Liberal Critique* (1990).

37. For a historical example, see American Bar Association Standing Committee on Education against Communism, *The New Czars vs. the Rule of Law* (1964); for a more recent example see M. Krygier, "Marxism and the Rule of Law: Reflections after the Collapse of Communism," *Law and Social Inquiry* 15 (1990): 633; for more critical views see A. Hutchinson and P. Monahan, eds., *The Rule of Law: Ideal or Ideology* (1987).

38. J. Singer, "Legal Realism Now," *California Law Review* 76 (1988): 465; J. Boyle, "The Politics of Reason: Critical Legal Theory and Local Social Thought," *University of Pennsylvania Law Review* 133 (1985): 685; G. Peller, "The Metaphysics of American Law," *California Law Review* 73 (1985): 1151; R. Coombe, "'Same as It Ever Was': Rethinking the Politics of Legal Interpretation," *McGill Law Journal* 34 (1989): 603.

39. R. Dworkin, *Law's Empire* (1986); Burton, "Reaffirming Legal Reasoning."

40. In the 1990s, for example, there appeared innumerable law review articles on large-scale legal reform in Eastern Europe and the then disintegrating Soviet Union. Taken together they illustrate the close connection seen between the rule of law idea and the difference between "us" and "them." For a sample of this literature, see "Symposium: Transitions to Democracy and the Rule of Law," *American University Journal of International Law and Policy* 5 (1990): 965; "Symposium: Approaching Democracy: A New Legal Order for Eastern Europe," *University of Chicago Law Review* 58 (1991): 439; J. Quigley, "The New World Order and the Rule of Law," *Syracuse Journal of International Law and Commerce* 18 (1992): 75.

41. V. Kerruish, *Jurisprudence as Ideology* (1991); A. Hutchinson, *Dwelling on the Threshold: Critical Essays on Modern Legal Thought* (1988); M. Tushnet, "Legal Scholarship: Its Causes and Cures," *Yale Law Journal* 90 (1981): 1205.

42. B. Bix, *Law, Language, and Legal Indeterminacy* (1993); Peller, "Metaphysics"; Singer, "Legal Realism." Compare also J. Singer, "Should Lawyers Care about Philosophy?" *Duke Law Journal* 1989 (1989) ("Objectivists believe that there are right answers to our most fundamental questions about truth and justice, and that we can discover the answers to these questions by thinking in the right way" [p. 1752]), and R. Unger, *The Critical Legal Studies Movement* (1986) ("Objectivism is the belief that the authoritative legal materials—the system of statutes, cases, accepted legal ideas—embody a defensible scheme of human association. . . . The laws are not merely the outcome of contingent power struggles" [p. 2]), with the view of objec-

tivism as a linguistic ideology in G. Lakoff, *Women, Fire, and Dangerous Things: What Categories Reveal about the Mind* (1987) ("The objectivist view rests on a theory of categories . . . that is taken for granted as being not merely true but obviously and unquestionably true" [p. xvii]).

43. A. Sarat and T. Kearns, eds., *The Rhetoric of Law* (1994); P. Goodrich, *Legal Discourse: Studies in Linguistics, Rhetoric, and Legal Analysis* (1987); G. Wetlaufer, "Rhetoric and Its Denial in Legal Discourse," *Virginia Law Review* 76 (1990): 1545; G. Frug, "Argument as Character," *Stanford Law Review* 40 (1988): 852.

44. D. Sugarman, ed., *Legality, Ideology, and the State* (1983); A. Hyde, "The Concept of Legitimation in the Sociology of Law," *Wisconsin Law Review* 1983 (1983): 379.

45. J. Balkin, "The Crystalline Structure of Legal Thought," *Rutgers Law Review* 39 (1986): 1; J. Balkin, "Nested Oppositions," *Yale Law Journal* 99 (1990): 1669; Duncan Kennedy, "A Semiotics of Legal Argument," *Syracuse Law Review* 42 (1991): 75; J. Paul, "The Politics of Legal Semiotics," *Texas Law Review* 69 (1991): 1779.

46. R. Coombe, "Room to Manoeuver: Toward a Theory of Practice in Critical Legal Studies," *Law and Social Inquiry* 14 (1989): 69.

47. On the historicity of the concept of property, see Cribbet, "Concepts in Transition"; C. Rose, *Property;* C. Donahue, "The Future of the Concept of Property Predicted from Its Past," in J. Pennock and J. Chapman, eds., *Property* (1980); M. Horwitz, "Transformation in the Conception of Property in American Law," *University of Chicago Law Review* 40 (1973): 248; F. Philbrick, "Changing Conceptions of Property in Law," *University of Pennsylvania Law Review* 86 (1938): 723; R. Schlatter, *Private Property: The History of an Idea* (1951); K. Vandevelde, "The New Property of the Nineteenth Century: The Development of the Modern Concept of Property," *Buffalo Law Review* 29 (1980): 325.

48. R. Gordon, "Unfreezing Legal Reality: Critical Approaches to Law," *Florida State University Law Review* 15 (1987): 199.

49. R. Gordon, "Historicism in Legal Scholarship," *Yale Law Journal* 90 (1981): 1017.

50. Boyle, "Politics of Reason," p. 696.

51. Peller, "Metaphysics," p. 1153.

52. Gordon, "Unfreezing Legal Reality," pp. 199–200.

53. Duncan Kennedy, "Form and Substance in Private Adjudication," *Harvard Law Review* 89 (1976): 1685; Unger, *Critical Legal Studies;* and sources mentioned in note 54 below.

54. See, for example, J. Feinman, "Contract Law as Ideology," in *The Politics of Law*, ed. D. Kairys (1990); F. Olsen, "The Family and the Market: A Study of Ideology and Legal Reform," *Harvard Law Review* 96 (1983): 1497; G. Alexander, "History as Ideology in the Basic Property Course," *Journal of Legal Education* 36 (1986): 381; M. Tushnet, *Red, White, and Blue: A Critical Analysis of Constitutional Law* (1988); M. Kelman, "Interpretive Construction in the Substantive Criminal Law," *Stanford Law Review* 33 (1981): 591; David Kennedy, "A New Stream of International Law Scholarship," *Wisconsin International Law Journal* 7 (1988): 1.

55. M. Sandel, ed., *Liberalism and Its Critics* (1984); M. Ryan, *Politics and Culture:*

Working Hypotheses for a Post-Revolutionary Society (1989). As John Gray sees it, "It is characteristic, and perhaps definitive, of liberalism that it should seek to ground the historical contingencies of liberal practice in a foundation of universally valid principles. . . . For a liberal, then, a liberal society is not merely one of the options open to human beings, but a moral necessity." *Liberalisms* (1989), p. 239. For related discussions, see R. Gooden and A. Reeve, eds., *Liberal Neutrality* (1989); W. Kymlicka, "Liberal Individualism and Liberal Neutrality," *Ethics* 99 (1989): 883.

56. B. Weissbourd and E. Mertz, "Rule-Centrism versus Legal Creativity: The Skewing of Legal Ideology through Language," *Law and Society Review* 19 (1985): 624.

57. P. Brooks and P. Gewirtz, eds., *Law's Stories: Narrative and Rhetoric in the Law* (1996); D. Papke, ed., *Narrative and the Legal Discourse* (1991); R. Cover, "Nomos and Narrative," *Harvard Law Review* (1983) 97: 4.

58. This formulation is taken from F. Benda-Beckmann, *Property in Social Continuity* (1979).

59. P. Bourdieu, "The Force of Law: Toward a Sociology of the Juridical Field," *Hastings Law Journal* 38 (1987): 837.

60. P. Schlag and D. Skover, *Tactics of Legal Reasoning* (1986).

61. J. Taylor, "On Construing the World," in J. Taylor and R. MacLaury, eds., *Language and the Cognitive Construal of the World* (1995); N. Goodman, *Ways of Worldmaking* (1978).

62. P. Bohannan, "The Differing Realms of the Law," in *Law and Warfare: Studies in the Anthropology of Conflict*, ed. P. Bohannan (1967).

63. A. Sarat and T. Kearns, eds., *Law's Violence* (1994); R. Cover, "Violence and the Word," *Yale Law Journal* 95: 1601 (1986).

64. P. Bourdieu: "Law is the quintessential form of symbolic power of naming that creates the things named and creates social groups in particular. . . . It would not be excessive to say that [legal discourse] *creates* the social world, but only if we remember that it is the world which first creates law." "Force of Law," pp. 839–840.

65. S. Fish, *Doing What Comes Naturally: Change, Rhetoric, and the Practice of Theory in Literary and Legal Studies* (1989); D. Cornell, "'Convention' and Critique," *Cardozo Law Review* 7 (1986): 679.

Chapter 2

1. S. Campbell, *The Slave Catchers: Enforcement of the Fugitive Slave Law, 1850–1860* (1970); T. Morris, *Free Men All: The Personal Liberty Laws of the North, 1780–1861* (1974); L. Gara, "The Fugitive Slave Law: A Double Paradox," *Civil War History* 10 (1964): 229.

2. See J. Mellon, ed., *Bullwhip Days: The Slaves Remember. An Oral History* (1988); N. Yetman, ed., *Life under the "Peculiar Institution": Selections from the Slave Narrative Collection* (1970); and especially G. Rawick, ed., *The American Slave: A Composite Autobiography* (1972–1979).

3. J. Rawley, *The Transatlantic Slave Trade: A History* (1981).

4. Often, and for understandable reasons, notions of race and race relations are reduced to synonyms for black, white, and black-white relations, or, somewhat more broadly, to relations between white people and other races such as Native Americans. There is, however, an important but little studied history of relations among nonwhite peoples in the United States. For a recent example with geographical significance, see K. Mulroy, *Freedom on the Border: The Seminole Maroons* (1993).

5. I. Berlin, "Time, Space, and the Evolution of Afro-American Society on British Mainland North America," *American Historical Review* 85 (1980): 44.

6. Ibid.

7. R. Wade, *Slavery in the Cities: The South, 1820–1860* (1964); L. Graham, *Baltimore: The Nineteenth-Century Black Capital* (1982); M. Johnson and J. Roark, eds., *No Chariot Let Down: Charleston's Free People of Color on the Eve of the Civil War* (1984); C. Green, *The Secret City: A History of Race Relations in the Nation's Capital* (1967).

8. H. Jaffa, *The Crisis of the House Divided: An Interpretation of the Issues in the Lincoln-Douglas Debates* (1959).

9. See chapter 3.

10. E. Genovese, *Roll, Jordan, Roll: The World the Slaves Made* (1972).

11. The allusion is to E. Genovese, *The World the Slaveholders Made: Two Essays in Interpretation* (1969); M. Sobel, *The World They Made Together: Black and White Values in Eighteenth-Century Virginia* (1987). I should acknowledge here my heavy reliance on secondary literature. This section is intended as a geographic reading of the political history of slavery. Moreover, while part of my point is to draw attention to variety and variability, the narrative cannot escape the general tenor of "typicality" in so brief a presentation.

12. E. Thompson, *Plantation Societies, Race Relations, and the South* (1975), p. 35.

13. By "politics" here, I mean the micropolitics that occur within specific relations and constellations of power. In the present context, I refer to the moves and countermoves of accommodation, resistance, and retribution that marked what Genovese has termed the "reciprocal dependency" that defined the relation of master-slave. Interestingly, he employs the key terms of legal discourse to characterize this politics: "The slaves accepted the doctrine of reciprocity, but with a profound difference. To the idea of reciprocal duties they added their own doctrine of reciprocal rights. To the tendency to make them creatures of another's will they counterposed a tendency to assert themselves as autonomous human beings. And they thereby contributed, as they had to, to the generation of conflict and great violence." *Roll, Jordan, Roll*, p. 91.

14. On spatial arrangements, see T. Singleton, ed., *The Archeology of Slavery and Plantation Life* (1985); J. Michie, *Richmond Hill Plantation, 1810–1868: The Discovery of Antebellum Life on a Waccamaw Rice Plantation* (1990).

15. But note Genovese's claim that "the slaves as well as the masters created the law . . . but even one right, imperfectly defended, was enough to tell them that the pretensions of the master class could be resisted." *Roll, Jordan, Roll*, p. 30.

16. Ibid., p. 339.

17. Ibid., p. 67.

18. Thompson, *Plantation Societies*, p. 36.

19. See Singleton, *Archeology*; Michie, *Richmond Hill*. Consider the words of planter H. N. McTyeire: "Some masters have a code of laws as well understood as if written. Their household and plantation servants are well governed communities. A tribunal exists where complaints are referred, grievances redressed and disputes settled. All transactions of a social nature proceed upon settled principles. . . . The lowest findings of justice and judgment are not despised. This is worthy of all praise." "Plantation Life—Duties and Responsibilities," *DeBow's Review* 29 (1860): 357, quoted in J. Breeden, ed., *Advice among Masters: The Ideal in Slave Management in the Old South* (1980), p. 87.

20. Genovese, *Roll, Jordan, Roll*, p. 5. Again this contradiction is conceptualized in legal terms: "Paternalism's insistence upon mutual obligations, duties, responsibilities, and, ultimately, even rights—implicitly recognized the slaves' humanity." *Roll, Jordan, Roll*, p. 5.

21. Ibid., p. 5.

22. A feel for some of these more extensive "neighborhoods" can be gotten from local histories such as C. Joyner, *Down by the Riverside: A South Carolina Slave Community* (1984); and T. Rosengarten, *Tombee: Portrait of a Cotton Planter* (1986). See also E. Miller and E. Genovese, eds., *Plantation, Town, and County: Essays on the Local History of American Slave Society* (1974).

23. See, for example, L. Litwack, *Been in the Storm So Long: The Aftermath of Slavery* (1979), p. 23; Rawick, ed., *American Slave*, vol. 7, p. 117.

24. "I never permit my servants to leave the plantation, unless on business, or to attend church. Neither do I permit other negroes to visit my place. I have seen the inconsistency, as well as every owner of slaves, of their visits; therefore, I prohibit it." Tattler, "The Management of Negroes," *Southern Cultivator* 8 (1852): 162–164, quoted in Breeden, ed., *Advice*, p. 249.

25. On the "self-hiring" of slaves, see M. Tushnet, *The American Law of Slavery, 1810–1860: Considerations of Humanity and Interest* (1981).

26. Breeden, ed., *Advice*, p. 43.

27. Genovese, *Roll, Jordan, Roll*, p. 472.

28. Ibid., p. 472.

29. H. Henry, "The Police Control of the Slave in South Carolina" (1914).

30. See, for example, Alabama Slave Code of 1852, sec. 2043, in W. Rose, ed., *Documentary History of Slavery in North America* (1976), p. 187.

31. Tushnet, *Law of Slavery*.

32. As illustrated by this testimony of Ruby Pickens Tartt, the patrollers were one of the principal topics of the slave narratives: "Ef de white folks give de niggers a pass, den dey could go, and ef dey was to go 'thout one dem Patterrollers would have 'em a-runnin thoo de woods jes' lack dey was a lot of deer, and ef dey ever cotch 'em, dey'd take 'em to dey Marster and he'd jes' natcherly wear 'em out. . . . And I knowed a women name Tishie, Miss Mollie's house sarvent. She run away 'case dey so mean to her, I reckon, and de cullud folks harbored her and hid her up in de grain house wid de peas and sech lac', stedder down in de corn crib. And who ever 'twuz 'trayed her I ain't sayin' but a crowd uv dem Patterrollers come and got

'er one night, and tuck her away, and I ain't nebber seed Tishie no mo'." Rawick, ed., *American Slave*, vol. 4, p. 220.

33. See Alabama Slave Code of 1852, secs. 1008, in W. Rose, ed., *Documentary History*, p. 179.

34. O. Taylor, *Negro Slavery in Arkansas* (1958), p. 210; C. Mooney, *Slavery in Tennessee* (1957); Henry, "Police Control."

35. "So central to the concerns of the white people in the black belt states was the problem of racial control that the very term applied to the area for which a patrol was responsible, the 'beat,' came to be applied to the smallest area of civil administration. What was a 'township' in New England . . . in the Deep South was a 'beat.'" J. Williamson, *The Crucible of Race: Black/White Race Relations in the American South since Emancipation* (1984), p. 19.

36. H. Catterall, ed., *Judicial Cases concerning American Slavery and the Negro*, 5 vols. (1926–1936); for example, *State v. Cole*, 2 McCord's Rpts. 117 (S.C. Ct. App., 1822) ("a patrol indicted for 'riot' was considered to have 'invaded' sovereignty of plantation", cited in Catterall, vol. 3, pp. 320–321), and *Tennant v. Dendy*, Dudley's Rpts. 83 (S.C. Ct. App., 1837) ("The slave ought to be fully aware that his master is to him what the best administered government is to a good citizen, a perfect security from injury," cited in Catterall, vol. 3, p. 365).

37. Quoted in Breeden, ed., *Advice*, p. 330.

38. 15 Ark. 162 (1854), discussed in O. Taylor, *Slavery in Arkansas.*

39. "The patrollers had no jurisdiction over the Curry slaves. They were given permits by the Curry's to go and come and Emma said if one of those patrollers whipped one of ol' miss's slaves, she would have sure sued them." Mary A. Poole in Rawick, *American Slave*, vol. 6, p. 62. More generally see G. Fry, *The Night Riders in Black Folk History* (1975).

40. L. Gara, *The Liberty Line: The Legend of the Underground Railroad* (1961).

41. Berlin, "Time, Space."

42. J. Franklin, *A Southern Odyssey: Travelers in the Antebellum North* (1976); J. Blassingame, ed., *Slave Testimony: Two Centuries of Letters, Speeches, Interviews, and Autobiographies* (1977); R. Starobin, ed., *Blacks in Bondage: Letters of American Slaves* (1974).

43. Franklin, *Southern Odyssey*. Also see cases discussed in chapter 3.

44. F. Douglass, *My Bondage and My Freedom* (1855; reprint, 1987); S. Northup, *Twelve Years a Slave* (1853; reprint, 1968).

45. See chapter 3.

46. A. Kraditor, *Means and Ends in American Abolitionism: Garrison and His Critics on Strategies and Tactics* (1969); G. Sorin, *Abolitionism: A New Perspective* (1972); L. Perry and M. Fellman, eds., *Antislavery Reconsidered: New Perspectives on the Abolitionists* (1979).

47. E. Foner, *Free Soil, Free Labor, Free Men: The Ideology of the Republican Party before the Civil War* (1970).

48. D. Fehrenbacher, *The Dred Scott Case: Its Significance in American Law and Politics* (1978).

49. E. Thomas, *The Confederate Nation* (1979).

50. I. Berlin et al., *Slaves No More: Three Essays on Emancipation and the Civil War* (1992); E. Foner, *Nothing but Freedom: Emancipation and Its Legacy* (1983).

51. Berlin et al., *Slaves No More*. On the practice of "refugeeing," or the removal of slaves from Union lines, see Litwack, *Been in the Storm*, pp. 30–35.

52. W. Rose, *Rehearsal for Reconstruction: The Port Royal Experiment* (1964); E. Magdol, *A Right to the Land: Essays on the Freedmen's Community* (1977); J. Williamson, *After Slavery: The Negro in South Carolina during Reconstruction, 1861–1877* (1965).

53. Williamson, *After Slavery;* Litwack, *Been in the Storm*.

54. Litwack, *Been in the Storm*, p. 297; P. Kolchin, *First Freedom: Responses of Alabama's Blacks to Emancipation and Reconstruction* (1972).

55. Singleton, ed., *Archeology*.

56. Quoted in Litwack, *Been in the Storm*, p. 293.

57. Magdol, *A Right to the Land;* J. Mandel, *The Roots of Black Poverty: The Southern Plantation Economy after the Civil War* (1978); W. Cohen, *At Freedom's Edge: Black Mobility and the Southern White Quest for Racial Control* (1991).

58. Williamson, *After Slavery;* Litwack, *Been in the Storm;* C. Oubre, *Forty Acres and a Mule: The Freedmen's Bureau and Black Land Ownership* (1978).

59. The space referred to in the order should be seen as a "legal space" embracing other legal spaces, and the issuance of the field order an act of territoriality which effected a radical—if ephemeral—spatial redistribution of legal meaning.

60. Litwack, *Been in the Storm*, p. 404.

61. W. Cohen, *At Freedom's Edge;* Magdol, *A Right to the Land*.

62. Litwack, *Been in the Storm*.

63. Fry, *The Night Riders;* A. Trelease, *White Terror: The Ku Klux Klan Conspiracy and Southern Reconstruction* (1971); W. DuBois, *Black Reconstruction, 1860–1880* (1935).

64. Kolchin, *First Freedom;* G. Tindall, *South Carolina Negroes, 1877–1900* (1952); V. Wharton, *The Negro in Mississippi, 1865–1890* (1947).

65. Litwack, *Been in the Storm*, p. 311.

66. DuBois, *Black Reconstruction*.

67. H. Rabinowitz, *Race Relations in the Urban South, 1865–1890* (1980); H. Shapiro, *White Violence and Black Response: From Reconstruction to Montgomery* (1988).

68. Rabinowitz, *Race Relations*.

69. W. Cohen, *At Freedom's Edge*.

70. W. Cohen, *At Freedom's Edge;* Williamson, *After Slavery*.

71. N. Painter, *Exodusters: Black Migration to Kansas after Reconstruction* (1977); N. Crockett, *The Black Towns* (1979); K. Hamilton, *Black Towns and Profit: Promotion and Development in the Trans-Appalachian West, 1877–1915* (1991); F. Logan, *The Negro in North Carolina, 1876–1894* (1964); Tindall, *South Carolina*.

72. Painter, *Exodusters;* W. Cohen, *At Freedom's Edge*.

73. F. Logan, *North Carolina*.

74. Quoted in F. Logan, *North Carolina*, p. 127.

75. Ibid., p. 130.

76. Painter, *Exodusters*.

77. F. Logan, *North Carolina*, p. 130.

78. W. Cohen, *At Freedom's Edge*.

Chapter 3

1. T. Morris, *Free Men All: The Personal Liberty Laws of the North, 1780–1861* (1974); P. Finkelman, *An Imperfect Union: Slavery, Federalism, and Comity* (1981); D. Fehrenbacher, *The Dred Scott Case: Its Significance in American Law and Politics* (1978).

2. J. Franklin, *A Southern Odyssey: Travelers in the Antebellum North* (1976); Finkelman, *Imperfect Union*.

3. Finkelman, *Imperfect Union*, p. 4. See also J. Story, *Commentaries on the Conflict of Laws* (1834).

4. Story, *Commentaries*.

5. *Lemmon v. the People*, 20 N.Y. 562, 578 (1860) (statement of Charles O'Conor, attorney for Appellant).

6. *Somerset v. Stewart*, 20 Howell 1 (1772); see also W. Wiecek, "*Somerset*: Lord Mansfield and the Legitimacy of Slavery in the Anglo-American World," *University of Chicago Law Review* 42 (1974): 141.

7. *Aves v. Commonwealth*, 18 Pick. 193, 204 (1836) (citing *Somerset v. Stewart*, 20, Howell 1).

8. A "slippery slope argument" is one that counsels restraint lest the action warned against—in this case the limited right of a slaveholder to compel obedience in England—lead inexorably and inevitably to dire consequences. The step to be avoided, if one has the chance, is the first step down a slippery slope.

9. "Addresses of the Liberty Party of Pennsylvania," in C. Cleveland, ed., *Antislavery Addresses of 1844 and 1845* (J. A. Bancroft: Philadelphia, 1867), p. 45, quoted in W. Wiecek, *The Sources of Antislavery Constitutionalism in America, 1760–1848* (1977), p. 212.

10. See *Commonwealth v. Chambre*, 4 U.S. (4 Dall.) 143 (1794); *Commonwealth v. Smyth*, 1 Browne 113 (1809); *Butler v. Delaplaine*, 7 Serg. & Rawle 378 (1821). These cases are discussed in Finkelman, *Imperfect Union*.

11. *Aves v. Commonwealth*, 18 Pick. 193 (1836).

12. *Aves v. Commonwealth*, 18 Pick. at 195.

13. Id.

14. Id. at 195.

15. Id. at 200.

16. Id. at 201.

17. Id. at 202.

18. Id. at 204 (emphasis in original).

19. Id. at 205.

20. Id. at 207–208.

21. R. Cover, *Justice Accused: Antislavery and the Judicial Process* (1975); W. Wiecek, "Abolitionists and the Problem of Unjust Laws," in L. Perry and M. Fellman, eds., *Antislavery Reconsidered: New Perspectives on the Abolitionists* (1979).

22. *Aves v. Commonwealth*, 18 Pick. at 215 (statement of Lemuel Shaw).

23. Id. at 210.

24. Id. at 212.

25. Id. at 212.

26. Finkelman, *Imperfect Union*.

27. 2 Stat. 103 (1793).

28. J. Stewart, *The Aims and Impact of Garrisonian Abolitionism, 1840–1860* (1969).

29. Morris, *Free Men All*.

30. P. Finkelman, "*Prigg v. Pennsylvania* and the Northern State Courts: Anti-Slavery Use of a Pro-Slavery Decision," *Civil War History* 25 (1979): 5.

31. Finkelman, "*Prigg v. Pennsylvania*"; *Prigg v. Pennsylvania*, 16 Peters 539 (1842).

32. *Prigg v. Pennsylvania*, 16 Peters at 558.

33. Id. at 569.

34. Id. at 585.

35. Id at 581.

36. Id. at 600.

37. Id. at 607.

38. Id. at 622.

39. Id. at 622.

40. Finkelman, "*Prigg v. Pennsylvania.*"

41. A. Bestor, "The American Civil War as a Constitutional Crisis," *American Historical Review* 19: 339.

42. C. Miller, *The Supreme Court and the Uses of History* (1969); J. Larson and C. Spillenger, "'That's Not History': The Boundaries of Advocacy and Scholarship," *Public Historian* 12 (1990): 33.

43. A crucial element of ambiguity that the Kansas-Nebraska Act brought to the fore concerned whether territorial legislatures had the power to prohibit or establish slavery. See A. Bestor, "State Sovereignty and Slavery: A Reinterpretation of Proslavery Constitutional Doctrine, 1846–1860," *Journal of the Illinois State Historical Society* 54 (1961): 148.

44. S. Kutler, *The Dred Scott Decision: Law or Politics?* (1967); Fehrenbacher, *Dred Scott.*

45. It is worth noting here the subtle spatiality of power revealed by the doctrines of "reattachment" and "reversion." *Reattachment* was, in Fehrenbacher's terms, a "substantive principle" that a "slave taken into a free state became free in the sense that his master lost the power to control him [as we saw in *Aves,* above], but upon his returning to a slave-holding state the status of slave reattached to him." This is related to but distinct from the "jurisdictional principle" of *reversion,* which concerned the question of which states' laws were to be applied in determining whether reattachment was applicable—that is, whether a "slave in returning to a slave-holding state reverted totally to its jurisdiction" or whether "the emancipa-

tory effect of the free state's laws would be enforced extraterritorially." Fehren-bacher, *Dred Scott*, p. 51.

46. Article 3, section 2, of the U.S. Constitution gives federal courts jurisdiction over cases between citizens of different states. Therefore "diversity of citizenship" between the parties allowed the Scotts to pursue their suit in federal courts. Of course, acceptance of the procedural claim (that the parties were citizens of different states) presupposed acceptance of the substantive claim (that the Scotts were not slaves).

47. *Scott v. Sandford*, 19 Howard 393 (1857).

48. Fehrenbacher, *Dred Scott*, p. 282.

49. Brief for Plaintiff at 14, *Scott v. Sandford*, 19 Howard 393, reprinted in P. Kurland and G. Casper, eds., *Landmark Briefs and Arguments of the Supreme Court of the United States: Constitutional Law*, vol. 3 (1975), p. 192.

50. Brief for Defendant at 5, *Scott v. Sandford*, 19 Howard 393, reprinted in Kurland and Casper, eds., *Landmark Briefs*, vol. 3, p. 232.

51. Fehrenbacher, *Dred Scott*, p. 367.

52. *Scott v. Sandford*, 19 Howard at 440.

53. Id. at 450.

54. See discussion of *Aves*, above.

55. *Scott v. Sandford*, 19 Howard at 519–523.

56. Fehrenbacher, *Dred Scott*, p. 409.

57. Wiecek, *Sources of Antislavery Constitutionalism* (1977). See also H. Hyman and W. Wiecek, *Equal Justice under Law: Constitutional Development, 1835–1875* (1982).

58. R. Kaczorowski, "To Begin the Nation Anew: Congress, Citizenship, and Civil Rights after the Civil War," *American Historical Review* 92 (1987): 45.

59. 16 Stat. 140 (1870), defining certain offenses motivated by racial or political animus as crimes against the United States; and 17 Stat. 13 (1871), the "Ku Klux Klan Act," defining certain offenses committed by armed men, in disguise and at night, as crimes against the United States.

60. That is, the defendants sought judicial invalidation of the indictments under which they were brought to trial. In these cases, the grounds offered were not simply that the indictments were vague or improperly drawn, for example, but that the legislation that prosecutors were working with was unconstitutional.

61. *The Slaughter House Cases*, 16 Wall. 36 (1873).

62. R. Kaczorowski, *The Politics of Judicial Interpretation: The Federal Courts, Department of Justice, and Civil Rights, 1866–1876* (1985). See also L. Miller, *The Petitioners: The Story of the Supreme Court of the United States and the Negro* (1966); C. Fairman, *Reconstruction and Reunion, 1864–1888*, vol. 3 of *The History of the Supreme Court of the United States* (1971).

63. *The Slaughter House Cases*, 16 Wall. at 81–82.

64. Id. at 77.

65. Id. at 79.

66. Id. at 95.

67. Id. at 121.

68. Id. at 129.

69. Kaczorowski, *Politics of Judicial Interpretation*, p. 173.

70. Ibid., pp. 173–174.

71. *United States v. Cruikshank*, 92 U.S. 542 (1876).

72. *United States v. Reese*, 92 U.S. 214 (1876).

73. Brief for Defendant at 26, *United States v. Cruikshank*, 92 U.S. 542, reprinted in Kurland and Casper, eds., *Landmark Briefs*, vol. 7 (1975), p. 407.

74. Brief for Defendant at 31, *United States v. Cruikshank*, 92 U.S. 542, reprinted in Kurland and Casper, eds., *Landmark Briefs*, vol. 7 (1975), p. 378.

75. Kaczorowski, *Politics of Judicial Interpretation*, p. 214.

76. *United States v. Cruikshank*, 92 U.S. at 550–551.

77. 18 Stat. 335 (1875).

78. J. Franklin, "The Enforcement of the Civil Rights Act of 1875," *Prologue* 6 (1974): 225; S. Spackman, "American Federalism and the Civil Rights Act of 1875," *American Studies* 10 (1978): 313; J. McPherson, "Abolitionists and the Civil Rights Act of 1875," *Journal of American History* 52: 496 (1965).

79. Franklin, "Civil Rights Act," p. 227.

80. Ibid., p. 232.

81. Ibid., p. 231.

82. *The Civil Rights Cases*, 109 U.S. 3 (1883). See also A. Westin, "The Case of the Prejudiced Doorkeeper," in J. Garraty, ed., *Quarrels That Have Shaped the Constitution* (1964).

83. *The Civil Rights Cases*, 109 U.S. at 30.

84. Id. at 21.

85. Id. at 23. Note also the use of the slippery slope argument that we first encountered in *Somerset* and *Aves*, discussed above.

86. *The Civil Rights Cases*, 109 U.S. at 55.

87. Id. at 56.

88. Id. at 42–43.

89. Id. at 56.

90. Id. at 40.

Chapter 4

1. B. Jackson, *The Waiting Years: Essays on American Negro Literature* (1976), pp. 3–4.

2. W. White, *A Man Called White: The Autobiography of Walter White* (1948); C. Rowan, *Dream Makers, Dream Breakers: The World of Justice Thurgood Marshall* (1993); J. Anderson, *A. Philip Randolph: A Biographical Portrait* (1972); C. Himes, *The Autobiography of Chester Himes* (1972).

3. J. Williamson, *The Crucible of Race: Black/White Relations in the American South since Emancipation* (1984).

4. C. Woodward, "*Strange Career* Critics: Long May They Persevere," *Journal of American History* 75 (1988): 858.

5. R. Logan, *The Betrayal of the Negro from Rutherford B. Hayes to Woodrow Wilson* (1965).

6. Williamson, *Crucible of Race*, p. 224.

7. H. Shapiro, *White Violence and Black Response: From Reconstruction to Montgomery* (1988).

8. C. Crowe, "Racial Massacre in Atlanta, September 22, 1906," *Journal of Negro History* 54 (1969): 150; R. Senechal, *The Sociogenesis of a Race Riot: Springfield, Illinois, in 1908* (1990).

9. See documents reprinted in J. Smith, ed., *Racial Determinism and the Fear of Miscegenation, Post-1900: Race and the Negro Problem* (1993), vol. 8 of *Anti-Black Thought, 1863–1925: "The Negro Problem."*

10. Williamson, *Crucible*; see also H. Rabinowitz, "Psychological Disorders, Socio-Economic Forces, and American Race Relations," *Slavery and Abolition* 7 (1986): 188.

11. W. Hall, ed., *The Rest of the Dream: The Black Odyssey of Lyman Johnson* (1988).

12. J. Cell, *The Highest Stage of White Supremacy: The Origins of Segregation in South Africa and the American South* (1982), p. 18.

13. Ibid., p. 3.

14. Ibid., p. 249.

15. C. Woodward, *Thinking Back: The Perils of Writing History* (1986), pp. 82–83.

16. L. Litwack, *North of Slavery: The Negro in the Free States, 1790–1860* (1961); R. Wade, *Slavery in the Cities: The South, 1820–1860* (1964); J. Williamson, *After Slavery: The Negro in South Carolina during Reconstruction, 1861–1877* (1965); H. Rabinowitz, *Race Relations in the Urban South, 1865–1890* (1980).

17. H. Rabinowitz, "More Than the Woodward Thesis: Assessing *The Strange Career of Jim Crow*," *Journal of American History* (1988) 75: 842, p. 844.

18. Woodward, "*Strange Career* Critics," p. 867.

19. Ibid., p. 861.

20. C. Woodward, *The Strange Career of Jim Crow* (1957); M. Berry, "Repression of Blacks in the South, 1890–1945: Enforcing the System of Segregation," in *The Age of Segregation: Race Relations in the South, 1890–1945*, ed. R. Haws (1978).

21. Cell, *White Supremacy*.

22. Rabinowitz, *Race Relations*.

23. Cell, *White Supremacy*, p. 230.

24. Ibid., p. 132; see also Rabinowitz, "More than the Woodward Thesis"; Woodward, "*Strange Career* Critics."

25. A. Meier, *Negro Thought in America, 1880–1915: Racial Ideologies in the Age of Booker T. Washington* (1963); F. Brodrick and A. Meier, eds., *Negro Protest Thought in the Twentieth Century* (1965).

26. See R. Hall, "Booker T. Washington: Separatist in Disguise," and S. Walker, "Booker T. Washington: 'Separatist' in Golden Chains," in *Black Separatism and Social Reality: Rhetoric and Reason*, ed. R. Hall (1977).

27. A. Meier and E. Rudwick, *Along the Color Line: Explorations in the Black Experience* (1976); W. DuBois, *The Souls of Black Folk* (1903).

28. C. Kellogg, *NAACP, A History of the National Association for the Advancement of Colored People* (1967); W. Hixon, *Moorfield Storey and the Abolitionist Tradition* (1972); B. Ross, *J. E. Spingarn and the Rise of the NAACP, 1911–1939* (1972).

29. C. Lofgren, *The Plessy Case: A Legal-Historical Interpretation* (1987); O. Olsen, ed., *The Thin Disguise: A Turning Point in Negro History:* Plessy v. Ferguson: *A Documentary Presentation*, (1967); C. Woodward, "The Case of the Louisiana Traveler," in J. Garraty, ed., *Quarrels That Have Shaped the Constitution* (1964).

30. *Plessy v. Ferguson,* 163 U.S. 537 (1896).

31. F. Henri, *Black Migration: Movement North, 1900–1920* (1976); C. Marks, *Farewell—We're Good and Gone: The Great Black Migration* (1989).

32. Figures cited from census reports in G. Wright, *Life behind a Veil: Blacks in Louisville, Kentucky, 1865–1930* (1985).

33. R. Rice, "Residential Segregation by Law, 1910–1917," *Journal of Southern History* 34 (1968): 179; G. Power, "Apartheid Baltimore Style: The Residential Segregation Ordinances of 1910–1913," *Maryland Law Review* 42 (1982): 289; B. Schmidt, "Principle and Prejudice: The Supreme Court and Race in the Progressive Era. Part 1: The Heyday of Jim Crow," *Columbia Law Review* 82 (1982): 444.

34. Power, "Apartheid Baltimore Style."

35. A. Hawkins, "A Year of Segregation in Baltimore," *The Crisis* 3 (1911): 27.

36. Ibid.

37. Ibid., p. 28.

38. Ibid., p. 30.

39. G. Stephenson, "The Segregation of the White and Negro Races in Cities," *South Atlantic Quarterly* 13 (1914): 1.

40. D. Kelleher, "St. Louis' 1916 Segregation Ordinance," *Missouri Historical Society Bulletin* 25 (1970): 239.

41. *St. Louis Post-Dispatch*, December 15, 1911.

42. *The Crisis* 10 (1915): 39; 11 (1916): 140; 11 (1916): 240.

43. *Atlanta Constitution*, June 11, 1913, p. 7.

44. *Atlanta Constitution*, June 6, 1913, p. 5.

45. Wright, *Life behind a Veil*, p. 4.

46. B. Jackson, *Waiting Years*, p. 3.

47. Ibid., p. 6.

48. Wright, *Life behind a Veil*, p. 103.

49. *Louisville Times*, October 21, 1913, p. 9.

50. *Louisville Times*, November 15, 1913, p. 6.

51. *Louisville Times*, December 17, 1913, pp. 6, 7.

52. C. Parrish et al., *The History of the Segregation Case and the Decision of the Supreme Court* (1918).

53. Wright, *Life behind a Veil*.

54. Parrish et al., *Segregation Case*.

55. *Louisville Times*, March 19, 1914, p. 9; *Louisville Courier-Journal*, March 19, 1914, p. 11.

56. Parrish et al., *Segregation Case*.

57. Ibid., p. 8.

58. Ibid., p. 9.

59. *Louisville Times,* May 11, 1914, p. 6.

60. Parrish et al., *Segregation Case;* Kellogg, *NAACP;* W. Hixon, *Moorfield Storey and the Abolitionist Tradition* (1972); B. Ross, *J. E. Spingarn.*

61. Schmidt, "Principle and Prejudice"; Wright, *Life behind a Veil.*

62. Schmidt, "Principle and Prejudice."

Chapter 5

1. M. Radin, "The Liberal Conception of Property," *Columbia Law Review* 88 (1986): 1667; C. Baker, "Property and Its Relation to Constitutionally Protected Liberty," *University of Pennsylvania Law Review* 134 (1986): 241; J. Nedelsky, *Private Property and the Limits of American Constitutionalism* (1990).

2. J. Paul, "The Hidden Structure of Takings Law," *Southern California Law Review* 64 (1991): 1393; F. Michelman, "Property, Utility, and Fairness," *Harvard Law Review* 80 (1967): 1165; R. Epstein, *Takings: Private Property and the Power of Eminent Domain* (1988).

3. J. Sax, "Takings and the Police Power," *Yale Law Journal* 74 (1964): 30.

4. See sources mentioned in notes 2 and 3 above. For a classic exposition in law, see *Pennsylvania Coal Co. v. Mahon,* 260 U.S. 393 (1922).

5. G. Alexander, "Takings, Narratives, and Power," Columbia Law Review 88 (1988): 1752; Paul, "Hidden Structure."

6. F. Cohen, "Dialogue on Private Property," *Rutgers Law Review* 9 (1954): 357; J. Singer and J. Beermann, "The Social Origins of Property," *Canadian Journal of Law and Jurisprudence* 6 (1993): 217.

7. T. Grey, "The Disintegration of Property," in J. Pennock and J. Chapman, eds., *Property,* Nomos, vol. 22 (1980) ("The specialist fragments the robust unitary conception of ownership into a mere shadowy 'bundle of rights.' Thus, a thing can be owned by more than one person, in which case it becomes necessary to focus on the particular limited rights each of the co-owners has with respect to the thing" [p. 69]); J. Penner, "The Bundle of Rights Picture of Property," *UCLA Law Review* 43 (1996): 711.

8. *Buchanan v. Warley,* 245 U.S. 60 (1917).

9. *State v. Gurry,* 88 A. 546 (1913).

10. Id. at 549.

11. Id. at 552.

12. *State v. Darnell,* 81 S.E. 338 (1914).

13. See the following by G. Stephenson: *Race Distinctions in American Law* (1911); "The Segregation of the White and Negro Races in Cities," *South Atlantic Quarterly* 8 (1914): 1; "The Segregation of the White and Negro Races in Rural Communities of North Carolina," *South Atlantic Quarterly* 13 (1914): 107; "The Segregation of the White and Negro Races in Cities by Legislation," *National Municipal Review* 3 (1914): 496.

14. *State v. Darnell,* 81 S.E. at 340.

15. Id. at 339.

16. *Carey v. City of Atlanta*, 84 S.E. 456 (1915).

17. Id. at 458.

18. *Buchanan v. Warley*, 177 S.W. 472 (1915).

19. Id. at 475.

20. Id. at 476.

21. Id. at 476.

22. Id. at 477.

23. *West Chester Railroad Company v. Miles*, 55 Pa. 209 (1867).

24. *Buchanan v. Warley*, 177 S.W. 472, 477 (1915).

25. *Hopkins v. Richmond*, 86 S.E. 139 (1915).

26. *Harden v. Atlanta*, 93 S.E. 401 (1917).

27. Id. at 403.

28. B. Schmidt, "Principle and Prejudice: The Supreme Court and Race in the Progressive Era. Part 1: The Heyday of Jim Crow," *Columbia Law Review* 82 (1982): 444.

29. Briefs are reprinted in P. Kurland and G. Casper, eds., *Landmark Briefs and Arguments of the Supreme Court of the United States: Constitutional Law*, vol. 18 (1975).

30. Because Moorfield Storey (with the assistance of John Davis) and Clayton Blakey filed separate briefs in 1916, the names of Storey and Blakey will be given in cites to these briefs to distinguish which brief is referred to. Thus the cite "Brief (Storey) for Plaintiff at 14, *Buchanan v. Warley*, 245 U.S. 60" refers to the brief prepared by Moorfield Storey with the assistance of John Davis and submitted to the Supreme Court for the plaintiff, Charles Buchanan, in 1916. The referenced material can be found at page 14 of this brief. No names are needed for the supplemental brief filed in 1917, since both Storey and Blakey contributed to it. Because both Chevalier and Beckley worked on the defendant's 1916 brief and 1917 supplemental brief, they are not named individually. Briefs, again, can be found in Kurland and Casper, eds., *Landmark Briefs*.

31. Brief (Storey) for Plaintiff at 12, *Buchanan v. Warley*, 245 U.S. 60 (1917) (quoting *Lochner v. New York*, 198 U.S. 45 (1904)).

32. Id. at 13.

33. Id. at 14.

34. Id. at 12.

35. Brief for Defendant at 24, *Buchanan v. Warley*, 245 U.S. 60.

36. Id. at 29.

37. Id. at 26–27.

38. Supplemental brief for Defendant at 147, *Buchanan v. Warley*, 245 U.S. 60.

39. Id. at 26–27 (quoting *Tanner v. Little*, 240 U.S. 369 (1915)).

40. Brief (Blakey) for Plaintiff at 44, *Buchanan v. Warley*, 245 U.S. 60.

41. Supplemental brief for Defendant at 129, *Buchanan v. Warley*, 245 U.S. 60.

42. Brief (Blakey) for Plaintiff at 22, *Buchanan v. Warley*, 245 U.S. 60.

43. Id. at 8.

44. Id. at 12.

45. Id. at 12.
46. Id. at 9 (quoting *Coppage v. Kansas*, 236 U.S. 1 (1914)).
47. Brief (Storey) for Plaintiff at 14, *Buchanan v. Warley*, 245 U.S. 60.
48. Brief for Defendant at 82, *Buchanan v. Warley*, 245 U.S. 60.
49. Id. at 101.
50. Id. at 103.
51. *The Slaughter House Cases*, 16 Wall. 36 (1873); brief for Defendant at 91, *Buchanan v. Warley*, 245 U.S. 60. See also chapter 3.
52. *Soon Hing v. Crowley*, 113 U.S. 703 (1885).
53. Brief for Defendant at 68, *Buchanan v. Warley*, 245 U.S. 60.
54. *Yick Wo v. Hopkins*, 118 U.S. 356 (1886).
55. Brief for Defendant at 41, *Buchanan v. Warley*, 245 U.S. 60.
56. *Hadachek v. Los Angeles*, 239 U.S. 394 (1915).
57. *Reinman v. Little Rock*, 237 U.S. 171 (1914).
58. Brief for Defendant at 74, *Buchanan v. Warley*, 245 U.S. 60.
59. *L'Hote v. New Orleans*, 117 U.S. 587 (1899).
60. Brief for Defendant at 94, *Buchanan v. Warley*, 245 U.S. 60.
61. *Plessy v. Ferguson*, 163 U.S. 573 (1896).
62. Brief for Defendant at 32, *Buchanan v. Warley*, 245 U.S. 60.
63. Id. at 22.
64. Id. at 47–48.
65. Id. at 54.
66. Id. at 66.
67. Brief (Storey) for Plaintiff at 12, *Buchanan v. Warley*, 245 U.S. 60.
68. *The Civil Rights Cases*, 109 U.S. 3 (1883); see also chapter 6.
69. Brief (Blakey) for Plaintiff at 32, *Buchanan v. Warley*, 245 U.S. 60.
70. Id. at 36; brief (Storey) for Plaintiff at 30, *Buchanan v. Warley*, 245 U.S. 60 (citing *McCabe v. Atchison, Topeka and Santa Fe*, 235 U.S. 151 (1914)).
71. Brief for Defendant at 10, *Buchanan v. Warley*, 245 U.S. 60.
72. Id. at 34.
73. Id. at 38.
74. Id. at 43.
75. Id. at 37.
76. Supplemental brief for Defendant at 131, *Buchanan v. Warley*, 245 U.S. 60.
77. Brief for Defendant at 5, *Buchanan v. Warley*, 245 U.S. 60.
78. Id. at 7.
79. Id. at 84.
80. Id. at 12–14.
81. Id. at 45–46.
82. Id. at 45.
83. Supplemental brief for Defendant at 137, *Buchanan v. Warley*, 245 U.S. 60.
84. Brief for Defendant at 10, *Buchanan v. Warley*, 245 U.S. 60 (the cited source of the "twilight zone" metaphor was Gilbert Stephenson: "Segregation legislation will, therefore, affect only those who live in the twilight zone between the distinctly

white and the distinctly colored communities," "The Segregation of the White and Negro Races in Cities by Legislation," *National Municipal Review* 3: 498 (1914)).

85. Id. at 20.

86. Id. at 115.

87. Id. at 15.

88. Id. at 52.

89. Brief (Blakey) for Plaintiff at 10, *Buchanan v. Warley*, 245 U.S. 60.

90. Id. at 42–43.

91. Id. at 18.

92. Supplemental brief for Plaintiff at 9–10, *Buchanan v. Warley*, 245 U.S. 60.

93. Id. at 37.

94. Id. at 29.

95. Brief (Blakey) for Plaintiff at 43, *Buchanan v. Warley*, 245 U.S. 60.

96. Supplemental brief for Plaintiff at 14, *Buchanan v. Warley*, 245 U.S. 60.

97. Id. at 22.

98. Id. at 22–23.

99. Id. at 23.

100. *Buchanan v. Warley*, 245 U.S. 60, 74.

101. Id. at 74.

102. Id. at 78.

103. Id. at 82.

104. Id. at 81.

105. Id. at 80.

106. Id. at 80.

Chapter 6

1. *Mays v. Burgess*, 152 F.2d 123 (1945).

2. By "state" in this context I mean the institutions of organized government, which in this case was the federal government.

3. *Mays v. Burgess*, 147 F.2d. 869 (1945), 152 F.2d 123 (1945).

4. *Buchanan v. Warley*, 245 U.S. 60 (1917).

5. *Mays v. Burgess*, 147 F.2d 869 (1945), 152 F.2d 123 (1945).

6. *Corrigan v. Buckley*, 271 U.S. 323 (1926).

7. *Shelley v. Kraemer*, 334 U.S. 1 (1948).

8. B. Schmidt, "Principle and Prejudice: The Supreme Court and Race in the Progressive Era. Part 1: The Heyday of Jim Crow," *Columbia Law Review* 82 (1982): 444; R. Kennedy, "Race Relations and the Tradition of Celebration: The Case of Professor Schmidt," *Columbia Law Review* 86 (1986): 1622.

9. J. Crow, "An Apartheid for the South: Clarence Poe's Crusade for Rural Segregation," in J. Crow, P. Escott, and C. Flynn, eds., *Race, Class, and Politics in Southern History* (1989); J. Kirby, "Clarence Poe's Vision of a Segregated Great Rural Civilization," *South Atlantic Quarterly* 68 (1969): 27; G. Stephenson, "The Segregation of the White and Negro Races in Rural Communities of North Carolina," *South Atlantic Quarterly* 13 (1914): 107.

10. *Harmon v. Tyler*, 273 U.S. 668 (1927).

11. *Richmond v. Dean*, 281 U.S. 704 (1930).

12. *Clinard v. Winston-Salem*, 6 S.E.2d 867 (1940).

13. C. Vose, *Caucasians Only: The Supreme Court, the NAACP, and the Restrictive Covenant Cases* (1959); T. Clark and P. Perlman, *Prejudice and Property: An Historic Brief against Racial Covenants* (1948).

14. G. Myrdal, *An American Dilemma: The Negro Problem and American Democracy* (1944).

15. F. Henri, *Black Migration: Movement North, 1900–1920* (1976); C. Marks, *Farewell—We're Good and Gone: The Great Black Migration* (1989); A. Harrison, ed., *Black Exodus: The Great Migration from the American South* (1991); J. Trotter, ed., *The Great Migration in Historical Perspective: New Dimensions of Race, Class, and Gender* (1991).

16. Ibid.

17. See, for example, G. Osofsky, *Harlem: The Making of a Ghetto* (1966); A. Spear, *Black Chicago: The Making of a Negro Ghetto, 1890–1920* (1967); K. Kusmer, *A Ghetto Takes Shape: Black Cleveland, 1870–1930* (1976); T. Cox, *Blacks in Topeka, 1865–1915* (1982); J. Trotter, *Black Milwaukee: The Making of an Industrial Proletariat, 1915–45* (1985); G. Wright, *Life behind a Veil: Blacks in Louisville, Kentucky, 1865–1930* (1985); Q. Taylor, *The Forging of a Black Community: Seattle's Central District from 1870 through the Civil Rights Era* (1994). More generally, see the multivolume set edited by K. Kusmer, *Black Communities and Urban Development, 1720–1990* (1991).

18. See, for example, S. French, "Toward a Modern Law of Servitudes: Reweaving the Ancient Strands," *Southern California Law Review* 55 (1982): 1261, who notes that "the law of easements, real covenants, and equitable servitudes is the most complex and archaic body of American property law remaining in the twentieth century" and who quotes others as describing "the law in this area" as "an unspeakable quagmire"; and C. Rose, "Servitudes, Security, and Assent: Some Comments on Professors French and Reichman," *Southern California Law Review* 55 (1982): 1403, who discusses easements and covenants as "a symbol of the mindless formalism of traditional property law." The point for the present discussion is that such devices contribute further to the complexity and ambiguity of the legal landscape. They are therefore particularly vulnerable to interpretive restructuring.

19. D. McGovney, "Racial Residential Segregation by State Court Enforcement of Restrictive Agreements, Covenants, or Conditions in Deeds Is Unconstitutional," *California Law Review* 33 (1945): 5; see also the case of *ex parte Lawes*, 193 P.2d 744 (1948).

20. *Gondolfo v. Hartman*, 49 F. 181 (1892).

21. *Corrigan v. Buckley*, 271 U.S. 323 (1926).

22. *Shelley v. Kraemer*, 334 U.S. 1 (1948).

23. J. Searle, *Speech Acts: An Essay in the Philosophy of Language* (1969).

24. See, for example, *Grady v. Garland*, 89 F.2d 817 (1937).

25. See Vose, *Caucasians Only*.

26. See annotations in 54 *American Law Reports* 814 (1928) and 4 *American Law Reports* 2d 1111 (1949).

27. *Black's Law Dictionary*, 5th ed., abr., s.v. "equity"; see also P. Hoffer, *The Law's Conscience: Equitable Constitutionalism in America* (1990).

28. *Fairchild v. Raines*, 151 P.2d 260, 262 (1944).

29. *Hundley v. Gorewitz*, 132 F.2d 23, 24 (1942).

30. *Grady v. Garland*, 89 F.2d 817, 819 (1937).

31. *Mays v. Burgess*, 147 F.2d 869 (1945).

32. *Fairchild v. Raines*, 143 P.2d 528 (1944).

33. *Lettreau v. Ellis*, 10 P.2d 496 (1932).

34. *Clark v. Vaughn*, 292 P. 783 (1930).

35. *Grady v. Garland*, 89 F.2d 817 (1937).

36. *Hundley v. Gorewitz*, 132 F.2d 23 (1942).

37. *Gospel Spreading Association v. Bennetts*, 147 F.2d 878 (1945).

38. *Fairchild v. Raines*, 151 P.2d 260 (1944).

39. For some sense of the controversy, see M. Gardner, "Race Segregation in Cities," *Kentucky Law Journal* 29 (1941): 213; "Equitable Servitudes—Defenses—Change of Conditions as Affecting Covenants Not to Sell to Negroes," Note, *Harvard Law Review* 44 (1931): 989; "Change in Character of Neighborhood as Affecting Restrictive Covenants," Note, *Virginia Law Review* 18 (1932): 439; "Real Property—Cancellation of Restrictive Covenant Where Change of Character in Neighborhood Makes Restriction Useless," Note, *University of Pennsylvania Law Review* 85 (1937): 740; "Equity-Restrictive Covenants against Alienation," Note, *Georgetown Law Review* 25 (1937): 1040; "Negro Restrictions and the 'Changed Conditions' Doctrine," Note, *University of Chicago Law Review* 7 (1940): 710.

40. *Clark v. Vaughn*, 292 P. 783 (1930).

41. Id. at 785.

42. Id. at 786.

43. Id. at 786.

44. Id. at 787.

45. Id. at 787.

46. *Grady v. Garland*, 89 F.2d 817 (1937).

47. Id. at 819.

48. Id. at 819.

49. Id. at 820.

50. *Fairchild v. Raines*, 143 P.2d 528 (1944).

51. Id. at 531.

52. *Fairchild v. Raines*, 151 P.2d 260 (1944).

53. Id. at 262.

54. Id. at 265 (emphasis in original).

55. Id. at 265 (emphasis in original).

56. Id. at 266.

57. *Grady v. Garland*, 89 F.2d 817 (1937).

58. *Hundley v. Gorewitz*, 132 F.2d 23 (1942).

59. *Hurd v. Hodge*, 162 F.2d 233 (1944).

60. C. Green, *The Secret City: A History of Race Relations in the Nation's Capital* (1967).

61. Vose, *Caucasians Only*; G. McNeil, *Groundwork: Charles Hamilton Houston and the Struggle for Civil Rights* (1983).

62. *Shelley v. Kraemer*, 334 U.S. 1 (1948).

63. Vose, *Caucasians Only*, p. 80.

64. *Grady v. Garland*, 89 F.2d 817, 819 (1937).

65. *Hundley v. Gorewitz*, 132 F.2d 23, 24 (1942). For a fuller treatment, see D. Delaney and M. Emanatian, "'Unnatural Barriers': Why Metaphor Matters" (forthcoming).

66. Id. at 24.

67. Id. at 25.

68. *Mays v. Burgess*, 147 F.2d 869 (1945).

69. Id. at 871.

70. For an examination of Edgerton's jurisprudence, see S. Rosenweig, "The Opinions of Judge Edgerton: A Study in the Judicial Process," *Cornell Law Quarterly* 37 (1952): 149; and F. Frankfurter, "Judge Henry W. Edgerton," *Cornell Law Quarterly* 43 (1958): 161. See also H. Edgerton, "Legal Cause," *University of Pennsylvania Law Review* 72 (1924): 343, as well as his account of "a liberal judge" as having "a tolerance for change" and "an effective sympathy with the underdog" in H. Edgerton, "A Liberal Judge: Cuthbert W. Pound," *Cornell Law Quarterly* 21: 7 (1935). It is worth noting that in the last-mentioned piece, he wrote that a liberal judge "can and must be guided by ideas of justice and social advantage. . . . A liberal judge has a heterodox picture of a good society . . . when he is called upon to determine where the balance of social advantage lies. . . . he allows . . . more weight to the interests of the propertyless and working classes . . . [and gives] less weight than the orthodox judge to the interests of conventional male Americans and more weight . . . to the interests of women, radicals, irregulars, foreigners and criminals" (p. 12).

71. *Mays v. Burgess*, 147 F.2d 869 (1945).

72. Id. at 869.

73. Id. at 878.

74. *Mays v. Burgess*, 152 F.2d 123 (1945).

75. Id. at 125.

76. Id. at 126.

77. Id. at 126.

78. *Hurd v. Hodge*, 162 F.2d 233 (1944).

79. Id. at 234.

80. Id. at 237 n. 11 (finding that "the rule of *Hundley v. Gorewitz* applies").

81. Id. at 236.

82. Id. at 243–244.

83. Id. at 245 (quoting Robert Weaver's "Housing in a Democracy," *Annals of the American Academy of Political and Social Sciences* 244: 45 [1946]).

84. Id. at 245.

85. Id. at 246 (quoting "Remarks of the President in Making the Wendell Wilkie Awards for Journalism," press release, Feb. 28, 1947).

86. Green, *Secret City*, p. 248.

87. J. Anderson, *A. Philip Randolph: a Biographical Portrait* (1972).

Chapter 7

1. *Hurd v. Hodge*, 334 U.S. 24 (1948).

2. *Shelley v. Kraemer*, 334 U.S. 1 (1948).

3. *Brown v. Topeka Board of Education*, 347 U.S. 483 (1954).

4. J. Kushner, "Apartheid in America: A Historical and Legal Analysis of Contemporary Racial Residential Segregation in the United States," *Howard Law Journal* 22 (1979): 547.

5. D. Bell, *And We Are Not Saved* (1987).

6. See, for example, J. Calmore, "Spatial Equality and the Kerner Commission Report: A Back to the Future Essay," *North Carolina Law Review* 71 (1993): 1486; H. McGee, "Afro-American Resistance to Gentrification and the Demise of Integrationist Ideology in the United States," *Urban Lawyer* 23 (1991): 25.

7. T. Morrison, *Playing in the Dark* (1992).

Bibliography

Abu-Lughod, J., et al., eds. *From Urban Village to East Village: The Battle for New York's Lower East Side.* Oxford: Blackwell, 1994.

Agnew, J., and J. Duncan, eds. *The Power of Place: Bringing Together Geographical and Sociological Imaginations.* Boston: Unwin Hyman, 1989.

Alexander, G. "History as Ideology in the Basic Property Course." *Journal of Legal Education* 36 (1986): 381–389.

———. "Takings, Narratives, and Power." *Columbia Law Review* 88 (1988): 1752–1773.

Altman, A. *Critical Legal Studies: A Liberal Critique.* Princeton: Princeton University Press, 1990.

Altshuler, A. *Community Control: The Black Demand for Participation in Large American Cities.* New York: Pegasus, 1970.

American Bar Association. Standing Committee on Education against Communism. *The New Czars vs. the Rule of Law.* Chicago: American Bar Association, 1964.

Anderson, J. *A. Philip Randolph: A Biographical Portrait.* New York: Harcourt Brace Jovanovich, 1973.

Aron, N. *Liberty and Justice for All: Public Interest Law in the 1980s and Beyond.* Boulder: Westview Press, 1989.

Baker, C. "Property and Its Relation to Constitutionally Protected Liberty." *University of Pennsylvania Law Review* 134 (1986): 741–816.

Baker, R. *Following the Color Line: American Negro Citizenship in the Progressive Era.* 1908. Reprint, New York: Harper and Row, 1964.

Balkin, J. "The Crystalline Structure of Legal Thought." *Rutgers Law Review* 39 (1986): 1–110.

———. "Nested Oppositions." *Yale Law Journal* 99 (1990): 1669–1705.

———. "Understanding Legal Understanding: The Legal Subject and the Problem of Legal Coherence." *Yale Law Journal* 103 (1993): 105–177.

Barnes, T., and J. Duncan, eds. *Writing Worlds: Discourse, Text, and Metaphor in the Representation of Landscape.* New York: Routledge, 1992.

Bartley, N. *The Rise of Massive Resistance: Race and Politics in the South during the 1950s.* Baton Rouge: Louisiana State University, 1969.

Bartolemew, A., and A. Hunt. "What's Wrong with Rights?" *Law and Inequality* 9 (1990): 1–58.

Beiner, R. *What's the Matter with Liberalism?* Berkeley: University of California Press, 1992.

Bell, D. *And We Are Not Saved: The Elusive Quest for Racial Justice.* New York: Basic Books, 1987.

———. *Faces at the Bottom of the Well: The Permanence of Racism in America.* New York: Basic Books, 1992.

———. *Race, Racism, and American Law.* 3d ed. Boston: Little, Brown, 1992.

Bell, H. "The Negro Emigration Movement, 1849–1859." *Phylon* 20 (1957): 132–142.

Benda-Beckmann, F. *Property in Social Continuity.* The Hague: Martinus Nijhoff, 1979.

Berlin, I. "Time, Space, and the Evolution of Afro-American Society on British Mainland North America." *American Historical Review* 85 (1980): 44–78.

Berlin, I., et al. *Slaves No More: Three Essays on Emancipation and the Civil War.* Cambridge: Cambridge University Press, 1992.

Berry, M. "Repression of Blacks in the South, 1890–1945: Enforcing the System of Segregation." In *The Age of Segregation: Race Relations in the South, 1890–1945,* edited by R. Haws, pp. 29–44. Jackson: University of Mississippi Press, 1978.

Bestor, A. "The American Civil War as a Constitutional Crisis." *American Historical Review* 19 (1964): 327–352.

———. "State Sovereignty and Slavery. A Reinterpretation of Proslavery Constitutional Doctrine, 1846–1860." *Journal of the Illinois State Historical Society* 54 (1961): 117–180.

Bix, B. *Law, Language, and Legal Determinacy.* Oxford: Clarendon Press, 1993.

Blassingame, J., ed. *Slave Testimony: Two Centuries of Letters, Speeches, Interviews, and Autobiographies.* Baton Rouge: Louisiana State University, 1977.

Blomley, N. "Text and Context: Rethinking the Law-Space Nexus." *Progress in Human Geography* 13 (1989): 512–534.

———. *Law, Space, and the Geographies of Power.* New York: Guilford, 1994.

Blomley, N., and G. Clark. "Law, Theory, and Geography." *Urban Geography* 11 (1990): 433–436.

Bohannan, P. "The Differing Realms of the Law." In *Law and Warfare: Studies in the Anthropology of Conflict,* edited by P. Bohannan, pp. 43–56. Garden City, N.Y.: American Museum of Natural History, 1967.

Bourdieu, P. "The Force of Law: Toward a Sociology of the Juridical Field." *Hastings Law Review* 38 (1987): 814–853.

Boyd, W. "Negro Colonization in the Reconstruction Era." *Georgia Historical Quarterly* 15 (1956): 360–382.

Boyle, J. "The Politics of Reason: Critical Legal Theory and Local Social Thought." *University of Pennsylvania Law Review* 133 (1985): 685–780.

Breeden, J., ed. *Advice among Masters: The Ideal in Slave Management in the Old South.* Westport, Conn.: Greenwood Press, 1980.

Broderick, F., and A. Meier, eds. *Negro Protest Thought in the Twentieth Century.* Indianapolis: Bobbs-Merrill, 1965.

Brooks, P., and P. Gewirtz, eds. *Law's Stories: Narrative and Rhetoric in the Law*. New Haven: Yale University Press, 1996.

Burton, S. "Reaffirming Legal Reasoning: The Challenge from the Left." *Journal of Legal Education* 36 (1980): 358–370.

Calmore, J. "Spatial Equality and the Kerner Commission Report: A Back to the Future Essay." *North Carolina Law Review* 71 (1993):1486-1518.

Campbell, S. *The Slave Catchers: Enforcement of the Fugitive Slave Law, 1850–1860*. Chapel Hill: University of North Carolina Press, 1970.

Castells, M. "Crisis, Planning, and the Quality of Life: Managing the New Historical Relationships between Space and Society." *Society and Space* 1 (1983): 3–21.

Catterall, H., ed. *Judicial Cases concerning American Slavery and the Negro*. 5 vols. Washington: Carnegie Institution, 1926–1936.

Cell, J. *The Highest Stage of White Supremacy: The Origins of Segregation in South Africa and the American South*. Cambridge: Cambridge University Press, 1982.

"Change in Character of Neighborhood as Affecting Restrictive Covenants." Note. *Virginia Law Review* 18 (1932): 439–443.

Clark, G. "The Geography of Law." In *New Models in Geography*, edited by R. Peet and N. Thrift, pp. 310–337. Boston: Unwin Hyman, 1990.

———. *Judges and the City: Interpreting Local Autonomy*. Chicago: University of Chicago Press, 1985.

Clark, T., and P. Perlman. *Prejudice and Property: An Historic Brief against Racial Covenants*. Washington, D.C.: Public Affairs Press, 1948.

Cohen, F. "Dialogue on Private Property." *Rutgers Law Review* 9 (1954): 357–387.

Cohen, M. "Property and Sovereignty." *Cornell Law Quarterly* 13 (1928): 8–30.

Cohen, W. *At Freedom's Edge: Black Mobility and the Southern White Quest for Racial Control*. Baton Rouge: Louisiana State University Press, 1991.

Coombe, R. "Room to Manoeuver: Toward a Theory of Practice in Critical Legal Studies." *Law and Social Inquiry* 14 (1989): 69–164.

———. "'Same as It Ever Was': Rethinking the Politics of Legal Interpretation." *McGill Law Journal* 34 (1989): 603–652.

Cornell, D. "'Convention' and Critique." *Cardozo Law Review* 7 (1986): 679–691.

Cosgrove, D., and S. Daniels, eds. *The Iconography of Landscape: Essays on the Symbolic Representation, Design, and Use of Past Environments*. Cambridge: Cambridge University Press, 1988.

Coutin, S. *The Culture of Protest: Religious Activism and the U.S. Sanctuary Movement*. Boulder: Westview Press, 1993.

Cover, R. *Justice Accused: Antislavery and the Judicial Process*. New Haven: Yale University Press, 1975.

———. "Nomos and Narrative." *Harvard Law Review* 97 (1983): 4–68.

———. "Violence and the Word." *Yale Law Journal* 95 (1986): 1601–1629.

Cox, T. *Blacks in Topeka, Kansas, 1865–1915: A Social History*. Baton Rouge: Louisiana State University Press, 1982.

Cribbet, J. "Concepts in Transition: The Search for a New Definition of Property." *University of Illinois Law Review* 1986 (1986): 1–42.

Crockett, N. *The Black Towns*. Lawrence: Regents Press of Kansas, 1979.

Crow, J. "An Apartheid for the South: Clarence Poe's Crusade for Rural Segregation." In *Race, Class, and Politics in Southern History*, edited by J. Crow, P. Escott, and C. Flynn, pp. 219–259. Baton Rouge: Louisiana State University Press, 1989.

Crowe, C. "Racial Massacre in Atlanta, September 22, 1906." *Journal of Negro History* 54 (1969): 150–173.

Cruse, H. *Plural but Equal: A Critical Study of Blacks and Minorities and the American Plural Society*. New York: William Morrow, 1987.

Davis, M. *Brutal Need: Lawyers and the Welfare Rights Movement, 1960–1973*. New Haven: Yale University Press, 1993.

Delaney, D. "Geographies of Judgment: The Doctrine of Changed Conditions and the Geopolitics of Race." *Annals of the Association of American Geographers* 83 (1993): 48–65.

Delaney, D., and M. Emanatian. "'Unnatural Barriers': Why Metaphor Matters (or, Linguistic Meets the Geo-Politics of Law)." In *Contributions in Cognitive Linguistics, Papers Read at the Third International Cognitive Linguistics Conference, Belgium*, edited by L. G. de Stadler. Berlin: Mouton de Gruyter, forthcoming.

Donahue, C. "The Future of the Concept Property Predicted from Its Past." In *Property*, edited by J. Pennock and J. Chapman, pp. 28–68. New York: New York University Press, 1980.

Douglass, F. *My Bondage and My Freedom*. 1855. Reprint, Urbana: University of Illinois Press, 1987.

DuBois, W. *Black Reconstruction, 1860–1880*. New York: Harcourt, Brace, 1935.

———. *The Souls of Black Folk*. 1903. Reprint, New York: Vintage, 1990.

Duncan, J., and N. Duncan. "(Re)reading the Landscape." *Environment and Planning* (D) 6 (1988): 117.

Duncan, J., and D. Ley, eds. *Place/Culture/Representation*. London: Routledge, 1993.

Dworkin, R. *Law's Empire*. Cambridge, Mass.: Belknap Press, 1986.

Edgerton, H. "Legal Cause." *University of Pennsylvania Law Review* 72 (1924): 343–375.

———. "A Liberal Judge: Cuthbert W. Pound." *Cornell Law Quarterly* 21 (1935): 7–45.

Epstein, R. *Takings: Private Property and the Power of Eminent Domain*. Cambridge, Mass.: Harvard University Press, 1988.

"Equitable Servitudes—Defenses—Change of Condition as Affecting Covenants Not to Sell to Negroes." Note. *Harvard Law Review* 44 (1931): 989–990.

"Equity—Restrictive Covenants against Alienation." Note. *Georgetown Law Journal* 25 (1937): 1040–1041.

Fairman, C. *Reconstruction and Reunion, 1864–1888*. Vol. 3 of *The History of the Supreme Court of the United States*. New York: Macmillan, 1971.

Fehrenbacher, D. *The Dred Scott Case: Its Significance in American Law and Politics*. New York: Oxford University Press, 1978.

Feinman, J. "Contract Law as Ideology." In *The Politics of Law*, edited by D. Kairys, pp. 172–184. New York: Pantheon, 1990.

———. "The Jurisprudence of Classification." *Stanford Law Review* 41 (1989): 661–717.

Felstiner, W., R. Abel, and A. Sarat. "The Emergence and Transformation of

Disputes: Naming, Blaming, Claiming. . . ." *Law and Society Review* 15 (1981): 631–654.

Fields, B. "Slavery, Race, and Ideology in the United States of America." *New Left Review* 181 (1990): 95–118.

Finkelman, P. *An Imperfect Union: Slavery, Federalism, and Comity.* Chapel Hill: University of North Carolina Press, 1981.

———. "*Prigg v. Pennsylvania* and Northern State Courts: Anti-Slavery Use of a Pro-Slavery Decision." *Civil War History* 25 (1979): 5–35.

Fish, S. *Doing What Comes Naturally: Change, Rhetoric, and the Practice of Theory in Literary and Legal Studies.* Durham, N.C.: Duke University Press, 1989.

Foner, E. *Free Soil, Free Labor, Free Men: The Ideology of the Republican Party before the Civil War.* New York: Oxford University Press, 1970.

———. *Nothing but Freedom: Emancipation and Its Legacy.* Baton Rouge: Louisiana State University Press, 1983.

Ford, R. "The Boundaries of Race: Political Geography in Legal Analysis." *Harvard Law Review* 107 (1994): 1841–1921.

Foucault, M. *Power/Knowledge: Selected Interviews and Other Writings, 1972–1977.* New York: Pantheon, 1980.

———. "Space, Knowledge, and Power." In *The Foucault Reader,* edited by P. Rabinow, pp. 239–256. New York: Pantheon, 1984.

Frankfurter, F. "Judge Henry W. Edgerton." *Cornell Law Quarterly* 43 (1958): 161–162.

Franklin, J. "The Enforcement of the Civil Rights Act of 1875." *Prologue* 6 (1974): 225–235.

———. *A Southern Odyssey: Travelers in the Antebellum North.* Baton Rouge: Louisiana State University Press, 1976.

Fredrickson, G. *The Arrogance of Race: Historical Perspectives on Slavery, Racism, and Social Inequality.* Middletown, Conn.: Wesleyan University Press, 1988.

French, S. "Toward a Modern Law of Servitudes: Reweaving the Ancient Strands." *Southern California Law Review* 55 (1982): 1261–1319.

Frug, G. "Argument as Character." *Stanford Law Review* 40 (1988): 869–927.

Fry, G. *Night Riders in Black Folk History.* Knoxville: University of Tennessee Press, 1975.

Gabel, P. "The Phenomenology of Rights-Consciousness and the Pact of the Withdrawn Selves." *Texas Law Review* 62 (1984): 1563–1599.

Gara, L. *The Liberty Line: The Legend of the Underground Railroad.* Lexington: University of Kentucky Press, 1961.

———. "The Fugitive Slave Law: A Double Paradox." *Civil War History* 10 (1964): 229–240.

Gardner, M. "Race Segregation in Cities." *Kentucky Law Journal* 29 (1941): 213–219.

Genovese, E. *Roll, Jordan, Roll. The World the Slaves Made.* New York: Pantheon, 1972.

———. *The World the Slaveholders Made: Two Essays in Interpretation.* Middletown, Conn.: Wesleyan University Press, 1969.

Goldberg, D. *Racist Culture: Philosophy and the Politics of Meaning.* Cambridge, Mass.: Blackwell, 1993.

Goodin, R., and A. Reeve, eds. *Liberal Neutrality.* London: Routledge, 1989.

Goodman, N. *Ways of Worldmaking.* Indianapolis: Hackett, 1978.

Goodrich, P. *Legal Discourse: Studies in Linguistics, Rhetoric, and Legal Analysis.* London: Macmillan, 1987.

Gordon, R. "Critical Legal Histories." *Stanford Law Review* 36 (1984): 57–125.

———. "Historicism in Legal Scholarship." *Yale Law Journal* 90 (1981): 1017–1054.

———. "New Developments in Legal Theory." In *The Politics of Law*, edited by D. Kairys, pp. 281–293. 2d ed. New York: Pantheon, 1990.

———. "Unfreezing Legal Reality: Critical Approaches to Law." *Florida State University Law Review* 15 (1987): 195–220.

Graham, L. *Baltimore: The Nineteenth Century Black Capital.* Lanham, Md.: University Press of America, 1982.

Gray, J. *Liberalisms: Essays in Political Philosophy.* New York: Routledge, 1989.

Gregory, D., and J. Urry, eds., *Social Relations and Spatial Structures.* New York: St. Martin's Press, 1985.

Green, C. *The Secret City: A History of Race Relations in the Nation's Capital.* Princeton: Princeton University Press, 1967.

Greenberg, J. *Crusaders in the Court.* New York: Basic Books, 1994.

Grey, T. "The Disintegration of Property." In *Property*, edited by J. Pennock and J. Chapman, pp. 69–86. Nomos, vol. 22. New York: New York University Press, 1980.

Hall, R. "Booker T. Washington: Separatist in Disguise." In *Black Separatism and Social Reality: Rhetoric and Reason*, edited by R. Hall. New York: Pergamon Press, 1977.

———. *Black Separatism and Social Reality: Rhetoric and Reason.* New York: Pergamon Press, 1977.

Hall, W., ed. *The Rest of the Dream: The Black Odyssey of Lyman Johnson.* Lexington: University of Kentucky Press, 1988.

Hamilton, K. *Black Towns and Profit: Promotion and Development in the Trans-Appalachian West, 1877–1915.* Urbana: University of Illinois Press, 1991.

Harrison, A., ed. *Black Exodus: The Great Migration from the American South.* Jackson: University Press of Mississippi, 1991.

Hawkins, W. "A Year of Segregation in Baltimore." *The Crisis* 3 (1911): 27–30.

Henri, F. *Black Migration: Movement North, 1900–1920.* Garden City, N.Y.: Anchor Press, 1975.

Henry, H. "The Police Control of the Slave in South Carolina." Master's thesis, Vanderbilt University, 1914.

Herod, A. *Afro-American Nationalism: An Annotated Bibliography of Militant Separatist and Nationalist Literature.* New York: Garland, 1986.

Himes, C. *The Autobiography of Chester Himes.* 2 vols. Garden City, N.Y.: Doubleday, 1972.

Hixon, W. *Moorfield Storey and the Abolitionist Tradition*. New York: Oxford University Press, 1972.

Hoffer, P. *The Law's Conscience: Equitable Constitutionalism in America*. Chapel Hill: University of North Carolina Press, 1990.

Horwitz, M. "Transformation in the Conception of Property in American Law." *University of Chicago Law Review* 40 (1973): 248–290.

Hunting, W. "The Constitutionality of Race Distinction and the Baltimore Negro Segregation Ordinance." *Columbia Law Review* 11 (1911): 24–35.

Hutchinson, A. *Dwelling on the Threshold: Critical Essays on Modern Legal Thought*. Toronto: Carswell, 1988.

Hutchinson, A., and P. Monahan, eds. *The Rule of Law: Ideal or Ideology*. Toronto: Carswell, 1987.

Hyde, A. "The Concept of Legitimation in the Sociology of Law." *Wisconsin Law Review* 1983 (1983): 379–426.

Hyman, H., and W. Wiecek. *Equal Justice under Law: Constitutional Development, 1835–1875*. New York: Harper and Row, 1982.

Jackson, B. *The Waiting Years: Essays on American Negro Literature*. Baton Rouge: Louisiana State University Press, 1976.

Jackson, P. "The Idea of 'Race' and the Geography of Racism." In *Race and Racism: Essays in Social Geography*, edited by P. Jackson, pp. 3–21. London: Allen and Unwin, 1987.

Jaffa, H. *The Crisis of the House Divided: An Interpretation of the Issues in the Lincoln-Douglas Debates*. Garden City, N.Y.: Doubleday, 1959.

Johnson, M., and J. Roark, eds. *No Chariot Let Down: Charleston's Free People of Color on the Eve of the Civil War*. Chapel Hill: University of North Carolina Press, 1984.

Josselson, R., and A. Lieblich, eds. *The Narrative Study of Lives*. Newbury Park, Calif.: Sage, 1993.

Joyner, C. *Down by the Riverside: A South Carolina Slave Community*. Urbana: University of Illinois Press, 1984.

Kaczorowski, R. *The Politics of Judicial Interpretation: The Federal Courts, Department of Justice, and Civil Rights, 1866–1876*. Dobbs Ferry, N.Y.: Oceana, 1985.

———. "To Begin the Nation Anew: Congress, Citizenship, and Civil Rights after the Civil War. *American Historical Review* 92 (1987): 45–68.

Kelleher, D. "St. Louis' 1916 Residential Segregation Ordinance." *Missouri Historical Society Bulletin* 25 (1970): 239–248.

Kellogg, C. *NAACP, A History of the National Association for the Advancement of Colored People*. Baltimore: Johns Hopkins University Press, 1967.

Kelman, M. "Interpretive Construction in the Substantive Criminal Law." *Stanford Law Review* 33 (1981): 591–673.

Kennedy, David. "A New Stream of International Law Scholarship." *Wisconsin International Law Journal* 7 (1988): 1–49.

Kennedy, Duncan. "Form and Substance in Private Adjudication." *Harvard Law Review* 89 (1976): 1665–1778.

———. "A Semiotics of Legal Argument." *Syracuse Law Review* 42 (1991): 75–116.

Kennedy, R. "Race Relations and the Tradition of Celebration: The Case of Professor Schmidt." *Columbia Law Review* 86 (1986): 1622–1661.

Kerruish, V. *Jurisprudence as Ideology.* London: Routledge, 1991.

Kirby, J. "Clarence Poe's Vision of a Segregated Great Rural Civilization." *South Atlantic Quarterly* 68 (1969): 27–38.

Kluger, R. *Simple Justice: The History of "Brown v. Board of Education" and Black America's Struggle for Equality.* New York: Knopf, 1976.

Kolchin, P. *First Freedom: The Responses of Alabama's Blacks to Emancipation and Reconstruction.* Westport, Conn.: Greenwood Press, 1972.

Koning, H. *The Conquest of America: How the Indian Nations Lost Their Continent.* New York: Monthly Review Press, 1993.

Kraditor, A. *Means and Ends in American Abolitionism: Garrison and his Critics on Strategies and Tactics.* New York: Pantheon, 1969.

Krygier, M. "Marxism and the Rule of Law: Reflections after the Collapse of Communism." *Law and Social Inquiry* 15 (1990): 633–663.

Kurland, P., and G. Casper, eds. *Landmark Briefs and Arguments of the Supreme Court of the United States: Constitutional Law.* Various volumes. Washington, D.C.: University Publications of America, 1975.

Kushner, J. "Apartheid in America: A Historical and Legal Analysis of Contemporary Racial Residential Segregation in the United States." *Howard Law Journal* 22 (1979): 547–685.

Kusmer, K. *A Ghetto Takes Shape: Black Cleveland, 1870–1930.* Urbana: University of Illinois Press, 1976.

———, ed. *Black Communities and Urban Development, 1720–1990.* New York: Garland Press, 1991.

Kutler, S., ed. *The Dred Scott Decision: Law or Politics?* Boston: Houghton Mifflin, 1967.

Kymlicka, W. "Liberal Individualism and Liberal Neutrality." *Ethics* 99 (1989): 883–905.

Lakoff, G. *Women, Fire, and Dangerous Things: What Categories Reveal about the Mind.* Chicago: University of Chicago Press, 1987.

Larson, J., and C. Spillenger. "'That's Not History': The Boundaries of Advocacy and Scholarship." *Public Historian* 12 (1990): 33–44.

Lazerson, J. *Against the Tide: Whites in the Struggle against Apartheid.* Boulder: Westview Press, 1994.

Lefebvre, H. *The Production of Space.* Oxford: Blackwell, 1991.

Lewis, G. "The Distribution of the Negro in the Coterminous United States." *Geography* 54 (1969): 411–418.

Litwack, L. *Been in the Storm So Long: The Aftermath of Slavery.* New York: Knopf, 1979.

———. *North of Slavery: The Negro in the Free States, 1790–1860.* Chicago: University of Chicago Press, 1961.

Llewellyn, K. *The Common Law Tradition.* Boston: Little, Brown, 1960.

Lofgren, C. *The Plessy Case: A Legal-Historical Interpretation.* New York: Oxford University Press, 1987.

Logan, F. *The Negro in North Carolina: 1876–1894*. Chapel Hill: University of North Carolina, 1964.

Logan, R. *The Betrayal of the Negro from Rutherford B. Hayes to Woodrow Wilson*. New York: Collier Books, 1965.

Lopez, G. *Rebellious Lawyering*. Boulder: Westview Press, 1992.

Macpherson, C. "The Meaning of Property." In *Property: Mainstream and Critical Positions*, edited by C. Macpherson, pp. 1–13. Toronto: University of Toronto Press, 1978.

———. "Property as Means or Ends." In *Theories of Property: Aristotle to the Present*, edited by A. Parel and T. Flanagan. Waterloo, Ont.: Wilfred Laurier University Press, 1979.

———. ed. *Property: Mainstream and Critical Positions*. Toronto: University of Toronto Press, 1978.

Magdol, E. *A Right to the Land: Essays on the Freedmen's Community*. Westport, Conn.: Greenwood Press, 1977.

Mandle, J. *The Roots of Black Poverty: The Southern Plantation Economy after the Civil War*. Durham, N.C.: Duke University Press, 1978.

Marks, C. *Farewell—We're Good and Gone: The Great Black Migration*. Bloomington: Indiana University Press, 1989.

Marquez, B. *LULAC: The Evolution of a Mexican American Political Organization*. Austin: University of Texas Press, 1993.

Marx, K. "On the Jewish Question." In *The Marx-Engels Reader*, edited by R. Tucker, pp.24–51. New York: Norton, 1972.

Massey, D. "Flexible Sexism." *Environment and Planning* (D) 9 (1991): 31–57.

Massey, D., and J. Allen, eds. *Geography Matters!* London: Cambridge University Press, 1984.

Massey, D., and N. Denton. *American Apartheid: Segregation and the Making of the Underclass*. Cambridge, Mass.: Harvard University Press, 1993.

Mather, L., and B. Yngvesson. "Language, Audience, and the Transformation of Disputes." *Law and Society Review* 15 (1981): 775–821.

McAdoo, B. *Pre–Civil War Black Nationalism*. New York: David Walker Press, 1983.

McGee, H. "Afro-American Resistance to Gentrification and the Demise of Integrationist Ideology in the United States." *Urban Lawyer* 23 (1991):25–44.

McGovney, D. "Racial Residential Segregation by State Court Enforcement of Restrictive Agreements, Covenants, or Conditions in Deeds Is Unconstitutional." *California Law Review* 33 (1945): 5–39.

McNeil, G. *Groundwork: Charles Hamilton Houston and the Struggle for Civil Rights*. Philadelphia: University of Pennsylvania Press, 1983.

McPherson, J. "Abolitionists and the Civil Rights Act of 1875." *Journal of American History* 52 (1965): 496.

McTyeire, H. "Plantation Life—Duties and Responsibilities." *Debow's Review* 29 (1860): 357. Reprinted in J. Breeden, ed. *Advice among Masters: The Ideal in Slave Management in the Old South*. Westport, Conn.: Greenwood Press, 1980.

Medcalf, L. *Law and Identity: Lawyers, Native Americans, and Legal Practice*. Beverly Hills, Calif.: Sage, 1978.

Meier, A. *Negro Thought in America, 1880–1915: Racial Ideologies in the Age of Booker T. Washington.* Ann Arbor: University of Michigan Press, 1963.

Meier, A., and E. Rudwick. *Along the Color Line: Explorations in the Black Experience.* Urbana: University of Illinois Press, 1976.

Mellon, J., ed. *Bullwhip Days: The Slaves Remember. An Oral History.* New York: Avon, 1988.

Mermelstein, D., ed. *The Anti-Apartheid Reader.* New York: Grove Press, 1987.

Merry, S. *Getting Justice and Getting Even: Legal Consciousness among Working Class Americans.* Chicago: University of Chicago Press, 1990.

Micheleman, F. "Property, Utility, and Fairness." *Harvard Law Review* 80 (1967): 1165–1258.

Michie, J. *Richmond Hill Plantation, 1810–1868: The Discovery of Antebellum Life on a Waccamaw Rice Plantation.* Spartanburg, S.C.: Reprint Co., 1990.

Miller, C. *The Supreme Court and the Uses of History.* Cambridge, Mass.: Harvard University Press, 1969.

Miller, E., and E. Genovese, eds. *Plantation, Town, and County: Essays on the Local History of American Slave Society.* Urbana: University of Illinois Press, 1974.

Miller, L. *The Petitioners: The Story of the Supreme Court of the United States and the Negro.* New York: Pantheon, 1966.

Minor, J. "Constitutionality of Segregation Ordinances." *Virginia Law Review* 18 (1912): 561–576.

Mitchell, W., ed. *The Politics of Interpretation.* Chicago: University of Chicago Press, 1983.

Mooney, C. *Slavery in Tennessee.* Bloomington: Indiana University Press, 1957.

Morris, T. *Free Men All: The Personal Liberty Laws of the North, 1780–1861.* Baltimore: Johns Hopkins University Press, 1974.

Morrison, T. *Playing in the Dark: Whiteness and the Literary Imagination.* Cambridge, Mass.: Harvard University Press, 1992.

Moses, W. *The Golden Age of Black Nationalism, 1850–1925.* Hamden, Conn.: Archon, 1978.

Mulroy, K. *Freedom on the Border: The Seminole Maroons.* Lubbock: Texas Tech University Press, 1993.

Myrdal, G. *An American Dilemma: The Negro Problem and American Democracy.* New York: Harper and Brothers, 1944.

Nedelsky, J. "Law, Boundaries, and the Bounded Self." *Representations* 30 (1990): 162–189.

———. *Private Property and the Limits of American Constitutionalism.* Chicago: University of Chicago Press, 1990.

"Negro Restrictions and the 'Changed Conditions' Doctrine." Note. *University of Chicago Law Review* 7 (1940): 710–716.

Northup, S. *Twelve Years a Slave.* 1853. Reprint, Baton Rouge: Louisiana State University Press, 1968.

Olsen, F. "The Family and the Market: A Study of Ideology and Legal Reform." *Harvard Law Review* 96 (1983): 1497–1578.

Olsen, O., ed. *The Thin Disguise: A Turning Point in Negro History: Plessy v. Ferguson: A Documentary Presentation.* New York: Humanities Press, 1967.

Omi, M., and H. Winant. *Racial Formation in the United States: From the 1960s to the 1990s.* New York: Routledge, 1994.

Oppenheimer, M. *The Sit-in Movement of 1960.* Brooklyn: Carlson, 1989.

Osofsky, G. *Harlem: The Making of a Ghetto.* New York: Harper and Row, 1966.

Oubre, C. *Forty Acres and a Mule: The Freedmen's Bureau and Black Land Ownership.* Baton Rouge: Louisiana State University Press, 1978.

Painter, N. *Exodusters: Black Migration to Kansas after Reconstruction.* New York: Knopf, 1977.

Papke, D., ed. *Narrative and the Legal Discourse.* Liverpool: Deborah Charles, 1991.

Parrish, C., et al. *The History of the Segregation Case and the Decision of the Supreme Court.* Louisville: privately printed, 1918.

Paul, J. "The Hidden Structure of Takings Law." *Southern California Law Review* 64 (1991): 1393–1548.

———. "The Politics of Legal Semiotics." *Texas Law Review* 69 (1991): 1779–1852.

Peller, G. "The Metaphysics of American Law." *California Law Review* 75 (1985): 1151–1290.

Pellow, D., ed. *Setting Boundaries: The Anthropology of Spatial and Social Organization.* Westport, Conn.: 1996.

Penner, J. "The Bundle of Rights Picture of Property." *UCLA Law Review* 43 (1996): 711–820.

Perry, L., and M. Fellman, eds. *Antislavery Reconsidered: New Perspectives on the Abolitionists.* Baton Rouge: Louisiana State University Press, 1979.

Philbrick, F. "Changing Conceptions of Property in Law." *University of Pennsylvania Law Review* 86 (1938): 691–732.

Pitten, R. "Negotiating Boundaries: Perspectives from Nigeria." In *Setting Boundaries*, edited by D. Pellow. Westport, Conn.: Bergin and Garvey, 1996.

Power, G. "Apartheid Baltimore Style: The Residential Segregation Ordinances of 1910–1913." *Maryland Law Review* 42 (1982): 289–328.

Pred, A. *Making Histories and Constructing Human Geographies: The Local Transformations of Practice, Power Relations, and Consciousness.* Boulder: Westview Press, 1990.

Prussin, L. *African Nomadic Architecture: Space, Place, and Gender.* Washington: Smithsonian Institution, 1995.

Quigley, J. "The New World Order and the Rule of Law." *Syracuse Journal of International Law and Commerce* 18 (1992): 75–110.

Rabinowitz, H. "More Than the Woodward Thesis: Assessing *The Strange Career of Jim Crow.*" *Journal of American History* 75 (1988): 842–856.

———. "Psychological Disorders, Socio-Economic Forces, and American Race Relations." *Slavery and Abolition* 7 (1986): 188–194.

———. *Race Relations in the Urban South, 1865–1890.* Urbana: University of Illinois Press, 1980.

Radin, M. "The Liberal Conception of Property." *Columbia Law Review* 88 (1986): 1667–1696.

———. *Reinterpreting Property.* Chicago: University of Chicago Press, 1993.

Rawick, G., ed. *The American Slave: A Composite Autobiography.* 19 vols. Westport, Conn.: Greenwood Press, 1972–1979.

Rawley, J. *The Transatlantic Slave Trade: A History.* New York: Norton, 1981.

"Real Property—Cancellation of Restrictive Covenant Where Change of Character in the Neighborhood Makes Restriction Useless." Note. *University of Pennsylvania Law Review* 85 (1937): 740–741.

Rice, R. "Residential Segregation by Law, 1910–1917." *Journal of Southern History* 34 (1968): 179–199.

Robben, A. "Habits of the Home: Spatial Hegemony and the Structuration of House and Society in Brazil." *American Anthropologist* 91 (1989): 570–588.

Rorty, A. *Mind in Action: Essays in the Philosophy of Mind.* Boston: Beacon Press, 1988.

Rose, C. *Property and Persuasion: Essays on the History, Theory, and Rhetoric of Ownership.* Boulder: Westview Press, 1994.

———. "Servitudes, Security, and Assent: Some Comments on Professors French and Reichman." *Southern California Law Review* 55 (1982): 1403–1416.

Rose, G. *Feminism and Geography: The Limits of Geographical Knowledge.* Minneapolis: University of Minnesota Press, 1993.

Rose, W. *Rehearsal for Reconstruction: The Port Royal Experiment.* Indianapolis: Bobbs-Merrill, 1964.

———, ed. *A Documentary History of Slavery in North America.* New York: Oxford University Press, 1976.

Rosenberg, G. *The Hollow Hope: Can Courts Bring about Social Change?* Chicago: University of Chicago Press, 1991.

Rosengarten, T. *Tombee: Portrait of a Cotton Planter.* New York: Morrow, 1986.

Rosenwieg, S. "The Opinions of Judge Edgerton: A Study in the Judicial Process." *Cornell Law Quarterly* 37 (1952): 149–205.

Ross, B. *J. E. Spingarn and the Rise of the NAACP, 1911–1939.* New York: Atheneum, 1972.

Rowan, C. *Dream Makers, Dream Breakers: The World of Justice Thurgood Marshall.* Boston: Little, Brown, 1993.

Ryan, A. *Property and Political Theory.* Oxford: Blackwell, 1984.

Ryan, M. *Politics and Culture: Working Hypotheses for a Post-Revolutionary Society.* Baltimore: Johns Hopkins University Press, 1989.

Sack, R. *Human Territoriality: Its Theory and History.* Cambridge: Cambridge University Press, 1986.

Sandel, M., ed. *Liberalism and Its Critics.* New York: New York University Press, 1984.

Santos, B. "Maps of Misreading: Toward a Postmodern Conception of Law." *Journal of Law and Society* 14 (1987): 279–304.

Sarat, A., and T. Kearns. "Beyond the Great Divide: Forms of Legal Scholarship and Everyday Life." In *Law and Everyday Life,* edited by A. Sarat and T. Kearns. Ann Arbor: University of Michigan Press, 1993.

———, eds. *Law in Everyday Life.* Ann Arbor: University of Michigan Press, 1993.

———. *Law's Violence.* Ann Arbor: University of Michigan Press, 1994.

———. *The Rhetoric of Law.* Ann Arbor: University of Michigan Press, 1994.

Sax, J. "Takings and the Police Power." *Yale Law Journal* 74 (1964): 36–76.

Schlag, P., and D. Skover. *Tactics of Legal Reasoning.* Durham, N.C.: Carolina Academic Press, 1986.

Schlatter, R. *Private Property: The History of an Idea.* London: Allen and Unwin, 1951.

Schlegel, J. "Notes toward an Intimate, Opinionated, and Affectionate History of the Conference on Critical Legal Studies." *Stanford Law Review* 36 (1984) 391–411.

Schmidt, B. "Principle and Prejudice: The Supreme Court and Race in the Progressive Era. Part 1: The Heyday of Jim Crow." *Columbia Law Review* 82 (1982): 444–524.

Senechal, R. *The Sociogenesis of a Race Riot: Springfield, Illinois, in 1908.* Urbana: University of Illinois Press, 1990.

Searle, J. *Speech Acts: An Essay in the Philosophy of Language.* London: Cambridge University Press, 1969.

Shapiro, H. *White Violence and Black Response: From Reconstruction to Montgomery.* Amherst: University of Massachusetts Press, 1988.

Singer, J. "Legal Realism Now." *California Law Review* 76 (1988): 465–544.

———. "Should Lawyers Care about Philosophy?" *Duke Law Journal* 1989 (1989): 1752–1783.

Singer, J., and J. Beermann. "The Social Origins of Property." *Canadian Journal of Law and Jurisprudence* 6 (1993): 217–248.

Singh, A., J. Skerrett, and R. Hogan, eds. *Memory, Narrative, and Identity.* Boston: Northeastern University Press, 1994.

Singleton, T., ed. *The Archaeology of Slavery and Plantation Life.* Orlando, Fla.: Academic Press, 1985.

Smith, J., ed. *Anti-Black Thought, 1863–1925.* 11 vols. New York: Garland, 1993.

Sobel, M. *The World They Made Together: Black and White Values in Eighteenth-Century Virginia.* Princeton: Princeton University Press, 1987.

Soja, E. *Postmodern Geographies.* London: Verso, 1990.

———. "The Spatiality of Social Life: Towards a Transformative Retheorization." In *Social Relations and Spatial Structures,* edited by D. Gregory and J. Urry. New York: St. Martin's Press, 1985.

Sorin, G. *Abolitionism: A New Perspective.* New York: Praeger, 1972.

Spackman, S. "American Federalism and the Civil Rights Act of 1875." *American Studies* 10 (1978): 313–328.

Spear, A. *Black Chicago: The Making of a Negro Ghetto, 1890–1920.* Chicago: University of Chicago Press, 1967.

Stampp, K. *America in 1857: A Nation on the Brink.* New York: Oxford University Press, 1990.

Starobin, R., ed. *Blacks in Bondage: Letters of American Slaves.* New York: New Viewpoints, 1974.

Stephenson, G. *Race Distinctions in American Law.* New York: D. Appleton, 1910.

———. "The Segregation of the White and Negro Races in Cities." *South Atlantic Quarterly* 13 (1914): 1–18.

———. "The Segregation of the White and Negro Races in Cities by Legislation." *National Municipal Review* 3 (1914): 496–504.

———. "The Segregation of the White and Negro Races in Rural Communities of North Carolina." *South Atlantic Quarterly* 13 (1914): 107–117.

Stewart, J. *The Aims and Impact of Garrisonian Abolitionism, 1840–1860.* New York: 1969.

Story, J. *Commentaries on the Conflict of Laws.* 8th ed. Boston: Little, Brown, 1883.

Straudenraus, P. *The African Colonization Movement, 1816–1865.* New York: Columbia University Press, 1961.

Sugarman, D., ed. *Legality, Ideology, and the State.* London: Academic Press, 1983.

"Symposium: Approaching Democracy—A New Legal Order for Eastern Europe." *University of Chicago Law Review* 58 (1991): 439–670.

"Symposium: Transitions to Democracy and the Rule of Law." *American University Journal of International Law and Policy* 5 (1990): 965.

Taylor, J. "On Construing the World." In *Language and the Cognitive Construal of the World,* edited by J. Taylor and R. MacLaury. Berlin: Mouton de Gruyter, 1995.

Taylor, O. *Negro Slavery in Arkansas.* Durham, N.C.: Duke University Press, 1958.

Taylor, Q. *The Forging of a Black Community: Seattle's Central District from 1870 through the Civil Rights Era.* Seattle: University of Washington Press, 1994.

Thomas, E. *The Confederate Nation.* New York: Harper and Row, 1979.

Thompson, E. *Plantation Societies, Race Relations, and the South.* Durham, N.C.: Duke University Press, 1975.

Tindall, G. *South Carolina Negroes: 1877–1900.* Columbia, S.C.: University of South Carolina Press, 1952.

Tobin, G., ed. *Divided Neighbors: Changing Patterns of Racial Segregation.* Newbury Park, Calif.: Sage, 1987.

Trelease, A. *White Terror: The Ku Klux Klan Conspiracy and Southern Reconstruction.* New York: Harper and Row, 1971.

Trotter, J. *Black Milwaukee: The Making of an Industrial Proletariat, 1915–45.* Urbana: University of Illinois Press, 1985.

————, ed. *The Great Migration in Historical Perspective: New Dimensions of Race, Class, and Gender.* Bloomington: Indiana University Press, 1991.

Tushnet, M. *The American Law of Slavery, 1810–1860: Considerations of Humanity and Interest.* Princeton: Princeton University Press, 1981.

————. "CLS: A Political History." *Yale Law Journal* 100 (1991): 1515–1544.

————. "Legal Scholarship: Its Causes and Cures." *Yale Law Journal* 90 (1981): 1205–1233.

————. *Making Civil Rights Law: Thurgood Marshall and the Supreme Court, 1936–1961.* New York: Oxford University Press, 1994.

————. *The NAACP's Legal Strategy against Segregated Education, 1925–1950.* Chapel Hill: University of North Carolina Press, 1987.

————. *Red, White, and Blue: A Critical Analysis of Constitutional Law.* Cambridge, Mass.: Harvard University Press, 1988.

Unger, R. *The Critical Legal Studies Movement.* Cambridge, Mass.: Harvard University Press, 1986.

Vandevelde, K. "The New Property of the Nineteenth Century: The Development of the Modern Concept of Property." *Buffalo Law Review* 29 (1980): 325–367.

Vose, C. *Caucasians Only: The Supreme Court, the NAACP, and the Restrictive Covenant Cases.* Berkeley: University of California Press, 1959.

Wade, R. *Slavery in the Cities: The South, 1820–1860*. New York: Oxford University Press, 1964.

Walker, S. "Booker T. Washington: 'Separatist' in Golden Chains." In *Black Separatism and Social Reality: Rhetoric and Reason*, edited by R. Hall. New York: 1977.

Walzer, M. "Liberalism and the Art of Separation." *Political Theory* 12 (1984): 315–330.

Wasby, S. *Race Relations Litigation in an Age of Complexity*. Charlottesville: University Press of Virginia, 1995.

Weissbourd, B., and E. Mertz. "Rule-Centrism versus Legal Creativity: The Skewing of Legal Ideology through Language." *Law and Society Review* 19 (1985): 623–659.

Westin, A. "The Case of the Prejudiced Doorkeeper." In *Quarrels That Have Shaped the Constitution*, edited by J. Garraty. New York: 1964.

Wetlaufer, G. "Rhetoric and Its Denial in Legal Discourse." *Virginia Law Review* 76 (1990): 1545–1597.

Wharton, V. *The Negro in Mississippi, 1865–1890*. Chapel Hill: University of North Carolina Press, 1947.

White, W. *A Man Called White: The Autobiography of Walter White*. New York: Viking, 1948.

Wiecek, W. "Abolitionists and the Problem of Unjust Laws." In *Antislavery Reconsidered: New Perspectives on the Abolitionists*, edited by L. Perry and M. Fellman. Baton Rouge: Louisiana State University Press, 1979.

———. "*Somerset:* Lord Mansfield and the Legitimacy of Slavery in the Anglo-American World." *University of Chicago Law Review* 42 (1974): 86–146.

———. *The Sources of Antislavery Constitutionalism in America, 1760–1848*. Ithaca: Cornell University Press, 1977.

Williams, P. "Alchemical Notes: Reconstructing Ideals from Deconstructed Rights." *Harvard Civil Rights–Civil Liberties Law Review* 22 (1987): 401–433.

———. *The Alchemy of Race and Rights*. Cambridge, Mass.: Harvard University Press, 1991.

Williamson, J. *After Slavery: The Negro in South Carolina during Reconstruction, 1861–1877*. Chapel Hill: University of North Carolina Press, 1965.

———. *The Crucible of Race: Black/White Relations in the American South since Emancipation*. New York: Oxford University Press, 1984.

Winokur, J. "The Mixed Blessings of Promissory Servitudes: Toward Optimizing Economic Utility, Individual Liberty, and Personal Identity." *Wisconsin Law Review* 1989 (1989): 1–98.

Wolch, J., and M. Dear, eds. *The Power of Geography: How Territory Shapes Social Life*. Boston: Unwin Hyman, 1989.

Wolff, M. *Lunch at the Five and Ten: The Greensboro Sit-Ins*. New York: Stein and Day, 1970.

Woodward, C. "The Case of the Louisiana Traveler." In *Quarrels That Have Shaped the Constitution*, edited by J. Garraty. New York: Harper and Row, 1964.

———. "*Strange Career* Critics: Long May They Persevere." *Journal of American History* 75 (1988): 851–868.

————. *The Strange Career of Jim Crow*. New York: Oxford University Press, 1957.
————. *Thinking Back: The Perils of Writing History*. Baton Rouge: Louisiana State University Press, 1986.
Wright, G. *Life behind a Veil: Blacks in Louisville, Kentucky, 1865–1930*. Baton Rouge: Louisiana State University Press, 1985.
Yetman, N., ed. *Life under the "Peculiar Institution": Selections from the Slave Narrative Collection*. New York: Holt, Rinehart and Winston, 1970.

Index